Introductory Methods in Population Analysis

Introductory Methods in Population Analysis

R.B. Mandal
Joseph Uyanga
Hanuman Prasad

CONCEPT PUBLISHING COMPANY, NEW DELHI-110 059

ISBN 81-7022-265-6 (H.B.)

Published 2007

Published and Printed by

Ashok Kumar Mittal
Concept Publishing Company
A/15-16, Commercial Block, Mohan Garden
New Delhi-110059 (India)

Phones: 25351460, 25351794
Fax: 091-11-25357103
E-mail: publishing@conceptpub.com

PREFACE

Population studies have recently received momentum not only in different disciplines but also in various parts of the Globe. This is because an ever-increasing population has endangered economic prosperity, creating such problems in unemployment. Population problems and issues are, therefore, not only one of the most important concern the world over, but they also cut across many disciplines ranging from Sociology to Economics and Geography. The administrator, the politician, the health worker and the environmental planner is occasionally faced with knotty population questions which require instant solutions.

This book addresses itself to the techniques of population studies and analysis. The introduction analyses, the meaning and scope of population studies, analysis of some statistical methods and the role of population planning in controlling growth of population. The second chapter deals with the theories of population growth, such as the theory of Malthus, theory of Karl Marx, Ester Boserup's concept of population, Lotka's theory of population, and the demographic transition theory. In the third chapter delineations have been made with special reference to the growth and distribution of population and urban development on a global scale. Chapter fourtth deals with population pressure in terms of underpopulation, overpopulation, optimum population and the carrying capacity of land. The Chapter, starting with the sources of population information, discusses methods in censuses, sample surveys, and population registers. It goes on to treat reporting procedure, international recommendations, defects and comparison of vital statistics with other sources of population data. It discusses migrations in their various ramifications and treats basic demographic measures with elaborate examples.

The problems of sex and age measures with particular reference to sex ratio, composition, rural-urban and regional differences are discussed in the sixth chapter. The chapter also deals with the methods in age composition, age definition, classification, errors, underenumeration, unknown ages, age pyramids as well as the factors which affect age composition. The seventh chapter opens with a discussion of the measures of calculating mortality–crude, specific and infant mortality rates – and ends with an indepth analysis, explanation and constructional issue of Life Tables.

The eighth chapter deals with fertility. Starting with the discussion of methods of birth registration, data evaluation, it goes on to discuss the possibility of using defective registration and delayed registration. Methods of measuring the general, crude, age-specific, parity-specific birth rates and net reproduction rate are discussed. The chapter also treats the use of census data to construct fertility measures, for instance, child-woman ratio, and the number of children ever born. In the ninth chapter several methods of population projection have been discussed.

Further, various cartographic techniques have been illustrated to enhance the scientific methods in population geography. The last chapter is concerned with the rank-size relationship of urban centres whose basis of delineation is the ranking of towns according to urban population.

The book is aimed at the general population, including community health workers, undergraduate students of economics, demography, statistics and population geography.

R.B. Mandal
Dar es Salaam
J.Uyanga
Calabar
Hanuman Prasad
Azamgarh

CONTENTS

ONE

INTRODUCTION

Until recently, the study of population was an underdeveloped branch of geography. Regional imbalances in the distribution of people on the earth's surface as well as their racial and social characteristics are facts which are commonly used in human geography and various social sciences. Glenn Trewartha, in his presidential address to the Association of American Geographers in 1953, pleaded the case for population geography and urged greater attention to it.[1]

The pattern of distribution of man on the earth's surface comes under the subject matter of population geography. Recently, population studies have been greatly emphasized because they provide a central theme around which revolve other geographic thoughts and ideas. Hence, population studies should be placed in the forefront of geographical research. With the increase in population in time and space, it is necessary to know not only the dynamic ideas about the place of population in geographic literature but also the quality and quantity of population in different parts of the globe. This is because in some areas the pressure of population on cultivated land is so high that it nullifies the pace of economic development of a region as well as jeopardises the measures of planning on both social and economic fronts.[2]

The human being is the only culture building architect on the earth's surface, and accordingly he adapts and creates an environment. At some places he is still learning to live in dispersed and nucleated communities while in others he creates a new social and economic order in the form of planned communities while in still others man feels suffocated in congested rural, urban and metropolitan areas.

Population as the creative element and surveyor of resources occupies a dominant position in geographical studies. The relationship between population and environment can be divided into three important groups:

a. Man utilizing the resources of nature as the creator of the natural environment;

b. Man utilizing the resources of nature by virtue of his working in the natural environment; and

c. Man utilizing the resources of nature because the human environment is the product of the physical environment.

Hence, the number of persons at a place is the focal point of geographical investigation. Without man, the Universe is resourceless because only those elements of nature are considered resources which are needed and utilized by man.

Altogether, nearly five billion persons inhabit the earth. Man is the dominant factor of economic geography as "he produces, manufactures, distributes, consumes and also destroys resources. Constantly active, he has moved from his prehistoric settlement of the grasslands and a few forest areas of the low latitudes, and now occupied most of the habitable parts of the earth and uses its resources to satisfy his needs".[3]

PURPOSE OF STUDY

This book aims at highlighting the general concepts, theories as well as the growth and distribution of the world population. In the second section, introductory methods are put forward with special reference to migration, sex and age, mortality, fertility and population estimates. In the third section, different techniques of spatial analysis have been dealt with, that is, techniques of mapping in population distribution, symbolising population data, grouping of population data and their representation of population growth.

MEANING AND SCOPE

Population analysis involves the study of people, their distribution, density, vital statistics, growth, movement, occupational structure, fertility, mortality, health planning and grouping of human settlements. The spatial variation of population concerns itself with three 'definite groups of facts' namely, (i) distribution, (ii) arrangement or pattern,and (iii) population migration.[4] In population study, geography deals with the areal differentiation of population distribution on the surface of the earth. The fourth group of factors relate to the trends of population growth within specific time limits and an understanding of regional differentiation of population on earth.[5] Hence, in the geographical context, the methods of population study should be oriented in such a way as to describe and interpret the areal differentiation in the number and density of population, and to highlight the relationship between population and facts of geographical resources, patterns of economic production and social conditions.[6] As regards needs and population planning, the factors which should be considered for population analysis are, (i) demographic factors, (ii) morbidity levels and patterns of population, (iii) socio-economic conditions, and (iv) the available resources in the field of health, for example, men, money and materials available to the society.

In the case of demographic studies, the geographers deal with 'the size, territorial distribution and composition of population, changes therein, and the components of such changes which may be identified as natality, mortality, territorial movement and social-mobility'.[7] The size of population refers to the number of persons in a region at a given time; territorial distribution means the arrangements of people in space and time; and the structure and composition of population refers to the distribution of population not only according to sex and age but also according to marital status, education, occupation etc. Thus, in a narrow sense, the method of population studies is the quantitative evaluation of the processes of births, deaths, marriage, migration and social mobility, whereas in a broader sense it includes social, economic, ethnic, psychological, geographical and political characteristics. Social characteristics include marital and family status, place of birth, literacy and educational attainment, religion etc. Economic characteristics refer to economic activity, employment status, occupation, industry and income. Ethnic characteristics refer to race and nationality, while geographic characteristics relate to climatic and environmental adaptability, colour of the body, texture of hair and population regions. On the whole, the demographic process includes population pressure on resources, population limitations on the family, rural and urban problems of population, manpower, maldistribution of income and the quality of population including intelligence, health and nutritional problems. The methodologies of population are mainly concerned with the components of population change and variation including social, economic, geographical, psychological and political factors. Trewartha widened the methodological scope of population studies by saying that numbers, densities and qualities of population provide the essential base for social science studies from which all other elements could be observed singly or collectively in order to arrive at a meaningful conclusion.

METHODS IN POPULATION ANALYSIS

The various methods used in population geography revolve around "the spatial aspects of population in the context of the aggregate nature of the places".[8] This is directed towards the understanding of traits of population of different places, their causes, consequences and above all, their interaction with physical and cultural elements. Population geography is, therefore, called "population study".

The methods of population study deal with the following points:

a. The use of natural resources, that is, environment, soil, space, time, energy, goods, techniques, money, information and other sources for the optimum population distribution over the earth's surface.

b. The spatial distribution, density, change and growth of population which depend on the economic conditions and the availability of food in any region.

c. The demographic attributes since the movement of people, fertility, mortality, age-sex structure and literacy play an important role in economic growth of inhabitants themselves.

d. People at a particular place and time provide an opportunity to make the best use of the available resources for the production of food, and labour in other jobs.

e. Population planning for regional economic development and welfare of the people.

There are various methods of explaining the concept of population density, which is generally expressed in terms of areal expansion and the ratio of resources available in a particular region for human living. This ratio shows the density of population. When the total population of a region is divided by the area, it gives the density of population per square kilometre. This is known as arithmetical density of population. But this is only a crude density of population, which does not highlight the internal distributional pattern and economic conditions of people in the region. In the same country, one area is densely settled whereas another area is sparsely settled; but there is no method to highlight these differences though the economic density pattern can be shown to some extent. The ratio of population in terms of any resource is called economic density of population, which gives the productive capacity of the area. When the total population is divided by the net sown area, the distributional pattern of agricultural resources in terms of population is apparent. This is known as the physiological density of population. Similarly, the number of persons employed in agricultural operations per square kilometer is known as the agricultural density of population.

The pressure of population has influenced man's attitude, values and behaviour. This can be explained in terms of population explosion, implosion and diversification. Population explosion is the phenomenal acceleration in the rates of population growth in a particular area, usually closely related with the decrease in the death rate and an increase in the birth rate, as is in the case of Shanghai in China and Tokyo in Japan. Population implosion is the increasing concentration of population in urban areas, or over smaller proportions of the earth's land surface. Population implosion has, of course, been created by population explosion, and both population implosion and explosion have generated population diversification, that is, the increasing heterogeneity of people by culture, values, religion, ethnicity and race, which share the same geographic area and increasingly the same territorial life space. The idea of population potential connotes the possible number of people who can live in a specific area with a reasonable standard of living in relation to the available resources in that region.

Overpopulation exists in a situation where per capita income is low and shows a decreasing trend in comparison with the increasing trend in population. Underpopulation is a case where population is increasing, resources are highly utilized but simultaneously per capita income and the level of consumption are increasing. Optimum population is said to occur when the available resources are highly utilized and the standard of living of people is also high.

The relationship between population and resources can be examined under the following aspects: per capita income, level of employment, the existence of diminishing returns, the volume and direction of migration, change in consumption patterns, life expectancy, changes in terms of international trade, and measures of population density.

In order to show the relationship between population and resources, Edward A. Ackerman [9] classified the whole world into five groups. These are:

a. The United States Type: developed technology, a case of under-population.

b. The European Type: developed technology, a case of over-population.

c. The China or Egypt Type: less developed technology, a case of over-population.

d. The Brazil Type: less developed technology, a case of under population.

e. The Arctic-Desert Type: less developed technology, a case of intensive over-population.

The mean centre of population in a region has been variously called the centroid or centre of gravity. After dividing the total horizontal tier moment by the vertical one, the fulcrum of a distribution can be calculated where each unit is considered to have equal weight on a hypothetical rigid level plane. According to Hart (1954)[10] it may be located by determining the point of intersection of the two lines along which the plane would balance. The median centre of population, or centre of convergence is the point where the whole population could be assembled with the minimum travel distance. The modal centre of population in space refers to the maximum surface density. In areas of large population size it coincides with the principal peak of the population potential. Population potential is a measure of influence of people at a distance where the influence is inversely proportional to distance. The standard distance deviation has been developed by Stewart and Warntz[11] as the dynamical radius of a population. It is found by dividing the mean centre Σ(Pr2) by the total population (P) and then by taking the square root of the resulting mean square:

$$Sr = \sqrt{\frac{\sum(Pr^2)}{P}}$$

Isolines of aggregate squared-distance deviations are concentric circles about the mean centre, regardless of the population distribution.

Population spacing is a measure of ecological distribution; it is the mean distance between nearest neighbours. This concept is based on the uniform and random distributions. The linear distribution map relates to the concept of spacing.

The change of population means growth or decline of the number of people in a region. In relation to settlement growth there are four stages of population arrangement in any space which are as follows:[12]

FIRST STAGE: Implanation of a nucleus of settlement by migrants attracted by special environmental qualities (resources, refuge, exploitable indegenous).

SECOND STAGE: Expansion of the settlement to the limit where land is exploitable with the available technology, the completion of the 'frontier' phase of 'free' land readily available.

THIRD STAGE: Completion for development from other people along border zones, influx of new migrants especially into new industrial and commercial districts.

FOURTH STAGE: Metropolitization: Population largely urban and suburban; commuting range brings most of the area within close contact of the centre; high mobility of population, much inter-regional contact and movement.

It has been found that population change also occurs on account of interaction of areal and demographic phenomena. The areal phenomena affecting population change include the annexation of territories from the previous boundary, while the demographic phenomena affecting population change are natural change and migration.

The index of change is a measure for estimating intercensal change in population. It can be calculated with the help of the following formula:

$$1C = \frac{P_1}{P_2}$$

where 1C is index of change, P1 is population of the last census and P2 is the population of the previous census. The regional indices can be easily compared with the national or state rates and can be plotted with the help of choropleth method to identify distributional patterns.

The location coefficient is another measure which takes into account population and area of the region for calculating the concentration of population distribution in the region. The formula:

$$LC = \frac{P_i}{A_i}$$

where LC is the location coefficient. This is the percentage of total population during 1971-81 in i th area and is the percentage of area contained in the ith sub-areal unit. In case the location coefficient for a district is unity, it means that the district has just the amount of population which it should have, if the total population were distributed in the different districts of the region in direct proportion to their areas. On the other hand, those districts which have values of more than one as locational coefficient are areas of population concentration. The index of concentration is given here:

$$1D = \frac{1}{2}\sum_{i=1}^{n}(X_i - Y_i),$$

where 1D is the index if concentration, is the percentage of population growth in the ith areal sub-unit and is the percentage of the area contained in that unit. In case the index is 0, it means that each territorial division has a population growth in proportion to its area. A higher index shows higher concentration.

In order to study the population growth and the size of population of a particular region in a decade, the location quotient has been estimated with the help of the given formula:

$$LQ = \frac{X_i}{Y_i},$$

where LQ is the location quotient, is the percentage of population change during 1961-71 in the i th area, and Y_i is the percentage of total population of the i th areal sub-unit in relation to the region as a whole. The index with a value of less than one is an under representation of the percentage of population change in the area and vice-versa.

The annual growth of population has been calculated on the basis of this formula which gives an average arithmetical growth rate:

$$r = \frac{(P_2 - P_1)/t}{(P_2 + P_1)/t} \times 100$$

where r is the annual growth rate, P_1 is the population of the region at a particular point of time, P_2 is the population of the region at another point of time and t is the time interval between P_2 and P_1. The population change as a demographic system may be observed if we consider that fertility, mortality and migration are the inner or formal variables of the system while social, economic, biological and topographical factors in relation to climate are the outer and the ultimate variables. These outer variables are largely responsible for population trends in respect of size, composition and distribution.

Similarly, the decadal change of urban population has been generally calculated on the basis of the following formula:

$$\text{Decadal growth rate} = \sqrt[t]{\frac{P_i}{P_o} - 1 \times 100}$$

where t is the number of years interval, P_1 is the last census population and P_0 is the previous census population.

Another method is the demographic coefficient. It is an index designed to give a measure of future population pressure in any region, for example c = d R, where c is the demographic coefficient, d is the density of persons per square kilometre, and R is the net reproduction rate. The same index after two generations is ç = d R^2. Another formula for demographic coefficient is c = dt; where t represents the rate of natural increase per 1000 inhabitants. This index can be plotted for each administrative unit and a choropleth map can be prepared.

Population dynamics is the study of population change and the components of such change are natality, mortality, migration and social mobility. The models of mortality are needed to build the system of marriage, fertility and migration. The analysis of mortality by sex and age is important from the socio-economic and demographic points of view for example, high infant and maternal mortalities prevailing in the region are indicators of socio-economic backwardness and poor health facilities. The simplest measure of mortality is the crude death rate. The crude death rate is defined as the number of deaths in a year per 1000 of the mid-year population. The formula is CDR = D/P X 100, where D is total deaths in a community during a given calendar year and P is the mid year population (July 1).

The fertility of population refers to the actual birth performance of a woman while fecundity refers to the physiological capacity to reproduce. Ones fertility is limited by ones fecundity. The reproductive span is 15-49 years. The factors determining fertility are the age of a woman, age of marriage, or of birth or parity, the duration of marriage, marital status, religion, literacy of the mother, occupation, income, employment, status of a female, infant mortality, sex aggressiveness, sex performance, fecundity, diet and climatic conditions. The measures of fertility are crude birth rate, general fertility rate and age cumulative fertility rate.

Fertility and mortality have a dominant impact on population growth. Coontz[13] has classified the theories of population geography based on fertility into three categories: biological, cultural and economic.

The biological theories stress that the law regulating human growth is basically the same as that regulating the growth of plants and animals- that demographic growth is not unique. The cultural theories of population growth emphasize the importance of man's character and culture in influencing its fertility. Economic theories of population growth emphasize the significance of economic relations in social change, particularly with reference to the demand for labour.

The migration of population is an important factor in population redistribution. This requires the analysis of volume, direction, characteristics and causes of migration which are useful in understanding trends in the population redistribution of a region. The migration of a person within a nation is called international migration. The time involved between the two migrations is known as the migration interval. On the other hand, the migrants who depart from a common area of origin and arrive at a common area of destination during a particular migration interval constitute a migration stream. The departure from the community of destination is termed as out-migration, while the arrival at the community of destination is termed in-migration. The net balance between arrival and departure is termed as net migration, whereas the study of difference in the rate of migration between various demographic, economic and social groups of population is 'differential migration'.

The method of population projection is dependent upon the analysis of past levels and trends of population growth and population change. Certain global methods such as the ratio, apportionment, and United Nations method can be used to project population, if the data for the previous census are available. Cohort survival or component methods of projecting population in general require the availability of both census and vital statistics data. They extrapolate the trends of each component of population change and the trend of area re-classification. Further, these are combined into a single projection. Population projection can also be calculated after considering the economic variables and population change. The use of probabilistic or stochastic models in population projection is of considerable importance but all these requires the use of computers.

In population planning, the countries of high fertility need a large number of institutions for maternal and child health care, whereas those with low mortality need facilities for taking care of those with degenerative diseases. Projections of populations by age, sex and other characteristics were expected to indicate the needs of the future. An idea about the level of mortality and morbidity would of help in planning the control of communicable diseases. Planning for population in urban and rural areas as well as different living conditions should be based on the differences in living patterns of population in different regions of the world. This indicates that any comprehensive scheme of economic planning should include within its scope population planning as well, because a rapidly growing population is the most fundamental obstacle to the economic development of a nation.

According to the regional method, the world or a country may be divided into population regions. This involves the regional study of population which is influenced not by political boundaries but by physical factors. This saves us from repetitive study of the same unit as the areas along the equator may constitute separate nations but the regional conditions and living conditions of people are the same everywhere. But the major limitation of this method is that no universal truth could be established about human behaviour which is an important factor in the study of population geography. The differences in human behaviour are to be found in social, political and economic surroundings.

Statistical methods include techniques of sampling, model building, cost-benefit analysis, multivariate analysis, and principal component analysis, etc. Since most of the methods of population projections involve mathematical computations, they also come under statistical techniques. On the earth-surface the representative items are generally chosen on the basis of random, systematic, clustered, multi-stage or purposive sampling.

In population analysis, cost-benefit analysis could be used as a cost-effective analysis. Cost-effective analysis involves difficulties in the method-wise estimation of costs relating to administration, organization, research, and assets and equipment. Hence the cost involved for a particular response of population, and the comparative cost-effective analysis of sub-national areas was bound to suffer from serious limitations. after considering the data for a large number of variables in factor analysis, multivariate and principal component analysis have been used in population analysis. with the advancement of high speed computers, complex models using the Markov chain and Monte Carlo Simulation techniques are extensively used in population analysis. These techniques are preferred because stochastic models or expected value models may not exist under general conditions of simulation model.

Two methods are generally used for the estimation of future population : (a) the macro approach in which projections, and (b) the micro approach in which projections are made for individual areas and then aggregated.

REFERENCES

1. Threwartha, G. T. "A Case for Population Geography", *Annals of the Association of American Geographers,* 43(1953) 71-97.
2. Mandal, R. B. "Nature of Population Geography", Dimensions in Geography; Associated Book Agency, Patna, 1979 p. 4.
3. Jones, C. F. and Darkenwald, G. G. *"Economic Geography;* The MacMillan, New York, 1964.
4. Fawcet, C. B. "Whither Population : Distribution and Trends Movement", *Geography,* XXII(1937) 14.
5. Prashad, Ayodhya, Chotanagpur: Geography of Rural Settlements, Ranchi University 1973.
6. Trewartha, G. T. 'A Case for Population Geography' *Annals of the Association of American Geographers* XLIII 1953,87.
7. Zelinsky, W. A Prologue to Population Geography New Jersy: 1966.
8. Ackerman, E.A. in Singh, K. N. and J. Singh: Bhoogol Ke Mul Tatwa, Tara

Publication, Varanasi 1973.
9. Hauser, P. M. and D. Duncan *The Study of Population,* 1954.
10. Hart, J.F. 'Central Tendency in Areal Distribution', Economic Geography, 30 (1954).
11. Stewart, J.Q. and Warntz, W. *'Macro-geography and Social Sciences', Geographical Review* 48(1958) 157.
12. Fielding, G.J. *Geography As Social Science,* New York, 1967.
13. Coontz, S.E. *Population Theories and Their Economic Interpretation,* 1957.

TWO

THEORIES OF POPULATION GROWTH

Population growth is a subject matter of general interest to anthropologist, economists, geographers, demographers and sociologists. Hence all these disciplines have contributed substantially in developing general concepts and theories relating to population studies.In this chapter only the simple understanding of some of the theories as developed by Malthus, Marxists, Ester Boserup, Lotka and others have been discussed in brief, in order to have a clearcut idea of the consequence of population growth and the issues involved in regional development and spatial integration.

The Theory of Malthus

It is a law of nature that all population at all times and places (unless deliberately checked) tend to go on expanding until they reach the 'limits of subsistence';after which, they are kept in check by 'vice and misery '. In other words, the population of the world tends to increase faster than the food supply and that unless fertility is controlled, famine, vice, disease, and war must serve as population checks.

The view that population growth can only have adverse consequence for the society is closely associated with Thomas Malthus.[1] Who did not deal with the effect of population growth on land use or on the structure of the agrarian society, but he certainly examined the effect of population growth on food supply. Malthus first put forward his views in 'An Essay on the Principles of Population ', published in 1798, and then extended it in a revised edition published in

1803. He argued that population has the capacity to increase at a geometric progression (3 x 3 = 9, 9 x 3 = 27), whereas food output only has the capacity to grow at an arithmetic progression (1 + 2 + 3 = 6). But as population did increase at a geometric progression there must exist checks to population increase. He recognized two categories: first, preventive checks, of which he considered only one, moral restraint or the deferment of marriage; and second, the positive checks, which included all the causes of a shortened life, but principally war, famine and disease.

Later on Malthusian cycle took the following course. Initially population is stationary, with birth and death rates being equal and income per capita at a subsistence level. Later for some reason if income per capita rises, this will allow people to marry earlier leading to a rise in the birth rate. In such a situation, people can buy extra food and become more resistant to diseases reducing the death rate. Consequently population begins to increase and in due course with the operation of the law of diminishing returns, the increase in food supply falls behind the increase in population. Income per capita also falls and as it does, marriage is once again deferred and fertility declines. In case per capita falls up to the subsistence level, death rate rises. Population growth ceases as fertility and mortality reach the same level, and income per head returns to the subsistence level. Malthus conclusion was that while population can increase, it will eventually always be halted by rising mortality as income per capita falls, and that period of temporary affluence will always be eroded by population growth and hence income per capita would be at subsistence level.

Malthus theory was much criticised by his contemporaries and subsequent writers. In particular he ignored the possibility of technological advances in agriculture allowing for a greater increase in food output. He did not anticipate that there might be birth control within marriage, or that men might defer marriage or have fewer children within marriage in order to achieve a better standard of living. Subsequent interpreters of this theory have been apt to emphasize that population growth is halted by rising mortality rather than falling fertility. Malthus allowed this as a possibility. It is said that Malthus ideas were received in France and played a major part in reducing France influence in world affairs. Malthus ideas also helped Darwin to formulate his theories. Malthus claimed that population tended to increase in geometrical progression. The growth of productivity of agriculture, on the other hand, he stated, could only grow in arithmetical progression but Malthus has given no evidence to support this statement.

Thus we may conclude with a converse of Malthus own original proposition, namely that, in a great many times and places, population is undesirably low, and may be increasing at a very low rate. The time comes, of course, when population growth does threaten to overtake 'means of subsistence', as understood in that time and place; and the consequence is that population growth itself provides the necessary stimulus, inducing the community to change its existing methods of producing or obtaining food for more productive methods, which will enable it to support a larger population. When Malthus wrote his first edition, the population of Britain was approaching 10 million, and, judging by what he knew of contemporary agricultural methods, he did not see how an increased number could be fed. But Malthus is to blame for being apparently unaware, throughout a long lifetime, of the agricultural, commercial and industrial revolution going on all around him, which not only enabled Britain to produce manufactured exports to purchase food grown elsewhere, but also to increase greatly agriculture production within the country.[2]

The Theory of Karl Marx

Lenin,the follower of Marx, in his celebrated book, 'Theory of the Agrarian Question' presented the following facts regarding population

1. According to Malthus 'the development of civilization and increase of population, food production is becoming more and more difficult'.[3] Lenin statedp[4] that it is silly to think that primitive men obtained all their requirements free from nature. In reality, primitive men had problems of existence and difficulties of fighting against nature. In conditions of increasing population, it is not difficult to produce food but it is difficult to obtain it for the population as the capitalist society concentrates land, machinery and money in fewer hands hampering higher production and the better utilization of

land.

2. Lenin completely rejected the Malthusian concept of overpopulation and in this connection Bulgakov's had to say, " the areas of overpopulation may be regarded as absolute poverty areas which face the problem of meagre production and not of distribution."

3. According to Malthus "economic progress and historical developments determined by geographical environment." This proposition has been rejected by the Marxists.[5] What Stalin has to say in this connection is as follows : The geographical environment is indispensable for the development of the society but it may not be a determining factor. In India, since the prehistoric period, three different social systems have been successively superseded, the primitive communal system, the religio-ritual system and the modern system. During these periods, the geographical conditions were more or less the same in India with slight variations. It is thus a fact that the geographical environment may not be the determining factor of social development and economic progress of the society.

4. It has also been said that population growth is the determinant of social system. But Marxists ask why the primitive communal system has been succeeded by the religio-ritual system and the latter by the modern system and not by the others. In such a situation the determining factors are the methods of procuring livelihood, the instruments of production and human abilities including experience and skill for boosting up the productive forces of the economy.

In this way, the theory of Marx completely rejected the theory of Malthus, keeping in view the changing conditions of society and geographical determinism.[6]

ESTER BOSERUP'S CONCEPT OF POPULATION

It is widely accepted that population growth may have positive effects upon agricultural change through the price mechanism. Indeed, some nineteenth-century writers thought that historically, all areas changed from extensive pastoralism to industrialization, intensive agricultural economies as a result of increase in population density.[7] More recently, Ester Boserup has argued that increasing population density is the major cause of agricultural change.[8]

The evidence for her model is based largely on the behaviour of peasants in Africa and Asia, and she specifically excludes modern commercial farmers using industrial inputs from her analysis. It is also based upon a number of implicit assumptions. First, population growth is independent of food supply, and it is this population growth that causes changes in agriculture, rather than as Malthus assumed, increases in the food supply that allow numbers to grow. Second, at any given stage of agricultural intensity (Table 2.1) farmers are satisfied with the amount of food per head they are producing and will only work harder to produce more if forced to do so by an increase in their numbers; they prefer to maximise leisure rather than profit. Third, farmers at any given stage of development are aware of a wide range of traditional farming techniques, but they use only those that require few labour inputs. Only with an increase in population they resort to more labour-intensive techniques in order to increase output. Fourth, there is intensification by which Boserup means increasing the proportion of total agriculturally usable land under crop cultivation rather than leaving it fallow. An increase in the cropped area and a decline in fallow is the result of an increasing population density.

The sequence of land use stages that results from population increase seems to be based mainly on the experience of farming in Africa and Asia (Table 2.1). In places where population density is low, satisfactory output could be òbtained from gathering and hunting. The second and the first arable stages are forest fallow. Wherever the forest is cleared with fire and simple tools, there is no cultivation of the soil, and the crops are sown for two years only. The land is then abandoned, the natural vegetation regenerates and the fertility of the soil is restored. The land may only be cultivated again after twenty five years of fallow as labour inputs are low and output per head is high. However, if population density increases, then farmers will have to reduce the length of the fallow and increase the period of cultivation of crops in order to produce the extra food supply. In bush fallowing, the fallow is shorter, fertility is not restored before the land is used again, leading to a fall in crop fields. To arrest this decline in yields extra-labour is expended on weeding and carrying manure. Thus, output per capita declines. Farmers, thus, will only change the system from forest fallow to bush fallowing in order to produce the extra food for the extra numbers. Therefore, intensification is a result of rising numbers. The switch to bush fallowing also requires the use of new implements. In bush fallowing, the fallow is occupied by grass, not trees, and the hoe is necessary to remove the grass roots before sowing. Similarly, in the transition from bush fallowing to short fallow the plough becomes necessary; again, there is an increase in labour needs not compensated by a proportional increase in crop yields, so that output per head falls again. In the final stages of annual cropping and multicropping, there is an increase not only in the tasks necessary to produce an annual crop, but in capital investment in the construction and maintenance of irrigation systems and drainage lines.

Hence, Boserup argues that the continuous reduction of fallow and the increased labour needed to maintain crop yields means a fall in output per head between each stage. Since it is assumed that farmers prefer leisure to extra work, the only reason why they will shift from one stage to another is to produce the extra food that the increasing numbers will require.

Several criticisms have been levelled against this model. Few believe that farmers are simply leisure maximizers. Wherever markets for agricultural products exists, farmers will increase labour inputs to increase yields and maximise profits; they may also increase the output to meet the demands for taxation.[9] In such a situation, there is no doubt that labour inputs will increase as the fallow is reduced. It is less clear that yields will fall with less successive reduction in fallow. The model also assumes that the new techniques adopted at each stage give an increased yield which cannot compensate for increased labour, and so labour productivity falls progressively. However, as yields in Europe doubled, it seems likely that in the stage from short fallow to annual cropping output per capita at least remained constant. Farmers, of course, had responses to population growth other than simply reducing the fallow. They could expand the area under cultivation, reduce the fallow, specialize in cash crops, emigrate, or limit their numbers. Recently, Boserup seems to have modified her original model, recognising that farmers may migrate into unoccupied areas rather than only reducing the fallow in their immediate territory, and that some technological advances can put off the decline in marginal returns.[10]

LOTKA'S THEORY OF POPULATION

Lotka's thoery is concerned with the evolution of a female population subject to constant fertility and age-specific mortality. No recognition is given to marriage. The latter is of no importance in the stable state: nuptiality is constant and, therefore, overall fertility too. In the initial phase, when population is fluctuating, there are imbalances in the size of male and female cohorts whose ages make them suited to marry each other; nuptiality and, consequently, fertility fluctuate as well.

Since we are dealing with the female population only, fertility is restricted to girls. It follows for purposes of computation, that the usual overall fertility which refers to both sexes together must be converted into fertility 'in terms of girls only'. This can be done by multiplying current overall fertility with 0.485 (sex ratio of 106) or with 0.490 (sex ratio of 104).

Lotka's essential conclusion is that a population which has been exposed forever to unchanging conditions of overall fertility and age-specific mortality tends towards a population with an unchanging age distribution and growth rate. They depend on the fertility and mortality conditions, but not on the initial age distribution. This population at the limit is characterised as stable. It is entirely unchanging except for its size which increases or decreases at a constant rate, that is to say, in geometric progression. Whenever the size remains constant, the stable population is called stationary. As a first approximation, the rate of increase of a stable population or intrinsic rate of natural increase, r depends only on the net reproduction rate, R_0 and on the average age ã, of the net fertility distribution. The relationship is expressed as follows:[11]

$$\log(1+r) = \frac{\text{Log } R_o}{\bar{a}}$$

If these results are valid for the female population, they can be applied to the whole population. The sex ratio of the stable population is unchanging and the two parts, masculine and feminine, grow at the same rate.

Table 2.1: The Characteristics of the Land Use Stages in Ester Boserup's Models

No	Type	Range of population density (per km^2)	Frequency of cropping %	Fallow Length	Type of Fallow	Tools of Use	Fertilizer	Labour needs	Productivity
1.	Gathering	0 — 4	0	-	-	-	-	Low	High
2.	Forest fallow	0 — 4	0 — 10	One or two crops and twenty-five years fallow	Secondary	Axe, fire dissing stick	Ash	Land clearance with axe and fire. No cultivation or weeding	High
3.	Bush fallow	4 — 64	10 — 40	Two or more crops, eight to ten years fallow	Small trees, bush	Hoe	Ash, vegetation, turfs mixed in soil	Less land clearance but some weeding	Falls as yields fall and weeding needed
4.	Short fallow	16 — 64	40 — 80	One or two crops and then one or two years fallow	Wild grasses	Plough	Manure and human waste	Extra preparation of seed-bed, extra weeding and carting manure	Falls as extra cultivation, extra weeding collecting and distributing manure, care of draught animals
5.	Annual cropping	64 — 256	80 — 100	One crop each year with a few months fallows	Legumes and roots	Plough	Manure, human waste, green manure marking and silting composts	Extra cultivation, weeding, terracing irrigation and water control	Falls as extra cultivation and weeding, collecting and distribution manure, constructing and maintaining irrigation terracing, water control, etc. distribution
6.	Multi-cropping	256 — 512	200 — 300	Two or more crops without any fallow			marking and	irrigation and	

Source: *The Dynamics of Agricultural change*, David Grigg London: Hutchinson, 1982, pp. 38 — 39.

THE THEORY OF DEMOGRAPHIC TRANSITION

The theory of Demographic Transition is a most widely accepted which explains population change over time. It states that population's fertility and mortality will both decline from high levels to low levels as a result of economic and social development. The decline in mortality usually precedes the decline in fertility, resulting in high population growth during the transition period.

For instance, Finland has passed through the four stages of demographic transition.[12] These are:

STAGE I: High birth rate, high death rate = little or no increase in the actual number of population.
(Finland in 1785-1790).
Birth rate 38 per 1,000.
Death rate 32 per 1,000.
Rate of natural increase 0.6 per cent.

STAGE II: High birth rate, falling death rate = high growth rate of population.
(Finland in 1825-1830)
Birth rate 38 per 1,000.
Death rate 24 per 1,000.
Rate of natural increase, 1.4 per cent.

STAGE III: Declining birth rate, relatively low death rate = decrease in the rate of growth of population.
(Finland in 1910-1915)
Birth rate 29 per 1,000.
Death rate 17 per 1,000.
Rate of natural increase. 1.2 per cent.

STAGE IV: Low death rate, low birth rate = very low rate of growth of population.
(Finland in 1970-1976)
Birth rate 13 per 1,000.
Death rate 10 per 1,000.
Rate of natural increase, 0.3 per cent.

CONCLUSIONS

To conclude, the theories of Malthus and Karl Marx are highly dependent upon population growth, its consequences as well as measures to curtail population growth. The theory of Bosèrup is closely related with the social evolution, resulting land use and the growth of population, whereas Lotka's theory as well as the theory of Demographic Transition are based on demographic coefficients and the differential stages of demographic transition.

REFERENCES

1. Malthus, T.R. : An Essay on the Principle of Population or a view of Its Past and Present Effects on Human Happiness (Edt. G.T. Bettany); London, 1890.
2. Clark, Colin : Population Growth and Land Use; London Macmillan:1967.
3. Readings in Land Utilization, *The Indian Society of Agricultural Economics*, Bombay, 1957, p.24.
4. Lenin, V.L., Theory of the Agrarian Question, International Publishers, New York, 1918.
5. Stalin, J., Dialectical and Historical Materialism, International Publishers, New York, 1940.
6. Mandal, R.B., *Land Utilisation: Theory and Practice,* New Delhi, Concept, 1982.
7. Nou, J., *Studies in the Development of Agricultural Economics in Europe*; Uppsala, 1967.
8. Boserup E., *"The Conditions of Agricultural Growth"*, The Economics of Agrarian Change Under Population Pressure, London, 1965.
9. Smith, P.E.L.,"Land Use, Settlement Patterns, and Subsistence Agriculture: A Demographic Perspective", in P.J.Ucko, R. Tringham and G. Dimbley (Edts.); Man, Settlement and Urbanism, London, 1972, pp. 409 - 425.
10. Boserup, E.; Population and Technology, Oxford, 1981.
11. Henry, Louis; Population Analysis and Models: Edward Arnold, Birkenhead: 1976.
12. Haupt, Arthur and Thomas, T. Kane : *Population Handbook*; Inc. Washington d.c., Population Reference bureau, 1980.

THREE

GROWTH AND DISTRIBUTION OF POPULATION IN THE WORLD

Among cultural factors, the study of population is of utmost significance. When the geographical analysis is conducted, the basic questions to be delineated are the number, distributional pattern and the controlling factors responsible for such a distribution of population.

For the human habitat, the varieties of physical and cultural environments have a varying impact on the living conditions of people, availability of food, protection from environmental hazards, taming of plants and animals, and the construction of shelters to safeguard against heat, cold and moisture.

Historically, a stage emerged when it was easier for some individuals or groups to move to new areas rather than to try within the existing culture. Hence, the beginning of migration brought about the spread of homosapien over most parts of the globe. In the process of migration, men encountered all sorts of physical environment, but only a few of them offered satisfactory habitats. Several parts of the globe were found to be uninhabitable until the cultural evolution made possible new ways of living. Even today, certain areas remain too undeveloped to support even temporary human living.

POPULATION NUMBERS

According to recent estimates (1987) the world population is somewhat over 5 billion. Of these, about 58 per cent are in Asia and 20 per cent in Europe, which together account for more than three-fourths of the population of the world. Africa has over 9 per cent, North America 7 per cent, South America 5 per cent and Australia 1 per cent of the world population.

Country-wise, the population of different countries, in 1981 was (in million) China 900, India 690, Japan 130, Bangladesh 70, Indonesia 30, Korea 50, Pakistan 60, Burma 30, Sri Lanka 10, United States 230 and Soviet Union 280. It is apparent that 50 per cent of the world's population resides in Southeast Asia alone. China alone has more than two times the population of the entire Western Hemisphere.

POPULATION GROWTH

In varying space and time, the world's population increases with varying rates. Moreover, the increase has been further accelerated especially during the past 125 years. Between 1850 and 1987, the world's population increased fourfold (1.17 billion to 5 billion) and it is estimated that by 2000 AD it will double again. For instance, in July 1982, the Statistics Bureau of China said the average annual increase of population since 1964 was 17 million, a yearly growth of 2.1 per cent. There were 30 million more men than women, or 106 males to every 100 females. Including children, there were 489 million females in comparison with 519 million males, a proportion of 48.5 per cent women to 51.5 per cent men.

In such a situation, if the increase in the world's population continues at the current rate, the figure will be 9 billion by 2000 AD. Every 30 seconds 117 babies are born in the world, 46 people die, the net increase being 71 new inhabitants. It means that each year there is and increase of 74 million people. Accordingly, in July 1987 the world's population was 5 billion. During the period 1980-84, the world's population increased at an annual rate of 1.7 per cent or at the rate of 17 persons per 1,000 population per annum.

Since 1972 the global population has increased from about 3.8 thousand million to an estimated 4.6 million in 1983. Most of this enormous and overwhelming rapid increase has occurred in the poor (the developing)nations, whose agricultural potential and natural environments have already been stressed to their limits and beyond. This spurt in population increase has been owing to the improvement in agricultural technology, industrial development, increased transportation linkages, improvement of nutrition and health care. This has also helped in lowering the mortality rate of children and life expectancy at birth (Table 3.1).

TABLE 3.1: TWO DECADES OF ECONOMIC DEVELOPMENT IN POOR COUNTRIES* WITH LARGE POPULATIONS

Country	Population (millions) 1979	GNP per capita average annual growth rate(%) 1960-1979	Life expectancy at birth 1960	1978
Bangladesh	88.9	0.1	43	49
Ethiopia	30.9	1.3	36	40
Burma	32.9	1.1	44	44
India	659.2	1.4	42	52
Vietnam	52.9	—	43	63
China	964.5	—	—	64
Pakistan	79.7	2.9	44	52
Tanzania	18.0	2.3	42	52
Zaire	27.5	0.7	40	47
Indonesia	142.9	4.1	39	53
Sudan	17.9	0.6	39	47
Egypt	38.9	3.4	46	57
Thailand	45.5	4.6	51	62
Phillipines	46.7	2.6	51	62
Nigeria	82.6	3.7	39	49
Peru	17.1	1.7	48	58
Morocco	19.5	2.6	47	56
Colombia	26.1	3.0	56	63
South Korea	17.5	3.5	54	63
Turkey	44.2	3.8	51	62
North Korea	37.8	7.1	54	63
Algeria	18.2	2.4	47	56
Mexico	65.5	2.7	58	66
South Africa	28.5	2.3	53	61
Brazil	116.5	4.8	55	63
Romania	22.1	9.2	65	71

* GNP per capita of less than US $2,000 in 1979

AFRICA'S FASTEST GROWING POPULATION

Since 1940, the world population has grown by over 50 per cent to 4.6 billion persons and will have reached 10 billion by the middle of the 21st century. These figures are quoted in a study recently published by the Population Reference Bureau, a private American organisation. The latest statistics of the United States reveal that Africa will be the most densely populated region in the world by the end of the 21st century. Population growth in the industrial countries and particularly in Europe is stagnating. In the Federal Republic of Germany, for instance, population is expected to decline by one-third between 1982 and 2020 AD.

Africa has the highest average growth rate of population of 2.9 per cent compared with 2.5 per cent in China, 2.9 per cent in India, 2.3 per cent in Latin America, 0.7 per cent in North America and 1.9 per cent in Asia. Nigeria's population alone will have trebled by 2020 AD to reach 258.1 million. Kenya has the highest average growth rate in Africa with 3.9 per cent followed by Libya with 3.5 per cent.

The population explosion in the Third World is held to be one of the most serious threats to successful development. In most States, the growth of food production, gross national product or productivity lags far behind population growth, resulting in a shortage of food supply. While it is possible to grow sufficient food stuffs on the existing crop land to prevent starvation, this would necessarily presuppose fundamental agricultural reforms.

THE ECONOMIC IMPACT OF POPULATION GROWTH

It has been found that in developing countries with high population concentration, per capita income is very low at about $130 per annum, whereas in developed countries it is very high at $1815 (Table 3.2). Hence, it is clear that there must be more equitable and effective sharing of the benefits of growth within both groups of developing and developed countries. The question is: how can the basic needs be satisfied if absolute poverty is to be overcome? The answers vary from country to country, culture to culture and from society to society. The possible solutions include:

a. Food with sufficient nutritional value to avoid the debilitating effects of malnutrition, and to meet the physical requirements of a productive life;

b. Shelter and clothing to ensure reasonable protection against the rigours of climate and environment; and

c. Public services that make available education, clean water and health care that all members of society need if they are to become fully productive.

Poverty which results from increasing population can also be tackled by enhancing productivity. This can be done by providing better access to credit, extension assistance and production inputs. The experience of Malaysia, Kenya, Malawi, Taiwan, Koera, Nigeria and other countries demonstrates that the productivity of small farms can be significantly enhanced through such programmes and the World Bank is committed to achieve this objective through its new rural development projects.

TABLE 3.2 GROWTH OF GNP IN DEVELOPING COUNTRIES

Region	Population (millions) 1975	Percentage Annual growth rate(%) 1951-1975	GNP per capita ($) 1950	1975
South Asia	830	1.8	85	130
East Asia	337	3.9	170	435
Sub-Saharan Africa	309	2.0	175	285
Latin America	309	2.6	550	1050
North Africa and Middle East	158	5.0	385	1300
Southeren Europe	117	4.9	555	1815

Source: Economic Impact,No. 31, 1978,p.83.

Table 3.2 shows that in 1975 the regions with large populations such as South Asia (830 million) are those with low per capita incomes in comparison with regions in other parts of the globe. Among developing countries, the lowest population has been found in Southern Europe (117 million) even if the annual growth rate is as high as 4.4 per cent and the per capita income is also highest ($1815) in 1975. What this means in effect is that in developing countries it is the rate of population growth which nullifies the pace of economic as well as planned development of the region.

POPULATION DISTRIBUTION

The distribution of population over the globe is most uneven.

The Himalayan mountains, the Antarctic and several other isolated islands in the world's oceans are entirely devoid of permanent human habitation. On the other hand, the island of Java has more than 2000 persons per square kilometre. These variations in the density of population are responsible for significant variations in cultural patterns and population distribution.

In the entire world, there are four clusters of population:
Eastern Asia, Southern Asia, Western Europe and East-Central North America.

Sparse population density is found in the greater part of Australia, the central and northern portion of Asia, the northern fringe of Europe, the Saharan portion of Africa, the northern portion of North America and the interior of South America. The cold lands of the world, the hot deserts and the Amazon Basin of South America and the Congo Basin of Africa are conspicuously empty.

AREAS OF HIGH CONCENTRATION

In Eastern Asia the three islands if Japan, the coastal regions of Korea, southern Manchurian, the North China Plain, the basins along the Yangtze River and the lower valley of Si River phenomenal number of people. According to July 1982 Census, the population of New China was 1,301,882,511 including Taiwan, British colony of Hong-Kong and Macao of South China. The number of people enrolled in the Chinese armed forces is 4.23 million. The Chinese population has grown by 314 million in eight years since the last census in 1964.

Near the Chinese coast, Western Taiwan and Northern Hainan are also areas of high population concentration. In Indonesia, a high density is found in Java, south-western Celebes, and the north-western Phillipines. In India, high density of population is found in the North Gangetic Plains, Malabar coast in the west and Caromandel coast in the east.

Most of the peoples of Asia are rural (73%) and their livelihood depends upon intensive cultivation of well-watered or irrigable alluvial lands. These areas are rather the result of an even spread of agricultural villages over the alluvial plain land. In Burma, the delta and the middle valley of the Irrawaddy are the foci; in Thailand, the lower valley of the Chao Phraya stands out; in South Vietnam, the delta of the Mekong and the small coastal plains on the South China Sea forms the centres of population concentration. In Java, high population density is found on the coastal plains and volcanic soils of exceptional fertility that play an important role in population distribution.

In Europe, high concentration is found around the southern end of the North Sea. In the British Isles, London forms the main centre. In the mainland of Europe, a heavily populated coastal zone extends from the south of the Siene in France to the mouth of the Elbe in Germany. From this coastal strip the zone of greatest numbers reaches island, along the southern margin of the plain of North Europe, into the Ukraine and southwards, along the Rhine River, into Switzerland. Besides this, there are major population concentrations found around Moscow and in the Po valley of northern Italy.

The third area of population concentration lies in the eastern part of North America. The greatest number of people live within the triangle whose points are Boston, Washington and Chicago. In the western part, the high concentrations are found in the Puget Sound-Willamatte Valley, the San Francisco embayment and the Los Angles area. Population density in North America varies from under four persons per square kilometre in the Rocky Mountains and the Canadian North through medium density in the central part of 100th meridian from north to south to higher density of more than 100 persons per square kilometre in the north-eastern lake side, Aplachian Plateau and coastal belts of New England and St. Lawrence river basin.

In the Southern part of USSR near the Black Sea, high concentration is found in areas of Chernozem soil and in Europe, the Flanders Plain, the Rhine delta, the middle Rhine-Ruhr area and the area around Dresden in Germany.

AREAS OF EXTREMELY LOW POPULATION DENSITY

The Antarctica is an area of zero population density per square kilometre in terms of permanent inhabitants. The situation is the same in the inner part of Greenland. Coastal areas have a density of two persons per square kilometre. The Atlantic Coast of North Africa, Arabia, Western Manchuria are also areas of scanty population. A similar condition is to be found in eastern and northern Siberia, over the Arctic fringe of Europe. In these areas the density is low on account of the lack of accessibility in the extreme climatic conditions.

Almost the same conditions of population distribution are to be found in southwest Africa, western parts of Australia, Patagonian portion of Argentina, the Great Basin and Rio-Grande areas of North America. In Alaska, Canada and Labrador owing to Sub-arctic and Tundra climates, sparse population density is found. In South America the Andean Plateaus, Guinea highlands and the Amazon basin are areas of very low population density.

WORLD'S URBAN POPULATION

The urban population on the globe has doubled in the past thirty years to 1800 million, so that four out of every ten persons live in the urban areas. The demographers at the United Nations characterise the movement to the cities as "the greatest mass migration in human history". If their projections materialise, more than half of the world's population will be living in cities in 2000 AD.

The population density found in cities presents dangers to human health in the form of epidemics. waterborne diseases and the concentration of wastes. Overcoming these dangers has required both ingenuity and substantial investment. All these have a profound impact on the size and the functioning of modern cities and questions are quite often raised about their long-term viability.

The trend of urban population growth in the past 30 years has been towards larger and larger metropolitan agglomerations, with an increasing concentration of people in the largest centres. In 1950 the combined population of all the "giant cities" - those with five million or more residents - was 47 million. In 1982 the "giant cities" had a population of 252 million, a figure that the United Nations projects will reach 650 million by the year 2000 AD. It is the poor cities in the developing countries which face the most serious difficulties in providing people with a decent level of living.

CURRENT TRENDS

Big cities have become a dominant aspect of modern living, witnessing a phenomenal growth rate. The city of five million people did not even exist until the beginning of twentieth century, apart from London. By the mid-century, six cities had five million people. In the eighties, there are 26 cities with a population of five million each and the United Nations predicts that there will be 60 such cities by 2000 AD. As the cities have increased in absolute number, they have also increased their share of the world's population. In 1920, only 14 per cent of the global population lived in the urban areas, but in 1982, 43 per cent of the world's population lived in cities. By the year 2000 AD, if this trend continues, the world will have an urban majority amounting to 3200 million people.

TABLE 3.3 URBAN POPULATION AS PROPORTION OF TOTAL WORLD POPULATION, 1980

Region	Population Living in Urban Areas (%)
North America	74
Australia	71
Europe	69
USSR	62
South America	61
Asia	27
Africa	26
Less Developed Countries	29
More Developed Countries	69
World	39

Source: Population Reference Bureau. Those figures are for urban population as defined by individual countries. The total is slightly lower than the UN/World Bank figure of 41%.

Table 3.3 shows that the highest percentage (74%) of Urban population is found in North America where the growth of towns and cities has been great. This means that in North America only 26 per cent of the people live in rural settlements of a dispersed type. The level of urbanisation in Australia is 71 per cent and in Europe it is 69 per cent. In Australia most of the white European migrants preferred to live in towns and cities of the coastal areas, whereas in Europe industrial development has heightened the growth of urbanisation. Asia (27%) and Africa (26%) are least urbanised continents because sedentary agricultural practices are more prevalent, the result being that 75 to 95 per cent of the population lives in the rural areas, and a marginal 5 to 25 per cent in urban centres of diffused character.

One of the most pressing problems of the world today is the rapid growth of cities: by the end of the century urban population will out number the rural population for the first time in human history. The cutting edge of this process is seen in the countless bustees and kampongs, favelas and ranchos of the Third World's swelling cities, where it is estimated that 75000 people arrive daily, creating massive needs for shelter, employment, clean water, health care and other services.

Table 3.3 shows that already most countries are predominantly urban. The present global figure for urbanisation is greatly affected by the figures of bulk rural population for the giant countries of Asia - Bangladesh, China, India, Indonesia, Japan, Korea. Burma, Malaysia, Thailand and Pakistan - that have low urbanisation levels, and more than half of the world's population live in these countries.

In China, in July 1982, over 800 million people were peasents while 207 million people lived in China's towns and cities. The urban population rose from 18.4 per cent in 1964 to 20.6 per cent in 1982. The population of Shanghai is 11.9 million, whereas the population of greater Shanghai is 16.9 million which includes the sprawling suburbs and the surrounding countryside of the municipality. Peking has a population of 5.6 million whereas greater Peking has 9.2 million.

The port city of Tianjen has a population of 7.8 million, of whom 5.1 million live in the urban core of metropolis. The highest population of 99.7 million was found in Sichuan State.

The phenomenal growth of urban population today is fueled not only by longer life spans but also by natural increase and migration. Four out of ten city dwellers are migrants. In Sub-Saharan Africa, where most of the cities are relatively small but growing very rapidly, migration from rural areas has a significant influence on city growth, whereas natural increase is more important in the Indian sub-continent and southeast Asia. The chief reason for the migration from the countryside, however, is not the attraction to urban amenities but the urban economy.

Barbara Ward[4] has written that the greatest "wandering of the people" in all of history, and our attempt "to get a coherent grip on the issue of the human habitat" is exceedingly difficult, since this habitat includes all aspects of human life.

CONCLUSIONS

It has been found that the world's population has been growing slowly but perceptibly over the years. A day will come when there will be a global explosion of population, but the question that crops up is: where will the food come from? One view is that the oceans which cover three-fourths of the Earth will be the source of food. Northern view suggests that with such a tremendous increase in population, the ice-cover of the North and the South poles together with the mountainous regions will melt, leading to a vast scale of marine transgression over the earth's surface. A large per cent of the world's population will die, and after the regression of the sea, a fresh civilization will start.

REFERENCES

1. Africa, 7th August 1982, p.32.
2. Kendall H.M. , Glendinning R.M. and MacFadden; *Introduction to Geography*; New York, Harcourt-Brace and World, Inc.; 1967 pp.371-373.
3. Newland K.; "City Limits", *Economic Impact* (1981/1) pp. 74-77.
4. Thornley Allan ; "Cida's Support for Human Settlements in Asia", Development Directions, May/June 1979, p. 7.

FOUR

THE CONCEPTS OF POPULATION PRESSURE

The concentration per capita availability of net sown area, and the density of population multiplied by the rate of population growth per thousand are among some of the measures of population pressures in a region.

The pressure of population, that is, the number of persons supported by land largely depends on the external environment and its utilization for human living. However, the term "population pressure" can often be misleading, as an agricultural region can support a larger number of people than a pastoral one, while an industrialized region can support a still larger number of persons than can an agricultural one. The concept of optimum population relates to the ideal number of people who can be sustained in a given area, in contrast to situations of overpopulation and underpopulation. Population explosion refers to the twentieth century worldwide trend of enormous and rapid population growth resulting from a birth rate which is much higher than the death rate. Population implosion, on the other hand, means a change in the distribution of population from a pattern of thinly dispersed groups dependent upon a variety of environments to relatively densely settled industrial or agricultural communities. Urbanization is the principal modern process of population implosion. Such an example is clearly found from the Rocky areas of North America to New England in the north-eastern part where maximum urban development has taken place.

OVER POPULATION, OPTIMUM POPULATION AND UNDER POPULATION

These three measures of population pressure are relative terms which may change in spatio-temporal dimensions, depending upon the demand patterns of the people and the economic development of an area. Let us suppose that there are three areas each having 100 hectares of land. In the first case, if 100 hectares of land has a capacity to provide the sustenance to 500 people we may call it an area of optimum population. In the second case, if 100 hectares support less than 500 people, then underpopulation exits, while if more than 500 people live over the same 100 hectares, a situation of over population arises (Fig. 4.1)

The situation, may, however, vary under different environments. For instance, in the case of a forest economy there may be only 100 persons per 100 hectares of land and yet the area may be considered over populated, because the forest area has the capacity to sustain much fewer persons.

Again, in an agricultural economy there may exist an optimum population with 500 persons living comfortably; while an industrial economy which has a capacity to support more than 500 people will be underpopulated. The fact is that an industrial economy can always support a larger number of people in comparison with forest and agricultural economies.

In view of what has just been said, if one wants to increase the population supporting capacity of a region, it is possible to convert the forest economy into an agricultural, commercial agriculture or an industrial one. So far as the agricultural economy is concerned, it may be transformed into either a commercial agriculture or an industrial one. In case of an industrial economy, the population supporting capacity may be raised by the diversification of the production, increasing the infrastructure facilities and industrial linkages.

Generally, "over population" is synonymous with poverty in crowded countries. However, when demographers speak about over-population or under-population, they have to first decide what the optimum (best) number is for the country. The French demographer Sauvy neatly summed up the relativity of the concept when he defined optimum population as "that which best assures the realization of a predetermined objective".[1]

The difficulties of defining optimum population have led other demographers to focus attention on another measure - the optimum rate of growth. This concept is more practical and useful one because it relates annual population increase to the index figures for production, capital formation, consumption or facilities such as housing, schools and other social services. This measure provides a clearer view of what ia an optimal population growth, because it links it to the immediate objectives of progress. Nevertheless, there remains the debatable assumption that in each country the "national goals" are agreed upon by the entire population.[2]

THEORY OF OPTIMUM POPULATION GROWTH

For the better part of the nineteenth century, food output and income per capita rose faster than population, which itself was increasing rapidly. Contemporaries believed that technological progress and investment, neither of which were considered by Malthus, had in fact invalidated his theory. Towards the end of the 20th century, there was renewed concern about the population growth but economists were interested, not in the inevitability of overpopulation, but in what could be considered the best or optimum population for the country to have. This was done by applying the newly discovered principles of marginal analysis to the relationships between output and population.[3]

Given resources, technology and capital, optimum population seeks to maximise output per head. If population is less than the average, output is less than the maximum, and any increase in the population will result in an increase in the total output, average output and, in some cases, marginal output. This is owing to the existence of increasing returns to the extra-labour inputs; the existence of such a condition has not ben widely investigated but presumably occurs in sparsely populated, recently settled areas, where extra population would allow improvements in transport, the spread of general overhead costs among a greater population, and the use of part of the population to clear new land for cultivation or to improve irrigation. One writer has argued that parts of Africa are underpopulated rather than overpopulated.[4]

At optimum population, marginal product equals average product per head but thereafter any increase in population caused output per head to decliner and marginal product falls below average output. At any population above the optimum level, diminishing return is operating, and although total output increases, output per head falls, because in terms of the optimum theory the country is overpopulated. However, at population level which are higher than the optimum, two special types of over population may be recognized. When population reaches the stage of overpopulation, marginal product is zero; with any subsequent addition to the work force each extra worker contributes a negative marginal product. Further, between optimum population and overpopulation any reduction in population would produce an increase in output per head. Modern economists have described those workers whose marginal product is zero as surplus population--a measure of underemployment. There have been many attempts to measure the degree of underemployment in contemporary Asian countries.[5]

When marginal productivity reaches zero, any further increase in population leads to a fall in total output as marginal productivity becomes negative: eventually average output per head falls to the subsistence level. Any further increase in population will lead to a rise in mortality. This point is clearly similar to the definition of overpopulation which can be derived from the Malthusi an theory where population growth is halted by rising mortality, and an equilibrium position is reached where fertility and mortality rates are equal.

The concept of optimum population then allows us to derive three definitions of overpopulation. In general terms any country is overpopulated which has a population greater than the optimum and thus an average output per head lower than the maximum possible. Two special cases can be identified. First beyond optimum population there is under-employment, which means that the removal of surplus population would lead to an increase in output per head. Second, in case of overpopulation marginal product becomes zero and not only does average output per head fall, but marginal productivity becomes negative and the total output declines.

The theory of optimum population has been criticized on the ground that it deals only with a static situation; as population increase beyond the optimum extra resources may be employed or a new technology adopted so that diminishing returns are offset and average output per head increases. But perhaps the major criticism is that the optimum population of an actual country has never been satisfactorily measured.

THE MEASUREMENT OF RURAL OVER-POPULATION

Several attempts have been made to measure rural overpopulation. In the 1930's investigations were made in eastern Europe, an area which was believed by many contemporary economists to be overpopulated. Two contrasting approaches to measure rural over population may be identified the production approach and the consumption approach.

Production Approach

The production approach is best exemplified by the work of W.B. Moore.[6] He calculated the net volume of agricultural output for each country in Europe in 1931-35 and expressed this in standard crop units. He estimated an index of productivity for Europe by dividing the total standard crop units by the total male labour force, and from this he worked out the number of workers needed to produce the output of each country. He then took the productivity of France as the norm and divided a second series of surplus population. As the agricultural productivity of France was higher the European mean seemed to be greater than in the first case. In both cases, countries with a surplus agricultural population were confined to eastern and southern Europe.

Consumption Approach

The second method of defining rural overpopulation is the consumption approach. Here an attempt is made to define the number of people that can be supported in a given area at a given standard of living. A good example of this approach is the work of Sen Gupta.[7], who calculated an index of population pressure for 335 districts in India in 1961. This index was:

$$1 = \frac{P - P_i}{A}$$

where 1 is the population pressure per km.^{2}, P_i is the number of rural inhabitants who could be supported at a given income per head, P is the actual rural population, and A is the total area in km.^{2}.

P_1 was determined by $P_1 = X/K$, where X was the gross value of agricultural production in the district, while K was the defined income. Sen Gupta took K to be the average earnings for those engaged in primary activities plus an amount 'needed to obtain a slight improvements in the standard of living'. From these calculations a relative measure of overpopulation and underpopulation for India has been obtained.

Neither the production nor the consumption approach compared the actual population with the optimum population: attempts to define overpopulation in terms of consumption have been apt to compare actual consumption levels with the subsistence and or near subsistence level rather than with an optimum consumption level. The surplus population has thus been far less if the comparisons were made with the maximum average output per head.

Two types of surplus population were recognized by P.N. Rosenstein-Rodan. In the first type, the number surplus to requirements with the existing agricultural technology is calculated. A second dynamic type is defined as the number surplus to requirements if an improved technology were to be introduced into the area.[8] This is clearly similar to the production approach pursued by W.E. Moore when he compared the labour available in each country with the labour which would be needed if French agricultural technology is in use.

CARRYING CAPACITY

'Carrying capacity' is known as the maximum sustainable size of a resident population in a given ecosystem. However, the term 'carrying capacity of the land' has a broader connotation because it recognizes other resources as well as agricultural production. Its focus restricted to the potential relationship between the environmental content of an area and its population. The evaluation of the carrying capacity of any region is meaningful in the geographical sense because it has a close relationship with the nature of population pressure found in an area.

Various attempts have been made by agronomists, geographers and anthropologists to measure the carrying capacity of parts of the tropics where shifting cultivation or bush fallowing is practiced.

Carrying capacity is defined as the maximum number of people that an area can sustain at a given subsistence level without the on set of land degradation. W. Allan,[9] one of the pioneer workers in this field, assumed that the inherent physical characteristics of the land determined the length of fallow. He then determined, by survey methods of the area that can be cultivated and the amount of fallow necessary to allow the regeneration of vegetation and hence soil fertility. From these data he calculated the area of crops and fallow necessary for a given soil type, and concequently the carrying capacity as a density. This could then he compared with the actual density. Similar calculations have been made for parts of Brazil and the New Guinea Highlands.

About these early works, there have been criticisms of the method and attempts to expand the concept in order to incorporate differing concepts of subsistence and varying levels of labour intensity.[10]

SIGNS OF OVERPOPULATION

The approaches of defining rural overpopulation so far discussed have received more criticism than praise.[11] This is because, they have not been based on any statistical information. Therefore many historians who describe contemporary events, rely on the existing evidences of overpopulation, adverse features of land use, and structure and technology which have been developed owing to population growth. However, these diagnostic characteristics may be the result of some other economic forces, such as the subdivision of fields, rising land values, rising prices of agricultural products, an increasing landless population, unemployment and falling real wages, retardation of technology, land use changes, an inferior diet and the use of marginal land after reclamation.

"The relative overpopulation becomes so much more apparent in a country, the more the Capitalist mode of production is developed in it. This, again, is the reason why, on the one hand, the more or less, imperfect subordination of labour to capital continues in many branches of production, and continues longer than seems at first glance compatible with the general stage of development. This is due to the cheapness and abundance of disposable or unemployed wage-labourers, and to the greater resistance, which some branches of production, by their very nature, render to the transformation of manual work into machine production. On the other hand, new lines of production are opened up, especially for the production of luxuries, and on this basis the relative overpopulation measured, often set free in other lines of production through the increase of their constant capital.[12]

PRESSURE OF POPULATION IN NORTH BIHAR

Generally, areas devoted to more intensive land use always develop a 'population pressure'. As is the case in North Bihar. The region supports a very large population which retards progress and is responsible for the operation of the vicious circle of economic stagnation and poverty.

In order to measure the pressure of population in northern Bihar, a concept of demographic coefficient has been employed.[13] It is an index designed to provide a measure of future population pressure in any region, for example, c = dR, where c is the demographic coefficient, d is the density of population per square kilometre, and R is the net reproduction rate. The same index after two generations is $c = dR^2$. Another formula for demographic coefficient is c = dt, where t represents the rate of natural increase per 1000 inhabitants.

On the basis of median and quartile, four categories of pressure areas have been demarcated. The first area is above the Q3 zone having 1,12,800 pressure value. The second zone lies in between

1,12,800 to 85,000. The third zone lies between 85,000 and 65,000 and the fourth zone is the area below 65,000 pressure value. The areas of high population pressure are found from Kishanganj in the north to Purnea in the south in a curvilinear narrow belt. The second zone begins from the north of Munger city to Begusarai and Barauni area. Except for the northern part of Sitamarhi district, the whole of Muzaffarpur and the old Darbhanga districts including Gopalganj are areas of high population pressure.

Low population pressure is found in Saran, Siwan, northwest Champaran and the northern part of Madhubani, especially Laukana, Laukahi and Ladania anchals. The entire Kosi belt is an area of low population pressure owing to the ravages caused by the Kosi river each and every year.

In Table 4.1, the pressure of population in North Bihar in terms of the availability of per capita net sown area has been shown. Per capita land above 0.17 hectare is found in Saran, Vaishali and Darbhanga districts whereas 0.13-0.16 hectare is found in Gopalgaris, Sitamarhi, Muzaffarpur, Madhubani and Begusarai districts. In these areas the land has been cultivated up to the farthest limit, hence in spite of high population density relatively better condition is found in comparison with East Champaran and Katihar districts where below 0.10 hectare per capita NSA is found. This adverse condition prevails on account of floods, waterlogging and the deposition of sand which make the land unfit for cultivation throughout the year.

TABLE 4.1 **PRESSURE OF POPULATION IN NORTH BIHAR (1981)**

Districts	Population in'00000	Net Sown Area in '000ha.	Gross Sown Area in '000ha.	Per Capita NSA	Per Capita GSA
Begusarai	11.47	131	186	0.11	0.16
Gopalganj	11.17	152	238	0.13	0.21
N.Bhagalpur	03.30	50	61	0.15	0.25
Katihar	09.42	169	236	0.17	0.25
Darbhanga	15.17	139	188	0.09	0.12
East Chamaparan	19.24	343	432	0.18	0.22
West Chamaparan	15.87	271	410	0.17	0.26
Madhubani	18.92	252	344	0.13	0.18
Khagaria	07.45	142	172	0.19	0.23
Muzaffarpur	19.09	237	232	0.12	0.17

Purnea	30.00	500	733	0.17	0.24
Saharsa	23.50	347	521	0.15	0.22
Samastipur	18.85	194	283	0.10	0.15
Saran	20.33	186	290	0.09	0.14
Sitamarhi	15.83	196	288	0.12	0.18
Siwan	11.27	173	297	0.15	0.26
Vaishali	13.49	138	198	0.10	0.15

Source: Department of Statistics and Evaluation, Government of Bihar, Patna.

LAND DISTRIBUTION IN OVERPOPULATED AREAS

The two alternative strategies for dealing with the population problems and land problem of a village have been employed. These will be based on the population projection of the village. Therefore, it is essential to project population after ten years interval by using the following formulae used in village viability assessment (V V A):

$$P_{future} = P_{now}\, 1 + \frac{Growth\,Rate}{100}$$

Therefore

$$P_{1992} = 1900\; 1 + \frac{3}{100}$$

$$= 1900\; 1 + 0.03$$

Take logs

$$\mathrm{Log}^{P}_{1992} = \log 1900 + 10 \log(1.03)$$

$$= 3.2788 + 10 \times 0.0128$$

$$= 3.2788 + 0.128$$

$$= 3.4068$$

$$P_{1992} = Anti\log 3.4068$$

$$P_{1992} = 2553\; population\; by\; 1992.$$

Therefore, the population after ten years, that is, in 1992 will be 2553 and there will be 511 families which consist of five resident members. This means an increase of 131 families by 1992 as opposed to 380 families in 1982.

According to the village viability assessment principle, each family must have 1.5 acres of land. Given 380 families in 1982, the amount of lánd cultivated is 570 acres at a population growth of 3% . Therefore, 511 families will need to cultivate 776.5 acres by the year 1992. Unfortunately the village has only a total of 770 acres of land. the following alternative has been suggested to the Regional Economic and planning Committee:

ALTERNATIVE 1: POPULATION CONTROL STRATEGY

In order to solve the problem of overpopulation it is essential to reduce the growth rate of population to a maximum limit of 2.5%, instead of the present growth rate of 3%. In the first five years of the planning horizon of ten years, the growth rate should be kept at 2.5%, and in the next five years it should be kept at 2%.

This suggestion is supported by the following formulae which will reduce the population growth to 2.5%.

$$P_{future} = P_{now}\, 1 + \frac{Growth\ Rate}{100}(future - now)\, years)$$

$$P_{1992} = 1900\, 1 + \frac{2.5}{100}(1992 - 1982)$$

$$= 1900\, 1 + 0.25^{(10)}$$

Take logs

$$logs\, P_{1992} = \log 1900 + 10 \log(1.025)$$

$$= 3.2788 + 10 \times 0.0107$$

$$= 3.3858$$

$$P_{1992} = Antilog\, 33858$$

$$= P_{1992} = 2431$$

If the population growth rate is reduced to 2.5%, there will be 2431 people and, therefore, 486 families will be able to cultivate 729 acres of land by 1992. This shows that further reduction in the growth rate of population is required by means of family planning measures.

This population control strategy through reduced growth rate must be done in the following ways. First, by encouraging family planning in all families through mass education and campaigns mainly by UMATI and MCH. By People should be made aware of the disadvantages of having large families, as it result in land fragmentation and therefore smaller size of plots owned by each family.

Second, various incentives should be introduced to ensure that family planning is adhered to. Child labour should be discouraged so that people do not consider having more children a potential source of labour. Two children per family should be considered the maximum member for a normal family. In fact, tax relief could be given to families with two children or under, while taxes could be levied on those families having more than two children. This will ensure that 1.5 acres of land will suffice for each family at a population growth rate of 2.5% (1982–1987) and (1987–1992) respectively. Therefore, with the population control strategy each family will be assured at least 1.5 acres of land for the planning horizon of ten years whereby traditional rights of land inheritance will be maintained.

ALTERNATIVE 2 : COLLECTIVISATION STRATEGY

The second alternative that can be adopted is collection; it is widely applied in Socialist countries. Collectivisation ensures that there is equal distribution of land among all families in a village. This implies that all the 770 acres of land should be brought under the ownership of the village (communally owned). In the process of collectivisation each family will guaranteed 1.5 acres, that is, 0.5 acre used for residential and food crop production (banana and vegetables) exclusively for individual use. The amount of land for this purpose will be 190 acres. Then there will be one acre for each family for communal production. In 1982 the total land used by the 380 families was 570 acres. The remaining 200 acres will have to be assigned to the increasing population and those who return to the village on retirements for the whole planning horizon of ten years.

Various methods will have to be employed to see that the collectivisation strategy through land distribution may succeed. First of all the government has to play a crucial role. In order to politicise the people so that they become aware of the usefulness of collectivisation, various campaigns will have to be launched by the government.

The second method will be the provision of incentives of various sorts. People should be assured of aid and assistance from the Government after collectivisation. They should be provided with ploughs, hybrid seeds, insecticides in order to improve farm production efficiency.

The third method should be to use the law, to prohibit further fragmentation of land below one-and-a-half acres per family. In case there are additional families they should be encouraged to engage in forestry job, bee keeping or small-scale industries.

Finally, there is need to establish a machinery composed mainly of a village manager, village chairman and elected ten cell leader (Balozi) all of whom compress development committee. Their role will be to work closely with the people in the overall development of the village, so as to ensure high productivity efficiency in the land allocated to each family and help in raising the general standard of living of the people of a village in Tanzania.

LEVEL OF LIVING

The level of living relates to existing standard of living according to the cultural image of a society. This distiction helps to understand the true nature of population pressure in many underdeveloped countries. Even if the production of underdeveloped countries meets the bare necessities of life, but population growth and the awareness that other people have higher standards of living creates a feeling of deprivation among people of the developing world. To alleviate such feelings requires higher production, per capita well above mere provision of food. But the point is that fast population growth can nullifies the gains in production eliminating all hopes for a more comfortable life. Such frustrations may led to social unrest or even class war between the rich and the poor.

CONCLUSIONS

It may be concluded that the pressure of population in any region may be measured in terms of underpopulation, optimum population and overpopulation. Besides providing a conceptual framework an attempt has been made to measure population pressure in North Bihar; further delineations have been made regarding the signs of population pressure, and the resulting problems of land distribution and the standard of living.

REFERENCES

1. Sauvy, A. *Theories generale de la Population*, Vol. 2 Paris, 1954, p. 221.
2. Broek, Jan O.M. and John W. Webb, *A Geography of Mankind*, New York, 1968.
3. Peacock, A.T., 'Economic Theory and the Concept of an Optimum', in J.B. Craggs, and N.W. Pirie (eds.), The Numbers of Man and Animals, Institute of Biology, London, 1955, pp. 1 - 7.
4. Stryker, J.D., Optimum Population in rural areas, empirical evidence from the France zone', *Quarterly Journal of Economics*; vol. 91 (1977) 177 - 93.
5. Robinson, W. C., 'Types of disquised rural underemployment and Some Policy implications', *Oxford Economic Papers* 21 (1969) 373 - 86
6. More, W.E., *The Economic Demography of Eastern and Southern Europe*; Geneva, 1945.
7. Sen Gupta, P. 'Population and Resource Development in India', in W. Zelinsky, L. Kasinski and R. Mangell Prothero (eds.), *Geography and a Crowing World*; Oxford, 1970, pp. 424 - 41.
8. Robenstein-Rodan, P.N. 'Disguised Unemployment and Underemployment in Agriculture', *Monthly Bulletin of Agricultural Economics and Statistics* 6 (1957), 1-7.
9. Allan, W., *The African Husbandman*, Edinburgh, 1965.
10. Carneiro, R.L. 'From Autonomous Villages to the State, a numerical estimate' in B. Spooner (ed.), *Population Growth: Anthropological Implications* (Boston, 1972); pp. 64 - 74.
11. Grigg, D.B. 'Population Pressure and Agricultural Change', *Progress in Geography*, 8 (1976), 135 - 76.
12. Marx, Karl, *Capital Moscow,* Progress, 1977,
13. Mandal, R. B., *Planned Development of Rural Settlements*; New Delhi, Concept, (1982)

Fig. 4.1

All the three have the capacity to give sustenance to 500 people, respectively

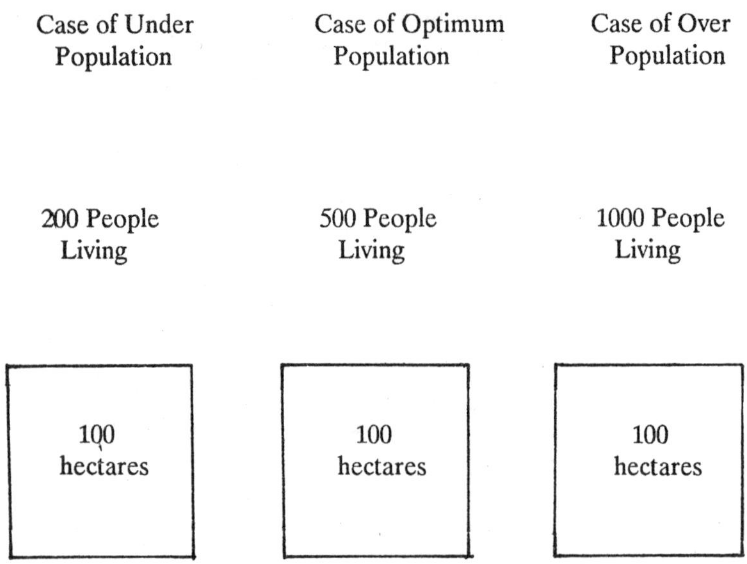

FIVE

DATA SOURCES AND INTRODUCTORY METHODS

The main sources of statistical data on population are: (a) censuses, (b) sample surveys, and (c) registration of migration and vital events, such as births, deaths, marriages and divorces.

CENSUSES AND SAMPLE SURVEYS

In accordance with international agreement a census is an enumeration of the population in a given area at a given time. Specific questions may be asked pertaining to certain characteristics of each person (age, sex, marital status, etc.) at the time the count is made. Thus, censuses provide data on the number and composition of population at a given time. Data on the number of persons in each subdivision of the area show the geographical distribution of population.

Sample surveys of the population may be undertaken to obtain information about certain groups, such as school/going age children, or to obtain information about the entire population on a sample basis. Special inquiries on population characteristics are described in Unit II of the Atlantica case study.

Censuses and sample surveys usually provide a general picture of the population at a given point of time. Sometimes, however, questions may be asked in a census or in a sample survey to obtain dynamic population data, such as the number of children born to each woman who is enumerated (a question asked to obtain information on past fertility), or the place of residence at some earlier date (asked to obtain data on migration).

REGISTRATION OF VITAL EVENTS AND MIGRATION

The occurrences most commonly registered are births, deaths, marriages, divorces, and international migratory movements. Statistics are compiled from such registers at intervals to measure the amount and rate of change in the population.

Census or survey data on the number and characteristics of the inhabitants at a particular time, and registration data on events occurring throughout a period, can be used together in demographic analysis to measure change in the population. The basic formula for estimating the total population of an area at any given moment is as follows: the population equals the number of persons at the time of the latest census, plus the number born since that time, minus the number that have died, plus the number that have migrated into the area. Registration data are most commonly used in combination with census or other data on the number of inhabitants to form rates or ratios. In the absence of usable registration data vital rates may be estimated from census data under some conditions. By the same time, registration data may be used in conjunction with census data for earlier dates to estimate the present composition of a population.

POPULATION REGISTERS

Some of the European countries, notably Denmark, Finland, Netherlands, Norway, and Sweden, and some Asian countries, have maintained population registers on a current basis for many decades. Recently, other European countries have advocated the establishment of population registers. In these registers are recorded the name, address, and some data on the characteristics of each individual in the population. Periodically, statistical reports containing information similar to that published in census reports may be compiled from such registers.

In countries which have population registers, generally every person gets registered at birth in the community of residence. A record is maintained there, listing the occurrence of all changes in the civil status and family composition. If he moves to another community, an official transcript of his birth and current civil and family status is sent to the new community.

To the extent that reporting is complete, population registers can provide the same data as population censuses. The difficulty is that reporting is seldom complete, because reliance is placed on the individual; and failure to report, especially on changes of residence, can lead to large errors over an extended period of time.

Most countries which maintain population registers also take population censuses at regular intervals. The census questionnaires are then used to correct and bring up-to-date information in the registers, especially with respect to the change of residence, though information on additions to the family and changes in marital status are also obtained. At the same time, the register is used to check and complete information of the census questionnaires regarding age, relationship with the head of household, etc.

Another difficulty with data from population registers is that definitions and concepts may differ from those needed for population research. For example, the old population registration system of Japan considered a person to belong to the place in which his family home was situated long with the resident of a new district according to the modern census definition.[1]

Apparently population registers have always been established primarily for purposes of administrative control, though in the case of those countries that have maintained population registers for centuries the original purposes may have been forgotten or revised. Among modern nations they have been established in recent years for such administrative purposes as food rationing, house rationing, settlement programmes, etc.

It seems that the quantity of administrative detail and office work required for recording each change of residence and status in modern mobile population involves too much expenditure of time and effort for population registers to be maintained for purely statistical purposes.

VITAL STATISTICS

By 'vital statistics' are meant the number of births, deaths, marriages, and divorces is an area.

A vital statistics system can be defined as "...including the legal registration, statistical recording and reporting of the occurrence of, and the collection, compilation, analysis, presentation, and distribution of statistics pertaining to vital events, which in turn include live births, deaths, foetal deaths, marriages, divorces, adoptions, legitimations, recognitions, annulments and legal separations."[2]

REPORTING PROCEDURE

Generally, a vital even such as a birth or death, is reported locally, in the registration office of the place where it occurs. At regular intervals each local registration office sends a statistical report on the number of each type of vital event that has been registered and on certain specified circumstances of the event (such as number of mothers at each age, number of infants of each sex, etc., in the case of births) to the central office which prepares and publishes the central statistical reports/vital statistics. This office is usually a division of the central statistical bureau of the country, though in many countries it is a division of the health department.

AVAILABILITY OF VITAL STATISTICS

The availability of vital statistics varies widely. According to the United Nations, 'this due to in part lack of uniformity and universality in national legislation. In some areas, registration is compulsory only for births and deaths; in others, it is compulsory for only a small part of the population (that is, European or non-indigenous population). In still other countries...there is no national provision for compulsory registration, but only municipal or state ordinances which do not cover the entire geographic area. Still other countries...have developed registration areas which comprise only a part of the country, the remainder being excluded for reasons of inaccessibility or because of economic and cultural considerations that make regular registration a practical impossibility."[3]

It may be pointed out that even where vital statistics are available for only part of a country, they serve as a nucleus for future development of a vital statistics system.

INTERNATIONAL RECOMMENDATIONS ON STATISTICAL REPORT ITEMS FOR BIRTHS AND DEATHS

The United Nations Statistical Office, after consultation with the Statistical Commission and Population Commission of the United Nations and the World Health Organization as well as the vital statistics offices of its member nations, prepared a list of recommended items to be included in the statistical report forms for births, deaths, fatal deaths, marriages, and divorces.[4]

ITEMS OF IMPORTANCE

The following items are considered to be of great importance as far as births and deaths are concerned:

(a) For births--attendant at birth, date of occurrence, date of registration, legitimacy, place of occurrence, sex, type of birth (single or Plural issue), date of birth of mother, number of children born to this mother, and mother's place of usual residence.

(b) For deaths--cause of death, certifier, date of occurrence, place of occurrence, date of decedent's birth, place of decedent's usual residence, and decedent's sex.

(c) For foetal deaths--date of occurrence, place of occurrence, date of registration, legitimacy, gestation period, sex, type of birth, date of birth of mother, number of children born to this mother, and mother's usual residence.

COMMENTS ON THE ITEMS: The recommended items for reporting of births and deaths have several things in common: These are:

(a) The date of occurrence of the event is required.

(b) The date of registration, as distinct from the date of occurrence is required, since delayed registration of births, deaths, and fatal deaths may seriously affect the statistics for any given period.

(c) The place of usual residence of the persons concerned, as distinct from the place of occurrence, is an item of great importance for the registration of all vital events. This is because so many people are away from a major vital event that data by place of occurrence rural parents and deaths of rural persons occur in city hospitals; the comparison of urban birth or urban death rates with rural birth and death rate requires that the place of usual residence be known.
(d) The date of birth of participants, or age in years if exact date of birth cannot be obtained, is of utmost importance for the interpretation of data on the number of events. For example, if there is an unusually small proportion of young women in a population because of a recent epidemic, and if these young women have the same number of children per woman during the year as is usual, then the total birth rate will be lower than usual. It is important in this case to know that the lower birth rate is a result of the usual age distribution among women and, therefore, is a temporary phenomenon and not indication of a major change in customs or family an patterns. Similarly, an increase or decrease in the number of marriages per total population may not mean a change in proportions of persons marrying. On the other hand, an increase in proportions marrying younger ages presages an increase in the birth rate. Almost all analysis of statistics on vital events requires knowledge of the ages at which they occur.

(e) The sex of the persons dying is of importance for the analysis of the causes of death and of age-sex structure of the population. The sex of infants born is of statistical importance primarily because a ratio of about 1.05 males to females is normal, and if the reported ratio differs much from that figure, it is an indication of poor registration of births.

DEFECTS IN THE REGISTRATION

An important consideration in evaluating the vital statistics of a country from its civil registration is the legal provision concerning them. If a fee is charged for registration, it is probable that registration will be less complete than otherwise. If family allowances or wages are increased with each addition to the family, birth registration may be very complete but death registration may not be. Any added incentive to register vital events tends to increase the completeness of the registration, and any inconvenience or fee tends to decrease it.

If the registration of both births and deaths is incomplete, and has been the data used for many purposes than it is better to use vital statistics of only a few urban centers where registration is good, than to use statistics for the country as a whole.

If births are more completely registered than deaths or vice-versa or if under-registration is selective in other respects such as age, sex, etc., the distortion is more serious.

Delays in registration may also have serious effects on vital statistics, especially in periods of rapid change in rates, and especially if the delay is longer than a year. Not only more or fewer vital events be recorded during the year than actually occurred, but they are related to the wrong population in the computation of rates.

COMPARISON WITH CENSUS DATA

If we have the population counts from two successive censuses, then the total number of births and deaths occurring during the intercensal period and the net migration during the same period should account for the change in the total population between the two censuses. One trouble with this comparison is that a country with poor vital statistics may also have rather poor censuses and very probably will have poor migration statistics. Another difficulty is that in a country where birth registration is as good or better than death registration, the indicated natural increase may equal the population increase measured by the censuses even though registration of both births and deaths in inadequate.

However, it is more usual to find that the reported births and deaths do not add up to anywhere near the increase (or decrease) found by the censuses, and that even the highest possible estimates of net migration cannot make up the difference.

If the census and the registration are both reasonably reliable, then the age-specific death rates should not be too different from the survival ratios indicated by the census. Thus, if the ratio of the group aged 40-50 years to the group aged 30-40 in the census 10 years earlier is 0.985, then the annual death rate should not be too far from 15 per 1000. However, even with perfect statistics there would be some difference between the survival ratios indicated by the censuses and the death rates because of changes in the rates during the intercensal period. Net migration also might alter the relationship.

CONSISTENCY OF THE VITAL STATISTICS

If the reported number of births or deaths varies markedly from year to year, especially if the movement is erratic (sometimes much larger and sometimes much smaller), and there are no known factors causing the variation, it is reasonable to consider the registration quite poor.

Also, if the reported numbers of vital events by age are very different from one year of age to the next, in the middle age range, this may be another sign of poor registration. In this case, however, the discrepancies may be owing to errors in age reporting. The data should be examined for successive years to see if the reported births by age of the mother and deaths by age regularly cluster around certain ages, which might be considered attractive ages.

It can be expected that the registration would show many more deaths for the first month of life than for later months; more for the first year of age than for later ages; and beginning somewhere about age 10, more for each later year of age. If this is not true, it can be assumed that registration of deaths is probably poor.

Examining the sex ratio at birth (ratio of the number of males to females) is another way of evaluating the adequacy of the birth registration. The sex ratio at birth should be about 1.05 or 1.06, since it is known that in most of the world about 5 per cent or 6 per cent more boys than girls are born. A ratio much different from 1.05 or 1.06 may indicate inadequate registration of one or both sexes.

REASONABLENESS OF THE DATA

Frequently the decision regarding the quality of registration data must be made on the basis of the reasonableness of the data in the light of what is known about general mortality and fertility levels in the country and the age-sex structure.

Apparent increases in fertility or mortality, especially in developing countries which have always had high fertility and mortality rates, are usually on account of improved registration of the events. Higher death rates in more prosperous areas of the country than in poorer ones are usually the result of better registration in the more prosperous areas. In many countries this is true also of birth rates, though a reversal here may reflect a true change in the rates, especially if an improvement in the economic situation and the spread of birth control practices are concomitant.

MIGRATION

Migration defined as a change of residence in which a recognized boundary of one type or another is crossed. The distinction between the migrant, who goes from one place to another and takes up residence in the second place, and the traveller, who may follow the same route but who soon returns to his residence in the first locality, is a fundamental one which must be maintained in any study of migration. Many itinerant workers have no homes other than the temporary quarters in which they live while working on each job. Such persons present special problems in the study of migration.

In practice, it is almost always necessary to treat international migrations and internal migrations separately because of differences in the sources and nature of data. Counts of international migrants, often classified by age and sex, are available for recent years in many countries. Such direct measurements are rarely, if ever, available for migrations within a country.

INTERNAL MIGRATION

There are several different types of internal migration. Rural-urban migration is the movement from rural to urban areas, often involving short distances. Inter-regional migrations take place between different regions of the same country. Expanding frontiers might be regarded as inter-regional movements of a special type; usually, however, they involve migration over shorter distances from areas which have been recently settled into areas which are still relatively uninhabited. Seasonal movements of itinerant workers, especially agricultural labourers, are usually ignored in general population studies, in part because they are difficult to measure.

It is customary to restrict the terms 'immigration' and 'emigration' to international migration and to use the terms 'in-migration' and 'out-migration' for internal migration.

The techniques used to estimate the size and composition of internal migrations may be the same regardless of the type of migration. Two types of census data may be used: data on place of birth and data on place of former residence. In addition, where birth and death registration are essentially complete, migration may be treated as a residual element of change; that is, derived from the basic formula of population growth.

The amount of total movement is not measured by a census. Some people move out of the area and then move back again before the census. The census, reports no movement in their cases. Those who have moved several times, while the census reports only one movement, either from their place of birth or from their place of residence at a given time only. Still others may have moved once or several times and then died before the census, so that no movement is reported for them in the census.

INTERNATIONAL MIGRATION

International migration that is, migration between different nations - is of two types with respect to any particular population. Immigrants arriving are international migrants. Emigrants departing are international migrants. Obviously, the immigrant in one country is an emmigrant for another country. This relationship is useful for purposes of conducting studies when emigration statistics are available by country of destination. If there are large differences - for example, between the number of emigrants from the United Kingdom destined for the United States (as reported by the United Kingdom) and the number of immigrants into the United States coming from the United Kingdom (according to the United States statistics) in the same year - something is wrong with one of the other, or both, of these figures.

SOURCES OF DATA

Data on international migration are collected in several ways by the different countries, including port statistics, frontier control data, passport data, local population registers, and statistics obtained in connection with enforcement of regulations concerning immigration, work permits for aliens, transport contracts for emigrants, etc. It is necessary to remember that the methods employed in collecting and tabulating such statistics can and do have some effects on their quality. The definitions and classifications employed can produce substantial differences in the results; sometimes, however, such differences may cancel each other out to a large extent.

Most countries publish immigration and emigration statistical reports on immigration and emigration. In addition, several of the issues of the United Nations Demographic Year Book which have appeared to date have included data on international population movements.

Most migrations work in both directions; that is, data on arrivals alone are not sufficient to study the effects of immigration on a population, because some of the immigrants returns to their places of origin and others go on to still other countries. Net migration, is more commonly of direct interest in population studies than gross movements to and from a country or between two particular countries. Nevertheless, net migration usually must be found from data on both immigration and emigration.

Statistics on migration between two countries which share a common land boundary are likely to be subject to much larger errors than those on inter-continental migrations. Errors are likely to be especially large if there are substantial difference in the levels of living between two countries and if the country with the higher level of living places some restrictions on immigration from its neighbour, causing much illegal unrecorded migration. Under such circumstances, it is extremely difficult to estimate the true magnitude of the net migration from either international migration statistics or census data.

SELECTIVITY OF INTERNATIONAL MIGRATION

Migration of all types draws more heavily on some parts of the population than on others. That is, migrations are selective of certain elements of the population from which the migrants are drawn. Intercontinental migrations usually draw most heavily upon males in the young adult ages. Exceptions to this general finding regarding age structure of migrants sometimes occur in the case of migration resulting from political occurrences; for example, refugee movements, transfers of population, etc.

BASIC DEMOGRAPHIC MEASURES

Good part demographic analysis is done with the aid of only a few very simple statistical measures.[5] Even very sophisticated analysis may employ only a few elementary devices. An important concern in analysis lies in understanding the limitations of the data, the methods by which the data were collected, the kinds of classifications used, and the manner in which the classifications may have affected the reported figures. Another concern in analysis is the effect on the population of economic, social, and cultural factors.

PERCENTAGE

A percentage is the size of one figure in comparison with another, translated into a proportion of 100 in order to make it easier to compare relationships between different sets of figures. For example,it is easier to see that the relationship of 152 to 608 is the same as the relationship of 719 to 2876 if both quantities are translated into percentages; it is found that in both cases the first number is 25 per cent of the second.

A percentage is obtained by dividing one figure by the other then moving the decimal point in the result of two places to the right (that is, multiplying by 100):

$$\text{Percentage} = \frac{a}{b} \times 100$$

The only problem is to decide which figure is to be related to the other, or whether each is to be related to the total of the two. For example, if the rural population of an area is 6,000,000, and the urban population is 4,000,000, then the following three statements are true:

(1) The rural population is 50 per cent larger than the urban population;

(2) The urban population is 66.7 per cent as large as the rural population;

(3) The rural population is 60 per cent of the total population and the urban population is 40 per cent of the total population.

In a cross-classification, the table is very different if percentages are presented one way instead of another. The table 5.1 presents figures on literacy for urban and rural populations. The three examples which follow show the different percentages which may be obtained from the same figures.

Table 5.1: Figures on Literacy for Urban and Rural Populations

	Total Population	No. of persons Literate	No. of persons Illiterate
Total	1,000,000	800,000	200,000
Urban	360,000	320,000	40,000
Rural	640,000	480,000	160,000

Example 1. Urban-rural distribution of literacy (in percentages).

	Total	Literate	Illiterate
Total	100	100	100
Urban	36	40	20
Rural	64	60	80

Example 2. Literacy and illiteracy in the urban & rural population (in percentages).

	Total	Literate	Illiterate
Total	100	80	20
Urban	100	89	11
Rural	100	75	25

Example 3. Literacy and urban-rural distribution of the population (in percentages).

	Total	Literate	Illiterate
Total	100	80	20
Urban	36	32	4
Rural	64	48	16

RATIO

A ratio expresses the size of one number in relation to the size of another number. For example, 140 is twice as large as 70; thus the ratio of 140 to 70 is 2. Likewise, 70 is one half the size of 140; thus the ratio of 70 to 140 is 0.5.

A percentage is one form of a ratio; it is a ratio based on 100. When we say that the ratio of 70 to 140 is 0.5, we are using a ratio based on 1. The same considerations which apply to percentages apply to all ratios; basically, the problem is to decide which number is to be expressed in terms of its size in relation to the other.

A ratio is obtained by dividing the number which serves as the basis of comparison into the number which is being compared to it. If the question is: how many units of A are there per unit of B the formula is:

$$\text{Ratio} = \frac{a}{b}$$

PROPORTION

A Proportion is a ratio in which the relative size of one number is expressed in terms of a total consisting of that number plus another number. That is, it is the relative size of a part compared with the size of the whole. The formula is:

$$\text{Proportion} = \frac{a}{a+b}$$

For example, if the rural population of an area is 300,000 and the urban population is 100,000, then the proportion of the total population which is rural is 0.75, or

$$\frac{300000}{300,000 + 100000} = 0.75$$

Of course this is usually obtained directly by dividing the total into the part, or

$$\frac{300,000}{400,000} = 0.75$$

Like other ratios, proportions are frequently multiplied by 100 and expressed as percentages; for example, the rural population is 75 per cent of the total population.

RATE

A rate is a ratio of one thing to another in a specified period of time. A birth rate is the ratio of births during a specified period of a group of population. Most often rates in population statistics are expressed in terms of years, but a rate may be computed for any other time period such as a week, month, quarter, decennium, etc.

Population rates are usually given as the number of events which occurred per 1,000 inhabitants. For example, if there were 40 births per 1,000 inhabitants during the year, the crude birth rate for the year was 40. Likewise, if there were 20 deaths per 1,000 inhabitants during the year, the crude death rate for the year was 20. If a given type of event is so uncommon that it would be necessary to use numbers to the right of the decimal point in a rate expressing its occurrence per 1,000 inhabitants per year, it may be preferable to base the rate on 10,000 inhabitants. For example; "the death rate from malaria was 57 per 10,000 inhabitants in 1940 whereas it had been

135 per 10,000 inhabitants in 1920; by 1955 it had dropped to 7 per 100,000 inhabitants."

The number of events which occurred during a given period is the numerator of a rate, and the population in which the events occurred in the denominator. For most vital statistics rate, the estimated population at the exact middle of the period is used. For example, the number of deaths reported in Madagascar in 1955 was 62,436, and the estimated midyear population in 1955 was 4,776,000; the crude death rate per 1,000 population was 13.1 or

$$\frac{62,436}{4,776} \times 1000 = 13.1$$

Care must be taken in the calculation of rates to be sure that the population in the denominator is really the population among which the events in the numerator occurred; or, as it is usually said, care must be taken to use the the population which was at risk of the event in the numerator. For example, if there is some remote area in a country, which is too far from any local registrar to report any deaths occurring in that area, then the reported deaths in the numerator exclude the area; therefore, the population in the area should be excluded from the denominator as well.

RATE OF GROWTH

If there are 100,000 people in an area at the beginning of the year and 110,000 at the end of the year, the increase is 10 per cent, that is, 10,000 additional people have been added to the population. If the population increases by 10 per cent the next year, it will increase by 11,000 and the population at the end of the year will be 1,21,000. If it increases by 10 percent the third year, there will be 12,100 more persons at the end of the year, and the total population will be 1,32,100. That is, if the rate of increase is 10 per cent each year a larger number of people are added to the population, because each year the 10 per cent is a percentage of a larger number.

If the analyst knows that the population was 1,00,000 at the beginning of the year and 1,32,100 at the end, then he can calculate that the average annual rate of increase during the three years as 10 per cent. Of course, it is unlikely that the increase each year was exactly 10 per cent; it was probably a little less than 10 per cent one year and a little more than 10 per cent another year. For example, it might have been 9 per cent (1,00,000 to 1,09,000) the first year, 10 per cent (1,09,000 to 1,19,000)the second, and 11 per cent (1,19,000 to 1,32,000) the third. An average annual rate of increase assumes a constant rate of increase each year, which is recognised to be at least a little fictitious in almost all cases.

If the population is known for two dates, then this average rate of increase can be found by the formulae:

$$P_2 = P_1 (1+r)^n$$

where P_2 is the population at the end of the period.

P_1 is the population at the beginning of the period.

r is the average rate of increase per unit of time.

n is the number of units of time - years, months, etc. - from the beginning to the end of the period.

A rate of increase is easier to calculate with logarithms. In terms of logarithms, the formulae just given are as follows:

$$\log P_2 = \log P_1 + n \log(1+r)$$

or

$$\log(1+r) = \frac{\log P_2 - \log P_1}{n}$$

For example, the computation of the rate of increase of the population of a country between the 1950 and 1960 censuses would give:

$$\text{Log}(1+r) = \text{Log}\,\frac{681,187 - \text{Log}\,531,818}{10}$$

Using a table of logarithms, we insert the logarithm of each of the two populations:

$$\text{Log}(1+r) = \frac{5.833158 - 5.725161}{10} = \frac{0.107997}{10}$$

$$\text{Log}(1 + r) = 0.010800$$
$$1 + r = 1.0252$$

$$r = 0.0252$$, or 2.5 per cent average annual rate of increase.

Rates of increase are frequently calculated for each Province or State and are compared with each other or with the rate of increase of the population of the nation as a whole. Comparisons may also be made of the respective rates of increase of the urban and the rural populations, or of other groups of the population.

As has been explained, the average annual rate of increase for any period of years assumes a constant rate of increase each year. If in fact, there have been major fluctuations in the rate of growth (such as a sudden spurt of growth in the few years immediately preceding the most recent census, or conversely a rapid growth at the beginning of the intercensal period and a leveling off towards the end) then the average annual rate of increase for the entire period gives a misleading impression. If there reason to believe that the rate of growth during part of the period was very different from the average rate for the entire period, it is probably better not to present figures for the average annual growth for the entire period. If the average annual rate is presented in such a situation, a note regarding the presumed changes in the rate of growth during the period should accompany it.

If the analyst knows the population at the beginning or end of a period, and knows the average rate of growth, then he can obtain an estimate of the population at any other time during the period by using the formula:

$$\text{Log } P_x = \text{Log } P_1 + n \text{ Log } (1+r)$$

For example, if we know that the population of a country was 531,818 in 1950 and that the rate of increase between 1950 and 1960 was 0.025, then it is possible to estimate that if growth between 1950 and 1960 was at a constant rate, the 1953 population was approximately 5,72,000:

$$
\begin{aligned}
\text{Log } P_x &= \text{Log } P_1 + n \text{ Log } (1+r) \\
&= \text{Log } 5{,}31{,}818 + 3 \text{ Log } (1 + 0.025) \\
&= 5.725161 + 3(0.010800) \\
&= 5.725161 + 0.032400 \\
&= 5.757561 \\
P_x &= 5{,}72{,}220 \text{ or, rounding to three significant} \\
&\quad \text{digits, } 5{,}72{,}000.
\end{aligned}
$$

If the analyst knows the present population and present rate of increase, he can estimate the length of the time it will take for the population to reach some given size if the rate of increase remains constant. In this case, the formula is expressed as:

$$n = \frac{\text{Log } P_x - \text{Log } P_1}{\text{Log } (1 + r)}$$

For instance, if the population in 1958 is 8,79,000, and the rate of increase is 2.5 per cent a year, then it can be estimated that the population will reach 1,000,000 in approximately 5 years if the present rate of increase continues:

$$
\begin{aligned}
n &= \frac{\text{Log } 1{,}000{,}000 - \text{Log } 879{,}000}{\text{Log } (1 + 0.025)} \\
&= \frac{6.000000 - 5.943989}{0.010724} \\
&= \frac{0.056011}{0.010724} \\
&= 5.2 \text{ years}
\end{aligned}
$$

REFERENCES

1. Irene B. Taeuber, *The Population of Japan*. (Princeton, New Jersey: Princeton University Press, 1958).
2. United Nations Statistical Office. *Handbook of Vital Statistics Methods* (Studies in Methods, Series F, No. 7), 1955.
3. United Nations, *Demographic Yearbook 1964*, 1965.
4. United Nations Statistical Office, *Principles for a Vital Statistics System*. (Statistical Papers, Series M, No. 19; ST/STAT/ SER.M/19), 1953.
5. Many other devices are available using more advanced statistical techniques.

SIX

SEX AND AGE

The importance of the sex composition of a population is so widely recognised that a classification of the population by sex is universally accepted in modern censuses. Few problems are associated with the collection of data on sex composition. The classification of each individual in the population as either male or female is simple and straight forward; it is probably subject to fewer reporting errors than any other item on the census questionnaire. Such errors as do exist in the tabulated data on sex composition are in fact caused entirely by the errors of coverage; that is, by the selective net under enumeration of the persons of one sex and of certain age groups.

SEX RATIO

Sex ratio is the basic tool for the analysis of the composition of population. It is defined as the number of males per 100 females. This measure is preferred to others, such as those which measure the number of females per 100 males, or the percentage of the total population made up of either males or females, because it is a conventional tool used in the population studies throughout the world.

Sex ratio is calculated by dividing the number of males by the number of females and then multiplying by 100; for example, the sex ratio of the total population of India[1] in 1961 is as follows:

$$\frac{Number\ of\ males}{Number\ of\ females} \times 100 = \frac{226,060,908}{212,713,821} \times 100$$

$$= 1.063 \times 100$$

$$= 106.3.$$

Three classifications reflecting variations in the sex ratio - age composition, rural-urban ratio and regional residence - are discussed here.

AGE COMPOSITION BY SEX

It is well established that males out-number females at birth (the sex ratio at birth is normally about 105.5). Therefore, a "young" population, in the sense that a population in which young persons make up an unusually large percentage of the total population, may be expected to have a high sex ratio. Such "young" populations are generally characterized by high birth rates (the example just given of India illustrates a country with a young population and a high birth rate). Conversely, a low sex ratio may be found in a population in which older persons make up an unusually large percentage of the total population.

The sex ratios in Table 6.1 illustrate the pattern that is expected for countries with an older population. According to age, males out-number females in the earlier age groups while females out-number males in the later age groups in most societies. The larger the death rate in a population, the younger the age at which women begin to be numerically preponderant.

TABLE 6.1 **SEX RATIO IN SWEDEN: 1960**

Age group	Males	Females	Sex Ratio
Total	3,738,881	3,756,435	99.5
0-4 years	259,950	245,281	106.0
5-9 years	274,208	259,278	105.8
10-14 years	312,550	297,639	105.0

15-19 years	303,288	290,994	104.2
20-24 years	235,839	230,406	102.4
25-29 years	219,838	215,572	102.0
30-34 years	236,320	233,828	101.1
35-39 years	268,828	264,694	101.6
40-44 years	270,523	265,476	101.9
45-49 years	268,942	264,831	101.6
50-54 years	261,154	260,761	100.2
55-59 years	226,190	235,224	96.2
60-64 years	190,538	205,538	92.9
65-69 years	152,478	173,330	88.0
70-74 years	115,862	137,806	84.1
75 years and above	141,965	175,777	80.8

Source: United Nations. Statistical Office, *Demographic Yearbook*, 1963. New york, 1964.

RURAL-URBAN DIFFERENCES

In Western civilizations, urban areas characteristically have lower sex ratios than the surrounding rural populations, at least in part, because rural-to-urban migration is ordinarily higher for females. In Eastern civilizations, the reverse is true.

REGIONAL DIFFERENCES

Areas which receive migrants from distant places are normally characterized by high sex ratios because long-distance migrations are ordinarily selective of males. Conversely, areas which lose migrants in long-distance migrations ordinarily have low sex ratios.

Frontier regions are characterised by particularly high sex ratios because frontier migrations are, as a rule, usually selective of males. The boisterous nature of a frontier society is often attributed to the relative lack of females in frontier populations.

AGE COMPOSITIONS

The classification of population by age, like its classification by sex, is universal in modern population censuses. There can be little doubt about the importance of the age composition of a population: almost all population characteristics and processes vary over a wide ranges of different ages. The bearing of children, for instance, is associated with only a limited part of the life span of women.The age composition of a population, by virtue of its relationship to the number of dependents per worker, is indirectly associated with the levels of living. The very young are economically inactive, and in some societies, a persons economic characteristics are a function of his age, in combination with other factors, throughout life. Marital status is closely associated with age.

The age composition of a population is so closely linked with its other characteristics that it is essential to take the age factor into account in comparing two or more populations which differ in age composition. Otherwise, apparent differences which are due only to variations in age composition may be ascribed to other factors such as rural-urban composition or ethnic composition.

DEFINITION OF AGE

Age is defined as the number of complete years which have elapsed since the birth of the individual. In other words, the data on age should refer to ages of individuals on their last birthday.

COLLECTION OF DATA

Data on age may be obtained by asking either for the exact date of birth or for the age at the last birthday. If the question is on the date of birth, then the processing operation must convert the responses to age in completed years. This approach is likely to yield more precise age data than a direct question on age, since such a question is more likely to receive approximate replies. If a considerable proportion of the population cannot give their exact date of birth, then it is better to ask for age in years.

Even if age in completed years is asked, the accuracy of reporting early ages may be improved upon by asking the age in completed months for children under one year of age, in order to be sure that children who are nearly one year old are not erroneously reported as having completed their first birthday.

CLASSIFICATION

The United Nations and the regional organizations recommend that at least one table for the whole country and its major administrative regions be presented by single years of age and sex. This table can provide information on the number of males and females in such categories as "preschool age", "school-going age", "voting age" and any other special age categories needed by the analyst. Data by single years of age are also useful for estimating the accuracy of age reporting.

Age data are classified by the five-year age groups for some tables by ten-year age groups for others. Grouping the single-year age data not only provides briefer tables but also serves to smoothen out the pronounced irregularities which appear in the single-year data because for the preference of years ending in certain digits.

The five-year age group tables that begin with age 0 usually separate the first group into (a) under one year, and (b) 1-4 years. Other groups are 5-9 years, 10-14 years and so on, to 75 years and over. The ten-year age group tables usually begin with 0-4 years, then continue with age groups 5-14, 25-34 etc. The purpose of this is to place the years ending in 0, such as 20, 30 etc., in the middle of the groups, since so many persons both over and under the ages ending in 0 report themselves at those ages.

ERRORS IN AGE COMPOSITION

Census data on age are subject to several types of errors. Selective net under-enumeration of infants and young adults, rounding off ages to "attractive" numbers, and deliberate misstatement of age all influence the quality of age data reported in the census.

The definition of the total population may also affect the age-sex composition of the enumerated population, since the groups which may be either excluded or included,such as the armed forces abroad or foreign armed forces stationed in the country, are usually of a select age group.

UNDER-ENUMERATION

Selective net under-enumeration usually leads to understating the figures for two types of persons. This defect is characteristic of virtually all censuses.

UNDER-ENUMERATION OF INFANTS AND YOUNG CHILDREN

Young children, especially those under one year of age, are usually under reported. This can be demonstrated on a national scale by comparing the number of persons reported to be under one year of age in one census with the number of persons born in the same year in the succeeding census (that is, persons ten years old in the second census if the two censuses were taken ten years apart). Of course, if vital statistics are known to be accurate, the most reliable method is to use data on births and infant deaths in the year preceding the census to estimate independently the number of children under one year who were alive on the census date.

Relatively few attempt have been made to date to measure precisely the extent to which infants and young children are omitted from censuses - mainly because other statistics on such persons are at least as incomplete as the census in most countries. On the basis of relatively complete birth and death registration data, it has been estimated that 8,02,000 persons under five years, or 4.7 per cent of the estimated total population of that age, were omitted from the 1950 U.S. Census of Population or were misclassified in some older age group. Of these children, 6,38,000 were less than two years old; they accounted for 9 per cent of the estimated total population of that age.[2] Studies in some other countries indicate considerably higher percentages of young children missed in the census - more than 15 per cent in some instances.

UNDERENUMERATION OF YOUNG ADULTS

Comparison of cohorts of persons born in the same five-year period from census to census in countries around the world which have taken repeated censuses indicated that young adults are characteristically selectively omitted from the censuses. This net underenumeration is more common among males than among females, and is in part responsible for variations between expected and observed sex ratios by age.

MIS-STATEMENT OF AGE

In every census there is a tendency towards the concentration of population in certain "attractive" ages. In most countries, the numbers for ages ending in 0 and 5 (and perhaps in the years ending in 2, 4, 6 and 8 to a lesser extent) are large relative to what may be expected; on the other hand, the numbers for ages ending in 1, 3, 7 and 9 may be relatively small. Such variations cannot be explained satisfactorily on the basis of differences in fertility or mortality or by the influence of migration. They occur at the same ages in census after census, and in country after country.

Special legal situations can lead to deliberate mis-statement of age. Thus, in a country in which the law specified that children legally become adults at the age of 18, there might be a tendency for persons a little under 18 years of age to report that they have passed their eighteenth birthday. Also, there might be a considerable tendency for persons a little under 65 years old to report that they have passed their sixty-fifth birthday in a country in which they become eligible for old age pension at the age of 65.

While conducting an analysis, any unusual clustering of population at certain ages should lead to the question as to whether there are legal or social benefits associated with those ages.The following points emerged in the course of the analysis:

1. The sex ratios by age in most countries led to the conclusion that adult women tend to understate their true ages.

2. The age distribution suggests that the very old people tend to overstate their ages.

3. There seems to be considerable reluctance in some areas to report age zero for persons under one year old, and consequent reporting of many of these infants as one year old (which is the reason why the age in months is sometimes asked for in the case of all infants under one year of age).

However, recent post-enumeration surveys of census accuracy, and checks of reported ages on census questionnaires against birth registrations for the same persons, indicate that errors in age reporting are more random than had been supposed. That is, it has been found that the ages of women, and very old persons and infants were about as likely to be overstated as understated. If this is true, then the observed inaccuracies in the age-sex distributions would be almost entirely attributable to selective under-enumeration in the census.

AGE RATIOS

The reliability of data on the age composition of five-year age groups is usually of more concern to the analyst than the accuracy of reporting of single years of age. It is possible to evaluate the data by age groups on the basis of age ratios. Generally, one would expect the number of persons in one age group to closely approach the mean of the number in each of the two adjacent age groups. An age ratio compares these two numbers by dividing the reported number of persons in the age group by the number "expected" on the basis of the number of persons reported in each of the adjacent age groups. The age ratio per 100 females aged 25-29, for example, is arrived at as follows:

$$Age\ ratio,\ females\ 25-29 = \frac{females\ 25-29}{\frac{1}{2}(females\ 20-24 + females\ 30-34)} \times 100$$

$$= \frac{200 \times females\ 25-29}{females\ 20-24 + females\ 30-34}$$

According to the 1960 data for Sweden, in Table 6.1 the age ratio for females 25-29 would be:

$$\frac{200 \times 215,572}{230,406 + 233,828} = 92.9$$

Age ratios can be calculated fro each age group (provided the intervals are equal) except in the case of the youngest and the oldest age groups.

Generally, age ratios should be studied for a series of age groups, preferably for the entire span of age for which they can be calculated. A ratio under 100 implies that either (a) members of the group were selectively under-enumerated or (b) errors in age reporting resulted in mis-classifying persons who belonged to the age group. A ratio of more than 100 suggests the opposite of one or the other, or both, of these conditions.

Tentative conclusions may be reached on the basis of the age ratios for a single census. The conclusions carry much greater weight, however, when it is found that the same pattern of age ratios is repeated in successive censuses, for in such cases the hypothesis that deviate from 100 are owing to true differences in age composition usually can be rejected.

UNKNOWN AGES

Persons for whom no age is reported often have been included in the tabulations by age in a special "age unknown" class. Some countries make it a practice to assign ages to individuals of unreported age, taking into account their other characteristics as well as characteristics of other members of their households. Such a system can take advantage of the available information to improve the quality of the data in this respect.

The United Nation recommends that: "Persons whose ages are not stated should be classified as a separate group, except where the number of such persons is negligible, when ages may be assigned to simplify tabulation. Such assignment should be to randomly select ages, appropriate to other characteristics of the individual and the household. If such allocation is employed, the method used and the number of cases should be clearly described in the census report."[3]

The "assignment to randomly select ages appropriate to other characteristics of the individual and of the household" must be done as a part of the processing of the questionnaires prior to tabulation.

The result is a table in which the problem of persons of unknown age has been solved by the statistical office; the "unknowns" do not appear as such in the table.

If the table presents a group of "ages unknown" (as it might if the group is at all large), then the user must decide how the "unknown" group should be treated in the analysis. Usually, it is assumed that the failure to report age is equally characteristic of all age groups. In that case, the unknowns are either, (a) eliminated from the distribution before calculating the percentages, or (b) distributed proportionately among the known ages. The choice between these two alternatives depends upon the use to be made of the data. If counts by age are to be used only to arrive at percentages, rates or ratios, the first alternative may be the wisest choice. If the absolute numbers are to be used for population estimates by age, then the second alternative is preferable.

If it is decided to distribute persons of unreported age proportionally among the known ages, the procedure is to (a) compute the percentage distribution of the population with known ages, and (b) apply these percentages to the total population including the "unknown"group.

AGE-SEX PYRAMID

The age-sex pyramid is a common graphic device for studying age structure. In effect, it records the history of a population through the lifetime of persons living at the time of the census. Wars, famines and migrations as well as the general levels of fertility and morality, all make their mark on the age structure of the population, and all are apparent on the age-sex pyramid.

Data on the composition of the population by sex and five-year age groups are preferred for the construction of age-sex pyramids. Pyramids based on data by single years overemphasize the rounding-off of ages to such an extent that it is often difficult to see more significant features. On the other hand, important features may be lost to a considerable extent if ten- year age groups are used.

Basically, an age-sex pyramid is a bar chart in which all the bars taken together represent 100 per cent of the population. The length of each bar (except for the oldest age group) is directly proportional to the percentage of the population made up of persons in the age-sex group it represents. Below is an age-sex pyramid illustrating the age-sex of the population of India in 1961: the data are shown in tabular form in Table 6.2.

Two, or even three age-sex pyramids may be partly superimposed in order to compare the age structure of two or three different populations or the same population at two or three different dates. If more than three populations are to be compared, separate pyramids are recommended.

FACTORS AFFECTING AGE COMPOSITION

The age composition of a population can be directly influenced only by the same factors (births, deaths and migration) which directly influence the total number of inhabitants. Other factors can create differences in age structure only through their influence on any of the three mentioned.

TABLE 6.2 AGE-SEX COMPOSITION OF INDIA: 1961

	Male		Female	
	Number	(%)	Number	(%)
Total	226,060,908	-	212,713,821	-
Reporting	225,966,228	51.5	212,632,190	48.5
0-4	33,176,745	7.6	32,905,030	7.5
5-9	33,063,452	7.5	31,588,298	7.2
10-14	26,263,602	6.0	23,021,533	5.2
15-19	18,590,021	4.2	17,275,998	3.9
20-24	18,190,157	4.1	19,126,173	4.4
25-29	18,524,705	4.2	18,042,886	4.1
30-34	15,981,218	3.6	14,849,246	3.4
35-39	13,598,888	3.1	11,856,553	2.7

40-44	12,082,312	2.8	10,770,047	2.5
45-49	9,733,150	2.2	8,320,033	1.9
50-54	9,127,783	2.1	7,977,199	1.8
55-59	5,281,481	1.2	4,547,684	1.0
60-64	5,705,175	1.3	5,530,815	1.3
65-69	2,471,975	0.6	2,378,447	0.5
70-74	2,155,503	0.5	2,258,070	0.5
75 and over	2,020,061	0.5	2,184,178	0.5
Unknown	94,680	-	81,631	-

Source: United Nations. Statistical Office, *Demographic Yearbook, 1964.* New York, 1965.

The general conformation of the age structure of the population, as it is reflected in the age-sex pyramid, is usually set by the levels of fertility, mortality and migration which have prevailed during the three or four preceding generations. It is the level of fertility rate which is the basic factor in determining the age structure of a normal population over a long period. Populations which have been characterized by high birth rates are also characterized by broad-based age-sex pyramids (the population of India, as shown in the Table 6.2, is an excellent example of this type). On the other hand, where birth and death rates have been relatively low for some time, the age-sex pyramid is characterized by a narrow base and steep sides.

Severe famines leave their mark on the age-sex pyramid by taking a higher toll of infants, young children and the aged of both sexes than of the population in the middle age group. Wars, however, reduce the number of male population in the young adult age group at the time of war.

In migratory movements, young adults are generally over represented. Long distance migrations usually involve more males than females, while shorter movements most often draw more heavily on the female population, particularly in the Western civilizations. As a result of migration ,the young adult age groups are deflated in the "sending" population and inflated in the "receiving" population.

REFERENCES

1. United Nations. Statistical Office. *Demographic Yearbook,* New York, 1964.
2. United States Bureau of the Census. *Estimates of the Population of the United States by Age, Colour and Sex, July 1955 to 1957.* Washington, 1958. (Current Population Reports, Series P-25, No. 170).
3. United Nations. Stastical Office. *Principles and Recommendations for National Population Censuses,* New York, 1958 (Statistical Papers, Series M, No. 27.).

SEVEN

MORTALITY

The basic measures for the study of mortality are death rates, crude death rates, age-specific death rates, etc. The idea of the "risk of dying" or "the probability of dying" is utilized for the construction of a life table. These probabilities in turn permit the computation of the expectation of life at different ages or the proportion of the population at one age that survives to another age.

DEATH RATES

Reliable death rates depend on the availability of reliable death registration data for the numerator and reliable population data for the denominator. Every effort should be made to evaluate the completeness of registration before interpreting the significance of death rate.

CRUDE DEATH RATE

The crude death rate is the simplest measure of the general level of morality in a population. It is the average number of deaths occurring during a year per 1,000 persons in the total population. It is found by dividing the total number of deaths which occurred during the year by the total population at the middle of the year and multiplying the result by 1,000. The formula is the following:

$$m = \frac{D}{P} \times 1000$$

where,

m = annual crude death rate,

D = number of deaths which occurred among the population of an area during a year,

P = midyear population of the same area during the same year

Crude death rates have an advantage of being simple to compute and easy to understand. They can be used as broad, general measures. They have the disadvantage of being very much affected by the age structure of the population, because of the marked differences in the death rates among the various age groups. Furthermore, a crude death rate for the total population of an area conceals very different mortality rates which are usually found in different regions, among different racial, ethnic and socio-economic groups, and in different type of areas of residence.

SPECIFIC DEATH RATES

Usually, it is desirable to introduce some refinements in the crude death rate, if registration is sufficiently complete to warrant the use of data. A specific death rate may be computed for segments of the population by age, sex, race, marital status, or other characteristics, provided that the data are available on both the number of persons in the population having that characteristic and the number of deaths occurring in that same group of persons.

SEX:- The death rate of females ia almost always lower than that of males for the span of life as a whole, though this is not always true for all age groups. Therefore, it is preferable to treat the two sexes separately in studying the death rates of any given area.

AGE:- Death rates differ greatly form one age to another, so that differences in age composition can seriously affect the crude death rate. Therefore, in the study of mortality, age composition should be taken into account whenever possible.

The death rate of a particular age group is referred to as an **age-specific death rate.** The arithmetic is exactly the same as it is for the crude death rate, except that data only for one age group are used:

$$m_x = \frac{D_x}{P_x} \times 1,000$$

where,

m_x = annual age-specific death rate for a population of age x.

D_x = number of deaths to population in age group x in an area during the particular year.

P_x = midyear population of age group x in the same area during the same year.

Age-specific death rates are usually prepared for five year age groups. These are fine enough to show the pattern of mortality by age, but not so detailed as to be made too erratic errors in age reporting. In order to limit the effect of infant mortality, it is preferable to include in a table of age-specific death rates both the age groups "under one year" and "one to four years".

The pattern of mortality by age is one of initially high rates in the first year of life (within the first year, mortality rates are highest in the first few days of life, very high in the first month and declines throughout the rest of the year). After the first year, the rates decline rapidly to a minimum, which usually occurs around the tenth year of life. After reaching this minimum, the age-specific death rates increase gradually upto about 40 years or 50 years of age, and then increases at a relatively rapid rate throughout the rest of life. Generally speaking, the decline in mortality rates in early life is quite abrupt in populations with low rates in general, and is more gradual in populations with high mortality.

Table 7.1 shows the age-specific death rates of Norway in 1955 and Mexico in 1950. As is usual in Western countries, the age-specific death rates of females are lower than those of males in all age groups except in the case of the extremely old. Here also, it is apparent that the differences in the mortality between the two countries are the greatest at the youngest ages.

It is usually desirable to make international comparisons on the basis of age-specific death rates by sex or on the basis of life table expectations of life by sex, in as much as measurements are free from the effects of differences in age-sex composition. In the absence of life tables for a particular country, it may be possible to make use of the United Nations model life tables.

INFANT\MORTALITY RATES

On account of the concentration of deaths in the first few years of life, the infant mortality rate (IMR) for deaths during the first year of life is calculated on the basis of the number of births during a year. Thus,

$$IMR = \frac{Deaths \text{ under } age \ 1}{Births} \times 1{,}000$$

or, in more precise language, the infant mortality rate equals

$$\frac{\text{number of death under one year of age which occured to the population of a given area during a year}}{\text{number of live birth which occurred among the population in the same area during that same year.}} \times 1{,}000.$$

Strictly speaking, the infant mortality rate is not necessarily an accurate measure because the deaths in the numerator do not occur among all the infants born during the year, which is in fact the population in the denominator. Many of the deaths during a calendar year are among infants born during the preceding year, and many of the infants born during the calendar year will die during the following year before they have reached one year of life. However, if the number of births does not change greatly from one year to the next, these factors cancel each other to such an extent that the reliability of the infant mortality rate is not seriously impaired.

TABLE 7.1 AGE-SPECIFIC DEATH RATES BY SEX IN NORWAY,1955 AND MEXICO, 1950

Age (Years)	Norway, 1955			Mexico, 1950		
	Both Sexes	Male	Female	Both Sexes	Male	Female
All ages	8.5	8.7	8.3	16.2	17.3	15.2
Under 1 year	21.1	23.5	18.6	138.8	150.4	127.0
1-4	1.3	1.5	1.1	27.8	27.5	28.2
5-9	0.5	0.6	0.3	4.5	4.5	4.5
10-14	0.4	0.6	0.3	2.4	2.5	2.3
15-19	0.7	1.0	0.4	3.6	4.1	3.2
20-24	0.8	1.2	0.4	5.1	5.9	4.5
25-29	1.0	1.3	0.7	6.1	6.9	5.4
30-34	1.2	1.5	0.9	7.2	8.1	6.4
35-39	1.6	2.0	1.3	9.1	10.5	7.8
40-44	2.2	2.6	1.8	9.9	11.5	8.4
45-49	3.2	3.8	2.7	12.8	15.0	10.7
50-54	5.5	6.9	4.2	15.3	17.6	13.1
55-59	8.8	11.3	6.4	21.0	23.8	18.1
60-64	13.6	16.6	10.8	28.9	31.7	26.5
65-69	22.2	25.7	19.3	42.8	44.5	41.1
70-74	36.4	41.1	32.7	62.9	66.0	60.1
75-79	63.8	68.5	60.0	89.1	89.8	88.5
80-84	107.8	110.1	106.1	120.7	119.4	121.8
85 years and above	218.5	215.8	220.4	246.8	229.2	260.6

Source: United Nations. Statistical Office. *Demographic Yearbook,* 1957. New York, 1957.

If there is much delay in birth registration, then the percentage of omissions of infant deaths is much greater than the omissions of of births, because infant deaths are very high in the first few days after birth. For example, in the Hispanic population of New Mexico, a one month delay in birth registration accompanied by a failure to report either the birth of infants who died before attaining one month of age would result in omitting from the statistics 42 per cent of all infant deaths (and 13 per cent of all deaths) but only 3 per cent of all births.[1]

LIFE TABLES

Life tables are one of the basic tools of demographic analysis in the countries for which they are or can be made available. A life table population is the population which would exist if the age-specific death rates prevailing at some particular time were to continue throughout the life span of all the individuals, with no change in the number of births each year and no migration. That is, a life table population is a theoretical population which never has existed and never will exist in reality. It is constructed to show what the effects of mortality on a population would be if it were not affected also by fertility and migration.

NATURE OF LIFE TABLES

A life table begins with a radix of 1,00,000 (or 10,000, etc.) births assumed to have occurred at a single moment. This theoretical cohort is reduced at each age, according to the death rates prevailing for that age, to arrive at the number of survivors at the beginning of the next age. The death rates and the size of the initial cohort determine all the other figures in the body of a life table.

The expectation of life at various ages and the survival ratios which may be determined, in a single step, from the survivors in each year of age or age group, are life table values of great use to demographers.

Complete life tables show all the life table functions by single years of age. Abridged life tables usually give the life table functions by five-year or ten-year age groups; some tables show life table functions for certain selected single years of age.

The construction of either complete or abridged life table is a complicated process; the process ordinarily should not be undertaken unless the basic population and mortality data from which they are constructed are known to be of reasonably good quality. Even the best data must be corrected for errors of coverage and classification before being used to construct life table. The preparation of life tables, although very important to population studies is in practice almost a field in itself and is therefore not treated fully in this discussion.

TABLE 7.2 ABRIDGED LIFE TABLES FOR MALE AND FEMALE POPULATION OF A COUNTRY

Age interval	Proportion dying	of 1,00,000 born alive		Stationary population		Average remaining lifetime
Period of life stated in years	Propotion of persons alive at beginning of age interval/dying during the interval	Number of persons living at beginning of age interval	Number of persons dying during age interval	The age Interval	All subsequent age intervals	Average number of years of life remaining at beginning of age interval
(1)	(2)	(3)	(4)	(5)	(6)	(7)
	$_nq_x$	l_x	$_nd_x$	$_nL_x$	T_x	e^o_x
MALE						
0-1	0.06660	100,000	6,660	95,338	6,153,656	61.5
1-4	0.02678	93,340	2,500	368,360	6,058,318	64.9
5-9	0.00875	90,840	795	452,210	5,689,958	62.6
10-14	0.00648	90,045	583	448,765	5,237,748	58.2
15-19	0.01064	89,462	952	444,930	4,788,983	53.5
20-24	0.01510	88,510	1,337	439,205	4,344,053	49.1
25-29	0.01559	87,173	1,359	432,465	3,904,848	44.8
30-34	0.01649	85,814	1,145	425,530	3,472,383	40.5

35-39	0.01922	84,399	1,622	417,940	3,046,853	36.1
40-44	0.02504	82,777	2,073	408,700	2,628,913	31.8
45-49	0.03600	80,704	2,905	396,255	2,220,213	27.5
50-54	0.05265	77,799	4,096	378,755	1,823,958	23.4
55-59	0.07685	73,703	5,664	354,355	1,445,203	19.6
60-64	0.11583	68,039	7,881	320,490	1,090,848	16.0
65-69	0.17320	60,158	10,419	274,740	770,358	12.8
70-74	0.25862	49,739	12,864	216,535	495,618	10.0
75-79	0.37529	36,875	13,839	149,775	279,083	7.6
80-84	0.52397	23,036	12,070	85,005	129,308	5.6
85 and over	1.00000	10,966	10,966	44,303	44,303	4.0
FEMALE						
	00.05519	100,000	5,519	96,137	6,491,157	64.9
1-4	0.02424	94,481	2,290	373,344	6,395,020	67.7
5-9	0.00777	92,191	716	459,165	6,021,676	65.3
10-14	0.00586	91,475	536	456,035	5,562,511	60.8
15-19	0.00924	90,939	840	452,595	5,106,476	56.2
20-24	0.01261	90,099	1,136	477,655	4,653,881	51.7
25-29	0.01355	88,963	1,1205	441,800	4,206,226	47.3
30-34	0.01491	87,758	1,308	435,520	3,764,426	42.9
35-39	0.01669	86,450	1,443	428,640	3,328,906	38.5
40-44	0.02048	85,007	1,741	420,680	2,900,266	34.1
45-49	0.02771	83,266	2,307	410,560	2,479,586	29.8
50-54	0.03891	80,959	3,150	396,920	2,069,026	25.6
55-59	0.05565	77,809	4,330	378,220	1,672,106	21.5
60-64	0.08561	73,479	6,291	351,665	1,293,886	17.6

65-69	0.13609	67,188	9,144	313,080	942,221	14.0
70-74	0.21809	58,044	12,659	258,570	629,141	10.8
75-79	0.33280	45,385	15,104	189,165	370,571	8.2
80-84	0.47885	30,281	14,500	115,155	181,406	6.0
85 and over	1.00000	15,781	15,781	66,251	66,251	4.2

Life tables are prepared from mortality rates based on vital statistics (for the number of deaths by age and sex) and census data (for the population by age and sex). A few appropriate life tables have been prepared on the basis of successive censuses in countries lacking reliable death registration data by comparing the population of each age-sex group as enumerated in the later censuses. Needless to say, this method can be applied only to populations in which the effects of migration during the period concerned were negligible. Even then, a number of rather arbitrary assumptions must sometimes be made to arrive at some of the life table death rates for certain ages. Under certain special circumstances life tables have been constructed from the results of a single census.

Life tables are usually based on current mortality rates. Frequently the mortality rates for the last three successive years, centered on a census year are averaged. Life tables based on current mortality rates are called current life tables, or occasionally cross-sectional life tables.

A historical life table may be constructed for a particular cohort born some 75 years or 85 years ago and followed through the years up to the present time. This type of life table, based on historical data about an actual cohort, in called a cohort life table or a generation life table. Such life tables are seldom constructed, since the mortality data are usually not available.

ABRIDGED LIFE TABLES

Table 7.2 illustrates an abridged life table in five-year age groups. Each of the columns in the table presents one of the life table functions for each age group.

The age interval shown in column 1 is the interval between the two exact ages stated at the beginning of two consecutive groups. For example, '20-24' means the five-year interval from the twentieth up to the twenty-five birthday.

Column 2--shows the proportion of the cohorts who are alive at the beginning of an indicated age interval and who will die before reaching the end of that age interval. For example, for males between 20-24 years, the proportion dying is 0.01510; this means that, out of every 1,000 males alive and exactly 20 years old at the beginning of the period, 15.1 will die before reaching twenty-fifth birthday. In other words, the n^ox values represent probabilities that persons who are alive at the beginning of a specific age interval will die before reaching the beginning of the next age interval. The column showing the proportion dying column forms the basis of the life table; the life table is so constructed that all other columns are derived from it.

The basic formula for deriving n^qx from n^mx (age-specific death rate of the population) is as follows:

$$n^q x = \frac{2n\left(n^m x\right)}{2 + n\left(n^m x\right)}$$

The n^qx differs from the ordinary age-specific death rate n^mx in that it is based on the life table population at the beginning of the age span to which it refers whereas the n^mx is based on the actual population at the mid-point of that period.

Column 3--shows the number of persons, starting with a cohort of 1,00,000 live births, who survive to the exact age marking the beginning of each age interval. The 1_x values are computed from the n^qx values, which are successively applied to the remainder of the original 1,00,000 persons still alive at the beginning of each age interval. Thus, out of 1,00,000 male babies born alive, 93,340 will complete the first year of life and enter the second; 90,840 will begin the fifth year; 88,510 will reach age 20; and 10,966 will live to age 85. (1_{x+n} = 1_x - n^dx; for example, column 3 for age group 10-14 equals column 3 for age group 5-9 years minus column 4 for age group 5-9 years).

Column 4--shows the number of people dying in each successive age interval out of 1,00,000 live births. Out of 1,00,000 males born alive, 6,660 die in the first year of life, 2,500 in the succeeding four years, 1,337 in the five-year period between the exact ages 20 years and 25 years and 10,966 die after reaching age 85. Each figure in column 4 is the difference between successive figures in column 3. (Column 4 is also equivalent to column 2 x column 3).

Column 5 and 6--The stationary population (n^Lx and T_x): Suppose that a group of 1,00,000 individuals such as those in columns 3 and 4 are born every year and that the proportions dying in each such group in each age interval throughout the lives of the members are exactly those shown in column 2. If there were no migration and if the births were evenly distributed over the calendar year, the survivors of these births would make up what is called a stationary population--stationary because in such a population the number of persons living in any given age group would never change. When an individual leaves the group, either by death or by growing older and enters the next higher age group, his place is immediately taken by someone entering from the next lower age group. Thus, a census taken at any time in such a stationary community would always show the same total population and the same numerical distribution of that population among the various age groups. In such a stationary population supported by 1,00,000 annual births, column 3 shows the number of persons who, each year, reach the birthday which marks the beginning of the age interval indicated in column 1, and column 4 shows the number of persons who die each year in the indicated age interval.

Column 5 shows the number of persons in the stationary population in the indicated age interval. For example, the figure given for males in the age interval 20-24 is 4,39,205. This means that in a stationary population of males supported by 1,00,000 annual births and with proportions dying in each age group always in accordance with column 2, a census taken on any date would show 4,39,205 persons 20--24 years old. For calculating column 5, the formula is:

$$5 \frac{1_x + 1_{x+5}}{2}$$

However, for the age groups O and 1--4, the formulae are:

$$L_o = 0.3l_o + 0.7l_1$$

$$_4L_1 = 4(0.5l_1 + 0.5l_5)$$

For the age group 85 and over, the formula is:

$$L_{85} = \frac{d_{85}}{m_{85}}$$

where m_{85} is the annual age-specific death rate of the population which is the source of the table.

Column 6 shows the total number of persons in the stationary population (column 5) in the indicated age interval and all subsequent age intervals. For example, in the stationary population of males referred to in the last illustration, column 6 shows that there would be at any given moment a total of 4,344,053 males who have passed their twentieth birthday. The total male population would be 6,153,656.

(Column 6 = L_x)

Column 7-- Thc average remaining lifetime (also called expectation of life) at any given age is the average number of years remaining to be lived by those surviving to that age on the basis of a given set of age-specific rates of dying. To arrive at this value, it is necessary to observe that the figures in column 5 can be interpreted in terms of a single life table cohort without introducing the concept of the stationary population. Each figure in column 5 represents the total time (in years) lived between two indicated birthdays by all those reaching the earlier birthday among the survivors of a cohort of 1,00,000 live births. Thus, the figure 4,39,205 (column 5) for males 20--24 is the total number of years lived between the twentieth and twenty-fifth birthdays by the 88,510 (column 3) who reached the twentieth birthday out of 1,00,000 males born alive.

The corresponding figure (4,344,053) in column 6 is the total number of years lived after attaining age 20 by the 88,510 persons reaching that age. The number of years divided by the number of persons (4,344,053 divided by 88,510) gives 49.1 years as the average remaining lifetime of males at age 20.

$$(Column\ 7 = \frac{column\ 6}{column\ 3}, \text{ or } \frac{T_x}{l_x}$$

COMPLETE LIFE TABLES

Complete life tables, in which the functions are given by single years of age, are constructed in the same manner as abridged life tables, with the value of n = 1. However, abridged life tables are generally constructed because most countries do not have reliable age-specific death rates by single years of age.

USE OF LIFE TABLES IN POPULATION ANALYSIS

In population analysis, the expectation of life and the survival ratios are the most used values which are calculated from life tables. For convenience, death rates might be calculated from the life table and used instead of age-specific death rates, but under most circumstances this would offer no special technical advantage.

EXPECTATION OF LIFE.

The expectation of life is the average number of years remaining to be lived by those surviving to that age. Generally, the expectation of life at birth for instance at age one, or at age ten is most useful in comparing the mortality of different populations; however, for some purposes, the expectation of life at other ages may be equally useful.

Differences in mortality of different age groups must be kept in mind in interpreting the expectation of life, especially when the expectation of life at birth is being used. If the average expectation of life at birth is 40 years, most of the deaths before age 40 occur in the first few years of life; those later than age 40 are spread out more evenly but none the less increase rapidly at older ages. A rather small proportion of deaths may occur around the fortieth year. Ordinarily the expectation of life is greater at age one than at age zero; a high point is reached somewhere between age one and five, after which the expectation of life declines with increasing age. Little significance should be attached to figures on expectation of life at advanced ages because of the small populations that are involved and the large age-reporting errors characteristic of those ages.

TABLE 7.3 EXPECTATION OF LIFE, TRINIDAD AND TOBAGO: 1900-1903 to 1957

	1900-1903		1910-1912		1920-1922		1930-1932		1945-1947		1957	AGE(yr.)
	Male	Female	Male	Female	Male	Female	Male	Female	Male	Female	Male	Female
0	36.73	38.75	38.97	40.95	37.59	40.11	44.51	46.95	52.98	56.03	59.88	63.35
1	43.23	44.81	44.99	46.73	43.57	45.52	50.92	52.34	57.07	59.46	63.22	65.87
2	45.08	46.56	46.51	48.22	45.11	47.56	51.42	52.97	56.91	59.37	62.69	65.26
5	44.65	45.93	45.54	47.30	43.87	46.40	49.56	51.34	54.54	56.93	60.14	62.66
10	41.12	42.60	41.69	43.56	40.14	42.64	45.50	47.11	50.06	52.44	55.42	57.94
15	37.29	38.82	37.73	39.65	36.09	38.63	41.04	42.81	45.50	47.91	50.78	53.16
20	33.63	35.41	34.12	36.35	32.34	35.28	36.97	39.06	41.20	43.83	46.15	48.41
25	30.32	32.57	30.75	33.54	29.04	32.23	33.23	35.55	37.13	40.05	41.47	43.78
30	27.09	29.88	27.46	30.71	25.82	29.13	29.48	32.08	33.10	36.24	36.86	39.21
35	23.89	27.08	24.30	27.68	22.68	26.15	25.78	28.61	29.13	32.52	32.35	34.63
40	20.88	24.06	21.33	24.65	19.85	23.37	22.35	25.16	25.29	28.70	27.97	30.21
45	18.07	20.95	18.38	21.54	17.21	20.40	19.17	21.83	21.67	24.93	23.79	26.04
50	15.46	17.99	15.59	18.42	14.66	17.42	16.13	18.66	18.34	21.47	19.72	21.92
55	12.96	15.09	12.98	15.33	12.18	14.55	13.31	15.65	15.32	18.34	16.03	18.26
60	10.62	12.31	10.49	12.50	9.89	11.85	10.78	12.86	12.53	15.37	12.85	14.74
65	8.51	9.83	8.28	9.95	7.88	9.49	8.61	10.39	10.11	12.67	9.91	11.78
65	6.80	7.84	6.53	7.81	6.36	7.56	6.89	8.28	8.18	10.06	8.93	10.69
75	5.50	6.32	5.23	6.17	5.24	5.99	5.60	6.53	6.59	7.65	7.64	8.61
80	4.33	4.96	4.05	4.98	4.41	4.89	4.53	5.16	5.12	5.74	6.05	6.27
85	3.21	3.70	2.91	3.88	3.61	3.94	3.91	4.20	3.86	4.53	—	—

Source: United Nations. Statistical Office. *Demographic Year book,* 1951 and 1963.New York, 1951 and 1964.

It must be remembered also that the life table average expectation of life at any age assumes a continues of the mortality rates of which the table is based. In a period of declining mortality such as the present one, it is probable that the average number of years lived by an actual group of persons now in the younger ages will be greater than the life table values for expectations of life at those ages.

Table 7.3 shows the life table expectations of life for Trinidad and Tabago at different periods throughout this century. It can be seen that most of the increases in expectation of life from 1900 to 1907 were at the younger ages.

SURVIVAL RATIOS

Survival ratios based on the l_x or the n^Lx columns of life tables provided the easiest means of 'aging' a population, a procedure which is especially important in preparing population estimates and projections (Table 7.4). A survival ratio is the ratio of the number of persons at a certain given period of time to the number in the same group at a previous period of time; it is expressed as a decimal. For example, five-year age groups by dividing the n^Lx value for each group into the n^Lx value for the succeeding age group. Similarly, ten-year survival ratios may be calculated from such abridged life tables by dividing the n^Lx value for each age group into the n^Lx value for the second succeeding age group. The following are n^Lx values and ten-year survival ratios, $\frac{5^L_x + 10}{5^L_x}$ from data for females in Table 7.2.

TABLE 7.4 SURVIVAL RATIOS AND n^Lx VALUES

Age interval	n^Lx	Survival ratio
15-19	452,595	0.9761
20-24	447,655	0.9729
25-29	441,800	0.9702

30-34	435,520	0.9659
35-39	428,640	0.9578
40-44	420,680	0.9435
45-49	410,560	0.9212

The notation $n^{s}x$ (see Unit III of the Atlantida Case Study on Population Data Controls) or P_x (United Nations Model Life Tables) may be used when applying a survival rate to a real population.

PRESENT TREND OF MORTALITY

A large percentage of the increase in population in the world has been brought about by decreases in mortality rates while fertility rates remained high. In Prehistoric and earlier historic periods both fertility and mortality were high. It seems probable that both the crude death rate and the crude birth rate through most of the period of history were above 40 per thousand or a little more.

The development of civilization at first brought a very slow and slight lowering of the death rates. The advent of modern medicine, increased sanitation measures, and public health programmes have resulted in rapid reductions of death rates, especially among the very young.

RANGE OF CRUDE DEATH RATES

At present, in the absence of serious under registration of deaths, death rate ranges from a low of about 6 or 7 to a high of something over 30. The upper limit of the present death rate is subject to considerable question, for the countries with the highest death rates are usually the countries with the least complete registration of deaths. It seems probable that in the recent past, death rates of 30--40 per thousand prevailed in most of the world. Crude death rates of 10 or less are probably a temporary phenomena, occurring in countries which have had recent sharp declines in infant mortality and which consequently have an unusually large percentage of population in the younger age groups in which mortality is at its lowest.

Even though relatively little faith can be placed in the precise figures given for the crude death rate of many countries, it is clear that the highest death rates in the world occur in the indigenous populations of Africa, and that these are followed closely by the death rates now prevailing in parts of Asia and Latin America. The lowest rates are to be found in Europe, Anglo America, Australia, and New Zealand. A worldwide decline in mortality is apparent from the crude death rates, even though the completeness of death registration in most of the world has increased in recent years.

TRENDS IN INFANT MORTALITY

The infant mortality rate now ranges from less than 20 in a few countries which have enjoyed unusally good health conditions for a prolonged period, to well over 200 in some aboriginal populations. A more normal range at the present time seems to be from about 20 to about 100.

TRENDS IN LIFE EXPECTANCY

The average expectation of life at birth ranges from about 25 years, or possibly a little lower in some aboriginal tribes, to about 75 years in some countries of Europe and North America. Low expectancies occur in Africa, and parts of Asia, and Latin America.

REFERENCE

1. Calculated from unpublished data furnished by the New Mexico Department of Public Health for Dr. W.W. Winnie's study of the Hispanic population of New Mexico.

EIGHT

FERTILITY

Fertility is concerned with the addition of new members to a population as a result of birth, that is, the actual performance of a population in bearing children. It is not to be confused with fecundity, which is the biological capacity of the population to bear children.[1]

Fertility, mortality, and migration are the three processes which may act to change the size of composition of a population. The first of these factors is probably of greater significance in industrialized nations rather than the other two factors. Whereas mortality rates appear to have fluctuated widely in area and through time during the past centuries and were largely responsible for the changing rates of population growth, at present, mortality rates are comparatively low and stable in many countries. The fertility rates, on the other hand, were probably high and relatively stable throughout the world until a few decades ago. In the 1980s they vary greatly among different countries.

Several types of data are used by demographers to study fertility. Vital statistics and population censuses provide most of these data. Special sources, such as baptismal records, may prove valuable either for basic data or for the evaluation of birth registration or census data under some circumstances.

EVALUATION OF BIRTH REGISTRATION DATA

Most countries maintain a birth registration system from which statistics are periodically compiled. However, birth registration is so incomplete in many countries that the data cannot be used for statistical purposes. Before relying heavily on birth registration data for the measurement of fertility, every effort must be made to determine the completeness of registration. If evidence of gross omission is found by comparing registration data with the infant population enumerated in a census or with baptismal records or other sources, or simply by arriving at a crude birth rate which seems impossibly low under certain circumstances, there is little point in going through a highly refined fertility analysis.

A preliminary evaluation may be accomplished fairly rapidly by comparing the number of infants enumerated in the census with the number of births reported in the year preceding the census (while taking into account that the infants enumerated are the survivors of those births). If this check indicates that the birth registration data are grossly deficient, it may be necessary to estimate births from census data on infants and young children. Analytical devices which rely upon registration data alone, without making use of census data or population estimates, should be approached with caution. The safest assumption is that deficiences in the registration do not occur in the same degree in all segments of the population.

INFANT POPULATION ESTIMATED FROM VITAL STATISTICS

Persons born during the twelve months preceding a census and who were still alive on the census date should be reported as children under one year of age in the census data. The number of surviving infants at the date of the census according to vital registration may be arrived at by deducting an allowance for infant mortality from the number of registered births. The United Nations has made a number of comparisons of the type under discussion by deducting 70 per cent of the infant deaths which occurred in the year before the census from the number of registered births.[2]

Not all the registered infant deaths should be deducted, because some of those deaths include infants born during the preceding year, and only those infants born on the first of the year preceding the census have suffered the full impact of infant mortality.

If birth registration is essentially complete, it may well be found that the number of surviving infants estimated in this way is greater than the number of infants enumerated in the census. Such a finding could be owing to the under-enumeration of infants in the census; it would not constitute conclusive evidence that birth registration is complete.

The only definite conclusion which may be arrived at by means of this comparison is that the reported number of registered births is probably incomplete by at least the number by which the infant population enumerated in the census exceeds the registered infant population.

If the birth registration data withstands this test, it does not mean that other tests can be omitted. On the contrary, it simply indicates that it would be worthwhile to perform such other tests as may be practical in the hope that they, too, will fail to confirm the hypothesis that birth registration data are deficient.

EFFECTS OF DELAYED REGISTRATION

The delay in birth registration may affect the quality of data on the number of births. It is often the case that a baby dies before his birth is registered and neither the birth nor the death is registered. Even though all surviving babies may be registered by the time they are one year or two years old, the practice of delayed registration of births is likely to result in some under-statement of the number of births in the statistics especially if infant mortality is high. Such errors do exist in birth registration which is otherwise essentially complete; appropriate adjustments can be made on the basis of data on the age of babies at the time their births were registered.

BIRTH RATES

Birth rates are expressed in several terms, such as the crude birth rate, age-specific birth rate, and parity-specific birth rates.

CRUDE BIRTH RATE

The number of births per 1,000 inhabitants, known as the crude birth rte, is the simplest measure of the rate at which a population is being replenished by births. It is arrived at by dividing the number of live births which occurred in one year by the number of inhabitants in the same population at the mid-point of that year, and multiplying the result by 1,000.3. That is,

$$\text{Annual crude birth rate} = \frac{\text{Number of live births in an area during a year}}{\text{Midyear total population in the same area in the same year}} \times 1000$$

Only live births should be taken into account in the numerator; the denominator should include the entire (but no more than) population in which the births occur. This last point is especially important in calculating birth rates for areas which do not comprise the entire nation. It is even more important when comparisons are made between rural areas and urban areas rather than in comparisons between larger territorial divisions. Births are ordinarily reported first on the basis of place of occurrence, which often is different from the usual place of residence of the mother. Whenever possible, data on births which are classified by place of residence of the mother should be used. If such data are not available, rural-urban comparisons should not be made because a varying numbers of births to rural mothers occur in urban hospitals.

While conducting an analysis it is usually preferable to treat each ethnic group in the rural population and urban population separately if data permit. Otherwise, the pronounced rural-urban fertility differentials which exist in many countries may be mistaken for inter-ethnic or other differentials.

In a situation where there are neither errors in reporting the number of births nor errors in the population base, the crude live birth rates range from about 15 (in the low-fertility countries of Europe) to approximately 50, or even higher, in the areas of highest fertility.

The crude birth rate is not a sufficiently refined measure of fertility for some purposes. In studying fertility differentials, the population analyst not only needs information whether country A has a relatively larger but he also needs to know the various factors that contribute to this difference. For example, in preparing estimates should know as much as possible about the past and present population variables that affect fertility; the determination and analysis of these factors require a more refined measure than that offered by the crude birth rate. Nevertheless, the crude birth rate is a powerful measure for determining the impact of present fertility on the total population; but it should be used only as a measure of the overall fertility.

GENERAL FERTILITY RATE

Statistically, the birth rate is a measurement of the probability or the 'risk' of giving birth to a living child. Obviously, it is not the total population that is 'at risk' but the female population of child bearing age. Consequently, differences in the crude birth rate may indicate nothing more than differences in the percentage of the population made up of women in the child bearing ages. The general fertility rate is the number of live births per 1,000 women in the child bearing ages. Most demographers use the female population in the age groups 15-44 or 15-49 as the base of this rate. The United Nations recommends that the age group 10-49 be used as the base.[4] The general fertility rate is given by the following formula:

$$\text{General fertility rate} = \frac{\text{Number of live births in an area during a year}}{\text{Midyear female population aged 15-44 in same area in same year}} \times 1{,}000$$

If virtually all births occur within marriage (including consensual unions) in the society under study, a further refinement may be introduced by limiting the denominator to females in the child bearing ages who are either married or living in consensual unions. Such refinements puts this rate into clearer focus because it eliminates from the denominator (which comprises females in the age group 15- 49) all those women who are unmarried, divorced or widowed. This rate might appropriately be referred to as the marital status-general fertility rate to distinguish it from the more common general fertility rate.

Either the general fertility rate or the marital-status-general fertility rate can be calculated on the basis of the male population in the age group 15-49 years, in which case the name of the rate would be preceded by the word "male".

AGE-SPECIFIC BIRTH RATES

Age specific birth rates differ from the general fertility rate in that both the numerator and the denominator are restricted and the age span is shortened. In most cases, age specific rates are calculated either for five-year age groups or by single years of age. The numerator is the number of live births to females of a specific age; the denominator is the number of women of that age.

$$\text{Annual age-specific birth rate} = \frac{\text{Number of live births to females of a specified age in an area during year}}{\text{Midyear female population of the same specified age in same area and same year}} \times 1{,}000$$

TABLE 8.1 AGE-SPECIFIC BIRTH RATES:UNITED STATES, 1936 and 1950, AND PANAMA AND PUERTO RICO 1950

Age group (years)	United States 1936	United States 1950	Panama 1950	Puerto Rico 1950
All ages*	52.5	80.3	114.2	135.0
10-14 years**	0.5	0.9	1.4	0.4
15-19 years**	45.1	79.4	123.6	99.2
20-24 years**	116.2	193.6	244.2	279.7
25-29 years**	105.0	163.3	211.3	260.3
30-34 years**	71.4	101.3	139.3	200.0
35-39 years***	45.7	51.2	82.1	143.1

40-44	16.0	14.5	26.2	53.1
45-49	1.8	1.1	8.3	11.7

*Rates based on live births to woman of all ages but computed on the female population aged 10 to 49 years.

**Rates based on live births to woman under 15 years of age but computed on the female population aged 10 to 14 years.

***Rates based on live births to woman aged 45 and over but computed on the female population aged 45 to 49 years.

Source of data: United Nations Statistical Office. *Demographic Yearbook. 1954.* New York, 1954.

Table 8.1 shows the age-specific birth rates for the United States in years 1936 and 1950, and for Puerto Rico and Panama in 1950. It is worth noting the relative differences between the 1950 rates for Panama and Puerto Rico on the one hand,and the United States on the other, are smallest in the ages of highest fertility and greater at older ages. However, the relative increases in fertility in the United States between 1936 and 1950 were greatest in the ages of highest fertility and at ages below, but were relatively small among older women. A comparison of the United States with the two other countries shows that the difference in fertility for all ages in 1950 are owing to differences in fertility in each of the age groups, especially after the age of 35; whereas the difference which arose between 1936 and 1950 in the United States was on account of a change in the fertility of women from 15 years to 34 years.

Age-specific birth rates can be further refined in the same manner as the general fertility rate. This refinement can be accomplished by limiting the base population to those women who are living as married.

PARITY-SPECIFIC BIRTH RATES

Parity-specific birth rates relate the number of births by birth order (that is, the first birth to a woman, the second birth to the same woman, etc.) to the number of women who have already born

$$\text{Annual parity-specific birth rate} = \frac{\text{Number of births of a given birth order occuring in an area during a year}}{\text{Midyear female population of appropriate parity group in same area in same year}} \times 1{,}000$$

year

Annual parity-specific birth rate = ——————————— x 1000
Midyear female population of appropriate parity group in same area in same year.

Parity specific birth rates may also be made specific for the age of the mother.

Sufficiently detailed data are rarely available for the computation of parity-specific birth rates by age, however, because corresponding population figures are not available except at the census period, and specific questions on the number of children ever borne would have to be asked of the female population. Therefore, the birth rate for birth order is usually calculated simply on the total female population between 10 years and 49 years. Rates computed in this manner are usually satisfactory for comparisons from one year to another in the same population, for crude comparisons of different populations.

GROSS REPRODUCTION RATE

The gross reproduction rate is the number of female babies that would be produced by the average woman who survived the entire reproductive period and who experienced the age-specific birth rates prevailing at the time for which the rate is calculated. It is calculated by adding together the age Specific birth rates of female births for all age groups, and converting the result to a rate 'per woman' by dividing by 1,000. That is, the gross reproduction rate is the sum of the age-specific birth rates, using only female births for the calculation of the rates.

In practice, the gross reproduction rate is usually calculated form data for both male and female births, and from age-specific birth rates for five-year age groups. When this is done, the age-specific birth rates for five-year age groups are added together and the total is multiplied by five (because there are only one-fifth as many rates as there would be if single-year age-specific birth rates were used). The product is then divided by 2.05 (because the "normal" sex ratio at birth is about 105 males per 100 females in most populations) to arrive at the gross reproduction rate.

This procedure is illustrated here:

Age of mother (years)	Number of recorded births	Enumerate female population	Age-specific birth rate per woman
10 - 14	90	156,362	0.00057
15 - 19	12,634	156,319	0.08082
20 - 24	20,046	141,711	0.14145
25 - 29	16,214	109,844	0.14760
30 - 34	10,043	78,469	0.12798
35 - 39	7,586	77,753	0.09756
40 - 44	2,618	60,875	0.04300
45 - 49	910	51,369	0.01771

In this illustration, the gross reproduction rate is equal to

$$\frac{\left(\sum \text{Sum } of\ age-specific\ birth\ rates\right)\times 5}{2.05} = \frac{0.65669\times 5}{2.05}$$

$$= 1.60$$

The gross reproduction rate is a single figure summary of all the age-specific birth rates of a population free form the influence of age composition. As such, it is a convenient means for comparing fertility performance independently of the effects of differences in age composition at different times or for different areas, provided reliable data are available. However, as is the case with all rates based on birth registration data, one often encounters cases in which large differences in the rate reflect differences in the completeness of birth reporting rather than true differences in fertility.

The gross reproduction rate can be calculated using the birth rates according to the ages of men in the population, though this type of rate is seldom used. However, if the births are to be male births only, then we have a rate which may be called the "male gross reproduction rate".

NET REPRODUCTION RATE

The gross reproduction rate does not take into account the effects of mortality on population or the replacement of population by fertility; it simply indicates the average number of female babies that would be born to a member of a cohort of women. Obviously, some women die before they have completed the child-bearing period; some, of course, die before the period begins. The net reproduction rate takes this into account. This rate is average number of female babies that would be born to each woman in a cohort of women - taking into account deaths among the new cohort of women throughout the child-bearing ages, using the age-specific death rates prevailing at a given time.

The net reproduction rate is calculated by multiplying the survival rate of each age as given in a file table by the age-specific birth rate for that age (taking into account only female births) and adding the products of the multiplication.

The following example illustrates the calculation of the net reproduction rate:

Age (years)	Age specific birth per woman	Female survival rate from birth to middle of age group	Expected survived births per woman.(2x3)
(1)	(2)	(3)	(4)
10 - 14	0.00057	0.83440	0.00048
15 - 19	0.08082	0.81607	0.06595
20 - 24	0.14145	0.78971	0.11170
25 - 29	0.14760	0.76080	0.11229

30 - 34	0.12798	0.73163	0.09363
35 - 39	0.09756	0.70219	0.06851
40 - 44	0.04300	0.67220	0.02890
45 - 49	0.01771	0.64161	0.01136

In this illustration, the net reproduction rate is equal to -

$$\text{(sum of expected births per woman)} \times 5 = \frac{4928 \times 5}{2.05} = 1.20.$$

The net reproduction rate is, thus, 1.20 in this example, which means that if the birth and death rates of that year continued, then 100 women in the child bearing ages would have 120 daughters who would survive to the same ages.

A net reproduction rate of 1.00 means, in theory, an exact replacement of the population; that is, on the average, each woman who reaches the child-bearing age succeeds in raising one daughter who survives to the child-bearing age.

The net reproduction rate has come to be used more cautiously in recent years. If birth rates change greatly from one year to the next, then the net reproduction rate cannot be used as a prediction of the population increase. Also, the net reproduction rate requires reliable death statistics as well as reliable birth registration data and accurate census enumeration by age.

Obviously, the net reproduction rate is a smaller number than the gross reproduction rate. The greater the mortality of females, the greater will be the difference between the two rates. In the afore mentioned example, the gross reproduction rate (the reproduction rate if all the female infants born survived to the child-bearing age) is 1.60 instead of 1.20.

CENSUS DATA ON FERTILITY

Birth registration data are too incomplete to be of much value for fertility analysis in many parts of the world. Even in countries in which birth registration is relatively complete, differentials in the completeness of birth registration make it somewhat risky to use rates dependent upon birth registration data for anything but gross comparisons. In some countries, the quality of the data is such that birth rates cannot even be used with safety to detect major differences in fertility.

Census data are also subject to errors; however, while these errors may change the counts considerably, many of them cancel each other in such a way that the rates constructed from the counts are affected relatively little. For this reason measurements of fertility based on census data alone may sometimes be more reliable than those based on vital statistics, in some areas.

CHILD WOMAN RATIO (FERTILITY RATIO)

The child-woman ratio, or fertility ratio, is the number of children under five years of age per 100 women in the age group of 15-44 both as enumerated in a census. The ratio is calculated as follows:

$$Child-woman\,ratio = \frac{children \text{ under } 5}{women\ 15-44} \times 100$$

The principal advantage of the child-woman ratio is that it can be derived from any census giving the population by age and sex. It requires no birth registration data, no census data on the number of children ever born, nor any special tabulations of any sort.

The child-woman ratio is influenced by coverage errors and by age reporting errors. Little research has been done to determine the extent to which such errors may affect the child-woman ratio. When a large percentage of a population in the first years of life is omitted from the census (as is frequently the case), the child-woman ratio may be seriously affected unless net omissions are proportionately as large in the female population in the age group 15 - 44 as among the children under five years of age. In any case, they are likely to be smaller than corresponding omissions from birth statistics.

The child-woman ratio does not have a "proportional" relationship to the crude birth rate because (a) it is influenced to a greater extent by infant and childhood mortality rates, and (b) it is independent of gross errors in the total population count, although it may be influenced somewhat by large errors in the female population aged 15 - 44 years. The extreme range of child-woman ratio is from about 30 - 50 years.

In using the child-woman ratio, extreme care must be taken to make sure that mothers and their children are classified in the same age group. For example, the child-woman ratio of the foreign-born women relate to the foreign-born and native-born children of these women.

NUMBER OF CHILDREN EVER BORN

Many recent censuses have included a question on the number of children ever born to enumerated women in certain age groups. In some countries, this question has been asked for all women or for all women over a certain age (such as 12 years); in others, it has been asked only for women who have been married. The question generally asked is: what is the number of children born alive to each woman upto the date of the census?

Census data on the number of children ever born can be used in a variety of ways as substitutes for birth registration data. Such data are sometimes preferable because (a) if children are classified in the wrong groups by urban-rural residence, then their mothers are also classified in the same wrong group, and (b) if a large number of children are omitted, then their mothers are also likely to be omitted. Responses to the question on the number of children ever born are probably subject to some memory bias; this is especially true of responses for older women and particularly in reporting children who have already died.

The most frequent use made of the tabulations on the number of children ever born is to show the proportion of women having had various number of children. This is particularly useful if the information is available for successive censuses. An increase in the total number of children per woman from one census to the next may result from larger numbers of women having two or three children each, even though fewer women have seven or eight each.

A common measure of fertility is the ratio of total number of children ever born to the women in the age group that has completed its child-bearing; that is the age-groups 45 - 49 or 50 -54. This gives the actual performance in the past of a particular cohort that has completed its fertility, or the "average size of a completed family".

PRESENT TRENDS IN FERTILITY

Fertility has been high in a large part of the world during most of history, and it is still high in most parts of the world. A very high fertility means, as a rule, a crude birth rate of 50 per thousand, or higher and an average of about six children to each woman who lives to the end of the reproductive period.

Comparative data on births in various regions of the world are misleading, because many of the countries with high fertility also have the least complete registration of births. Many of the figures presented on the number of births cannot be accepted as even indicative of the true fertility of the population. Child woman ratios (fertility ratios) from census data are a more reliable measure of fertility in many areas of the world.

In general, the picture is one of relatively low fertility in Western Europe, the United States, Canada, New Zealand and Australia and very high fertility in Africa, much of Asia and most of Latin America.

Where there have been declines in mortality, they have usually been followed by declines in fertility, but not until after a period of some years. The intervening period, of a decline in mortality but still high fertility, is a period of rapid population growth.

Fertility is usually lower in urban-industrial areas than in agricultural societies. Even in highly industrialised countries, fertility is higher in rural areas; and even in primarily agricultural countries fertility is lower in the cities. Until quite recently, fertility steadily and consistently declined with increasing industrialization and rising standards of living. Since World War II, there have been widespread increases in the birth rates in the industrialized nations; more recently, however, birth rates have been declining.

NOTES AND REFERENCES

1. It should be noted that the meanings of the apparent cognates of fertility and fecundity are reversed in some languages. In Spanish and French respectively, *fertilidad* and *fertilite* are used by demographers in the same sense that *fecundity* is used in English; *fecundidad* and *fecundite* are used in the sense as *fertility*.
2. United Nations. Statistical Office. *Handbook of Vital Statistics Methods*, New York, 1955. (Series F, No. 7)
3. In dealing with small populations, where "chance" variations in the number of births from year to year are significantly large, the number of births for a 3 or 5 year period may be divided by 3 or 5 respectively to arrive at a figure in which year-to-year variations have been minimised.

NINE

POPULATION ESTIMATES AND PROJECTIONS

Population is in a constant state of change, both in terms of size and characteristics. Periodic census enumerations obtain data on the size and composition of the population at the time of census. For many practical purposes, it is important to know the number and characteristics of people during the period between the two censuses and even after the last census.

POPULATION ESTIMATES

Population estimates are approximations of the size or composition of the population at the past or present dates. Estimates for dates between the two censuses are referred to as intercensal estimates. Such estimates may be nearly as reliable as the census counts themselves. The necessary assumptions usually are extremely simple and straight forward. Often they amount to nothing but the acceptance of the basic data adjusted for known errors, and the premise that any population changes in the size or in the composition generally occur in fairly regular patterns unless there is some indication to the contrary. The range of error is greatly limited by the availability of census data for both earlier and later dates; and if information on births, deaths and migration is complete and reliable for the intercensal period involved, the estimate made will be adequate.

The situation is somewhat different for post-censal estimates; that is, in the case of estimates for dates subsequent to the most recent census for which data is available. First, there is no later census to indicate the upper limit of the range within which the true figures usually lie. Second, post-censal estimates most commonly are made for dates so recent that vital statistics and other data bearing on population change during the period since the last census may not yet be available for the entire period. Post-censal estimates amount to estimates of the extent of change which has already taken place in the population. The assumption on which post-censal estimate is based may be much more complex than those involved in most intercensal estimates, especially if the estimate is for an area smaller than an entire nation. Nevertheless, if there has been a major change in the birth, death or migration rates which prevailed at the time of the last census there is also likely to be some hint of at least the direction of the change. Post-censal estimates for entire nations may be as reliable as the intercensal estimates if birth, death and migration statistics for the nation are of a high quality. On the other hand, such estimates for cities or administrative divisions of countries characterized by a large amount of internal migration often involve assumptions based on incomplete knowledge of the elements of population change and therefore may be subject to rather large errors.

POPULATION PROJECTIONS

Population projections are estimates of the total size or composition of the population at future dates. The assumptions involved in the population projections are always subject to much more doubt than those for population estimates, for they involve events which have not yet taken place. Occasionally, there are reliable indications of the nature of the assumptions on which a population projection should be based. More commonly, the range of possibilities for each known factor which may influence one or more of the components of population change is so great and hidden factors are so numerous, that the selection of the basic assumptions from among those which are possible may be little more than an educated guess. For this reason, two or more projections are commonly prepared on the basis of different set of assumptions so that the user may take the usual probable developments into account or may select the estimate based on the single set of assumptions best suited to his own needs.The word "projection" is used instead of "prediction" or "forecast" because the results are expected to hold true only to the extent that the assumptions are fulfilled.

For the purpose of this discussion, it is convenient to treat population estimates and projections together, since similar statistical techniques are involved in both.

QUALITY AND TECHNIQUES

The quality of population estimates and projections is dependent upon (a) the quality of the basic data, (b) the accuracy of the assumptions on which the estimate or projection is based, and (c) the validity of the techniques applied in manipulating the data in accordance with the assumptions. If the basic data are grossly incorrect, or the assumptions are not plausible, there is little hope that the estimate or projection would be correct no matter how good the statistical procedures applied. Consequently, no population estimate or projection should be published without a statement of the underlying assumptions (unless those assumptions are obvious from the procedures used).

Many of the techniques used to prepare population estimates and projections are essentially the same whether one is working with one or more segments of a population or working with the total. If the basic data are reliable, under certain circumstances, it is possible and desirable to treat each age-sex group separately in preparing estimates or projections for the entire populations. If this is done, estimates by age and sex are obtained as a by-product.

Demographers make use of a wide variety of techniques for preparing population estimates and projections. The most detailed methods for obtaining estimates and projections treat each of the components of population change separately, and are consequently referred to as component methods. Strictly, mathematical methods do not do this, but simply base the estimates and projections of population size on past growth performance; such methods are usually less reliable than the component method.

INTERPOLATION AND EXTRAPOLATION

Perhaps the most accepted method of estimating population which is strictly mathematical is that which assumes a constant rate of population change or constant increment to the population each year. Such estimates are more easily prepared than those of any other type. However, the basic assumption almost always proves to have been in error if any considerable period of time is involved. These techniques are most useful for the following purposes:

1. Estimating the size of population at the points of time between the censuses.

2. Estimating the size of population at times during the first year or so following the census.

3. Adjusting the population counts or estimates to midyear or other dates in the same or adjacent years.

Interpolation is the process of mathematically calculating the size of population at a point of time in between two dates at which its size is unknown. This may be done on the basis of either constant increments in number ("arithmetic" interpolation) or constant rates of increase ("geometric" interpolation). Extrapolation is the same process for years beyond the two known dates.

"Arithmetic" Interpolation and Extrapolation

In "arithmetic" interpolation, the difference between the size of population at two different dates is prorated on the basis of the time interval between the earlier known date and the estimate date. Thus, to arrive at the population of Mexico in 1958, the difference of 9,132,112 between the 1960 census population (34,923,129)and the 1950 census population (25,791,017) is multiplied by 0.8 and the product is added to the 1950 population to arrive at the figure of 33,096,706.

Arithmetic extrapolation is accomplished in the following three steps:

a. First, finding the average increment per year by dividing the total increase in population by the number of years between the last two censuses.

b. Second, finding the estimated increment upto the date of the estimate by multiplying the average annual increment by the number of years from the last census date to the date of estimate.

c. Finally, finding the extrapolated population on the estimate date by adding that increment to the population at the last census date.

"Geometric" Interpolation and Extrapolation

In "Geometric" interpolation, the average annual rate of increase between two dates for which the population is known is determined, and that rate is then applied to estimate the population at some point of time between the two dates. The calculations required to estimate the population of Mexico in 1958 on the basis of the average annual rate of increase between 1950 and 1960 censuses are as follows:-

(1) Average annual rate of increase, 1950 - 1960:

$$\log(1+r) = \frac{\log P_2 - \log P_1}{n}$$

$$= \frac{\log 34{,}923{,}129 - \log 25{,}791{,}017}{10}$$

$$= \frac{7.54311 - 7.41147}{10}$$

$$= \frac{0.13164}{10}$$

$$= 0.013164$$

$$1 + r = 1.0307$$

$$r = 3.07 \text{ per cent}.$$

2. Population in 1958 if the rate of increase had been constant from 1950 to 1960:

$$\log P_x = \log P_1 + n \log (1 + r)$$

$$= 7.41147 + 8(0.013164)$$

$$= 7.41147 + 0.105312$$

$$= 7.516782$$

$$P_x = 32{,}868{,}000$$

The same procedures are used for extrapolation as for interpolation. The only difference between the two, as explained earlier, is that interpolation in between two known values and extrapolation is for years later than the period between the two known values.

COMPONENT METHOD FOR ESTIMATES AND PROJECTIONS

It has already been emphasised that the size of the population can change only as a result of the combined effect of such population processes as fertility, mortality and migration. These are the basic factors responsible for change in any given area. Other factors, such as economic cycles and wars, can produce any population change only through their effects on one of the three basic population processes.

COMPONENT METHOD - DEFINITION

Procedures which take into account the components of population change individually are known as component method for estimating the population. In such procedures, each component is estimated or projected separately and is added to or subtracted from a base population to arrive at the population at some future date. The basic formula for the component method is:

$$P_2 = P_1 + B - D + I - E$$

where

P_2 is the population at the later date

P_1 is the population at the earlier date

B is the number of the births occurring between the two dates

D is the number of deaths occurring between the two dates

I (immigration) is the number of migrants arriving in the population between the two dates

E (emigration) is the number of emigrants departing from the population between the two dates

For estimating the present population, registered births and deaths as well as immigration and emigration statistics are added and subtracted, as the case may be, to the most recent census population figure. If registration and census data are reasonably complete, this method yields reasonably good population estimates; that is this type of estimate is just as good as the data that are used.

The component method of population projection is often applied by calculating the expected births and deaths in relation to each age and sex group of population. This is called the cohort procedure. Each age-sex group in the population is decreased in accordance with expected mortality rates. Each age group of women is assumed to give birth to children at a given rate, and the births are added to the population. The infants added to the population are then subjected to mortality rates along with the rest of the population. If net migration gains or losses are expected, the age-sex structure of the migrant population must be taken into account, and its mortality and fertility estimated. The assumption about each component of change should be examined carefully to make sure that they are compatible with known facts.

Projections are usually made for five-year age groups at five year intervals. If a ten-year projection is made, it is done by projecting the population forward in two five year steps.

The chief advantage of the cohort method is that it takes into account the age-sex structure of the population and the effect this will have on the population growth. If at any period of time there have been important changes in the age-sex structure as a result of war or a rapid reduction in either births,or deaths, a simple projection of past rates of growth may be particularly inadequate. The component method should give a more realistic picture of the probable future growth.

Another advantage, though sometimes a doubtful one, is that the component method permits the use of common sense assumptions about the probable effects on birth and death rates of such factors as government policy regarding birth control or immigration, or public health campaigns directed towards reducing mortality.

An incidental advantage of the component method is that it provides estimates of the future population by age and sex besides giving a total figure. For many purposes these estimates are indispensable; for example, calculations of the number of school going young children in the future are needed if schools have to be built and of the working-age population for effective economic planning. In an industrialized society a number of firms require estimates of number of the persons that will belong to particular age-sex groups; for example, in some countries, many firms are engaged in supplying services and equipment to infants.

FERTILITY COMPONENT

The fertility component in a population estimate sometimes may be determined directly from birth registration data, making appropriate allowances for under registration. In countries where family planning is common, fertility projections on a national basis are subject to much larger absolute errors than projections of either mortality or migration.

FERTILITY ESTIMATES FOR PAST PERIODS - This is a simple matter for the relatively few populations in which birth registration is complete and up-to-date. The number of births which occurred from the beginning to the end of the estimate period is simply added to the population at the beginning of that period. If separate estimates are being prepared for each age-sex group, births are usually handled on a year-to-year or quinquennial basis. In the first procedure, the population which is less than one year old at the end of each year in the estimate period may be determined by subtracting the number of infant deaths which occurred in the preceding 12 months from the number of births which occurred in the same period.1. When this is done, the population which is one-but-less-than-two years old in the second year is estimated by subtracting the deaths of children of that age during that year from the estimated population under one year old at the end of the preceding year, instead of applying life table rates. This process is continued to the end of the estimate period, the result being an estimate of the population born after the beginning of the estimate period by single years of age.

In the absence of reliable birth registration data, estimates of the number of births might be made on the basis of indirect indicators (for example, sales of some item used exclusively by babies)[2] or by applying estimated it may be sometimes necessary to project from census data the amount of change attributable to fertility. Such projections differ from fertility projections for future periods only in that (i) other conditions during the period are known at least in part, and (ii) the projected number of births can be compared with other measurements or estimates.

FERTILITY PROJECTIONS Such projections involve (i) arriving at a set of premises or assumptions about birth rates, (ii) applying those assumptions to the birth rate over the period of the projection in order to arrive at the number of births. For example, if the projection is based on a crude birth rate of 25, and it is estimated that the population at the mid-point of a certain year will be 1,000,000, the number of births projected for that years is:

$$Birth\,rate = \frac{births}{population} \times 1,000$$

$$Births = \frac{birth\ \ rate \times population}{1,000}$$

$$= \frac{25 \times 1,000,000}{1,000} = 25,000$$

The population base for the future year may be obtained by some cruder method, and then rechecked in view of the number of births found.

While preparing fertility projections, it is sometimes desirable to control population composition at least to the extent of basing birth rates on the female population in the reproductive ages. More elaborate control[3] may introduce some additional precision, but unless an unusual amount of confidence can be placed in the underlying assumptions, such refinements would ordinarily be meaningless in the light of much larger discrepancies which may be expected because the assumption about future conditions may prove to be incorrect.

Commonly, fertility is projected on more than one set of assumptions, and the user of the projection is given the choice of more than one population projection. The assumptions may be either simple or complex. For example, it might be assumed that the age-specific birth rates prevailing at the beginning of the projection period decline by ten per cent in the first ten years and by 15 per cent in the next ten years.

Little can be said in a discussion such as this (intended mainly for use by technicians from all over the world) concerning specific assumptions for fertility projections for specific countries or smaller areas. If birth control practices are widespread and birth rates are now low, future economic conditions may be expected to exert a strong influence on fertility, with births rising during periods of prosperity and falling during periods of economic depression. In areas of high fertility, on the other hand, economic cycles seem to have relatively little effect on the number of births. In populations of the latter type, account must be taken of the possible effects of the adoption and implementation of governmental policies favouring birth control and the influence of related cultural factors.

The cohort method may take into account past changes in fertility and infant mortality; these affect the number of women in the reproductive ages and consequently the numbers of future births.

MORTALITY

The projection of mortality can be nearly as difficult as the projection of fertility. Errors owing to faulty mortality assumptions can be especially large in populations subject to high death rates.

In most of the world, death rates are still relatively high, but may be expected to fall with the spread of public health programmes. In preparing projections for such populations, demographers are increasingly faced with the need to assess the impact on mortality of future public health programmes for which funds are not yet available at the time the projections are prepared.

Perhaps the greatest difficulty in estimating or projecting mortality lies in the fact that death registration is grossly incomplete in most countries of the world. It is often difficult to arrive at more than vague notions about the general levels of present mortality, much less to produce estimates which are sufficiently accurate to serve as a firm basis for population estimates and projections. Under such conditions, survival ratios based on model life tables such as those published in the United Nations Demographic Yearbook might prove to be a safer starting point for mortality projections than the available registration data.

The effect on population projections of error in mortality estimates is less than from errors of similar relative magnitude in fertility because mortality affects only a small proportion of each group whereas the fertility estimate determines the initial size of each whole age group. Also, in the case of many age groups and in many areas mortality rates are so low than even large errors in mortality projections would have little effect on the estimated population size.

MIGRATION

Migration is even less predictable than either fertility or mortality. The restrictions on international migration which have been adopted throughout the world keep absolute levels sufficiently low in most countries so that large relative errors in migration estimates produce relatively minor errors in the estimated or projected figures for the total population.

In estimates and projections for areas smaller than entire nations, migration is sometimes the largest component of change. It is ordinarily necessary to estimate population changes owing to internal migration either by simply extending migration rates known to have prevailed in the period preceding the last census or by the use of indirect indicators. The techniques for such indirect estimates of migration are complex, and detailed knowledge of the selectivity of migration and reliable statistics on other items which are necessary for the preparation of such estimates are not available in most countries. Therefore, students who feel they would find it profitable to study those techniques are referred to the specialized publications in which they are described in details.4

INDICATORS OF POPULATION SIZE

The available data are often inadequate to arrive at satisfactory estimates of the size of a population at recent dates by the component method. This is especially true where estimates are to be prepared for areas smaller than entire nations, in which migration may have been an important component of change. Under such circumstances, one must often resort to indicators of population size in order to arrive at estimates of the number of inhabitants. This and other methods obviously are not suitable for preparing detailed estimates of population composition.

Anything for which reliable counts are available and which is known to have a definite and relatively constant relation either to the number of individuals or to the number of households may be used as an indicator of population size. The major stumbling blocks in the use of indirect indicators are (i) the counts of the indicator are subject to error, and (ii) changes may take place in the ratio between the indicator and population. The number of registered births and deaths, the number of children enrolled in school, units of staple food items sold, the number of private users of electricity or telephone services, the number of pairs of shoes sold, or anything else closely related to the number of individuals or households for which counts are available as of both the census date and the estimate date, may be used to estimate the size of the population by means of simple proportions.

An example of this type of estimate for the population of Mexico as of 1958 is given here. In this case, the indicator is the number of registered births. The assumption underlying the estimate is that there was no significant change in the crude birth rate of Mexico between 1950 and 1958. Methods based on such assumptions about birth rates and death rates are referred to as 'vital rates' estimates.

$$Registered\,births, 1950 = 1,174,947$$

$$Census\,population, 1950 = 25,791,017$$

$$Registered\,births, 1958 = 1,447,578$$

$$Estimated\,population, 1958 = (1950\,population)$$

$$= \frac{(1958\,births)}{(1950\,births)}$$

$$= 25,791,017\ \frac{(1,447,578)}{1,174,947}$$

$$= 31,775,483$$

Changes in the relationships between indicators and population sometimes may be taken into account by 'borrowing' rates of change from other populations. For example, in estimating the population of a province in a country, the change in the death rate of the nation might be taken to be equally characteristic of the change in the death rate for the province during the same period.

CONCLUSION

The work of a population analyst is often directed primarily or even entirely towards the goal of arriving at the most reliable population estimates and projections possible on the basis of the data available to him. There may be a considerable amount of uncertainty even in population estimates for current dates. The widely varying estimates of the 1958 population of Mexico presented here as examples of different methods of preparing population estimates should serve as a warning. The person making the estimates and projection often must have serious doubts about their accuracy.

Perhaps, unfortunately, the users of population estimates and projections are not often as cautious as the person who prepared them about accepting the resulting figures as entirely accurate forecasts. There is considerable tendency on the part of the users to make use of the numbers given in the estimates and projections without giving the least attention to the reservations about the reliability of those numbers; such reservations should be clearly stated in the accompanying text.

The fact is that population projection for most countries are grossly inaccurate at least as often as they are correct, and that current population estimates may be subject to relatively large errors within a few years after the census date. This should not discourage the population analyst from making the best efforts (of which he is capable) to arrive at reliable estimates and projections. There is a pressing need for a knowledge of the present and the future size of the population not only on the part of governmental agencies, but also throughout the business community. Estimates and projections of one sort or another will be made by someone; it is usually better that they be made by a person who is aware of the many factors which are known to have an influence on the population processes and who has at his command a knowledge of the techniques available to take those factors into account in arriving at his estimates and projection.

BIBLIOGRAPHY

1. Barclay, George W. *Techniques of Population Analysis.* New York: Wiley, 1958.

2. Spiegelman, Mortimer. *Introduction to Demography.* Cambridge, Massachuetts; Harvard University Press,1968.

3. United Nations.Department of Economic and Social Affairs. *Methods of Estimating Population, Manual III: Methods for Population Projections by Sex and Age,* (ST/SOA/Series A, Population Studies, No.25), 1956.

4. United Nations. Statistical Office. *Handbook of Vital Statistics Methods* (Studies in Methods, Series F, No.7),1958.

GLOSSARY OF TERMS

Abridged life table: A life table covering the full range of life, with life table functions presented for age groups rather than single years of age (Chapter 3).

Age ratio: The ratio of an enumerated age group to the average of the two adjacent age groups (Chapter 2).

Age-sex pyramid: Age distribution by sex, graphically represented as a bar chart (Chapter 2).

Age-specific birth rate: A measure expressing the number of birth per 1,000 women of specified age (Chapter 4).

Age-specific death rate: A measure expressing the number of death per 1,000 population of specified age (Chapter 3).

Birth rate: A measure expressing the number of births in relation to the size of the population from which these births arose (Chapter 4).

Child-woman ratio: Number of children under 5 years per 1,000 women 15--44 years of age at a certain point in time (Chapter 4).

Cohort: In demographic analysis this term refers to a group of persons having in common a demographic experience or change of demographic status or classification during the same period of time.

Cohort-Component projection: A form of population projection in which the population at a future date is computed separately for each age cohort of the population by taking into account the changes in the size of each cohort resulting from births, deaths, and migration. The base of such a computation is a set of figures representing the distribution of the population by age and sex at a given date. The projected size of cohorts included in the base is affected only by death and migration, whereas the projected size of cohorts born after the base date is also affected by the number of births in each time period between the base date and the date to which the projection applies (Chapter 5).

Component projection:A method of projection in which the projected population is computed by adding or substracting from a base population the number of births, deaths, and migrants estimated to occur during the projection period. Whenever the computation is done separately for each age component projection (Chapter 5).

Crude birth rate: The ratio of the number of births to the total population during a period of time, usually a year. It is generally expressed as births per 1,000 total population. It is computed by dividing the number of births during a period of time by the population at the midpoint of that period, and multiplying by 1,000 (Chapter 4).

Crude death rate: The ratio of the number of deaths to the total population during a period of time, usually a year. It is generally expressed as deaths per 1,000 total population. It is computed by dividing the number of deaths during a period by the population at the midpoint of that period, and multiplying by 1,000 (Chapter 3).

Death rate: A measure expressing the number of deaths in relations to the size of the population in which these deaths occurred (Chapter 3).

Expectation of life: A measure (based upon a life table) of the expected average future life time (in years) of persons at a specified age. Conceptually, it equals the number of years of life remaining to all persons reaching a specified age in a life table,divided by the number of persons reaching that (Chapter 3).

Expectation of life at birth: A measure (based upon a life table) of the expected average length of life of a birth cohort. Conceptually, it is equal to the number of years of life remaining at birth divided by the radix of that life table (Chapter 3).

Extrapolation: Any mathematical process for estimating the value of a variable at points outside an interval for which known values of the variable exist. For example, if the population of a country is known as on 1 january 1965 and 1 january 1966, a mathematical computation which uses the known figures for the two dates to estimate the population as on 1 July 1966 is called extrapolation (Chapter 5).

Fertility ratio: See child-woman ratio.

General fertility rate: The number of children born during a year per 1,000 women of childbearing age at the mid-point of the year. The most common definition of childbearing age for purposes of from 15-44 years although other age ranges may be used if advantageous for particular purposes. The general fertility rate has sometimes been referred to as the age-limited birth rate (Chapter 4).

Gross reproduction rate: Average number of girl babies that would be born to each woman in a cohort of women subjected to the age-specific birth rates prevailing at a given time (Chapter 4).

Infant mortality: Mortality prior to age 1 (Chapter 3).

Infant mortality rate: A measure of infant mortality expressed as the number of infant deaths during a year per 1,000 live births during that same year. It should be noted that some of the infant deaths in the numerator of the infant mortality rate occur to infants born in the year prior to that for which the infant death rate is computed. Hence, the measure is only an approximation of the true risk of mortality during the year of birth (Chapter 3).

Interpolation: Any mathematical process for estimating the value of variable at points intermediate between two or more known values of the variable. For example, if the population of a place is known as on 1 january 1940, i January 1950,and two of all three of the known values to estimate the population on 1 July 1953 would be called interpolation (Chapter 5).

Life expectancy: See Expectation of life.

Life table: A tabular numerical representation of mortality and survivorship of a cohort of births at each age of life. The conventional life table is based on the assumption that as the cohort passes through life, it experiences mortality at each age in accordance with a predetermined pattern of mortality rates which do not change from year to year. The life table thus constitutes a hypothetical model of mortality, and even though it is usually based upon death rates from a real population during a particular period of time,it does not describe the real mortality which characterizes a cohort as it ages. There is another kind of life table in which the mortality patterns are derived from the experience of the same cohorts as they pass through different ages. Such tables are called "Cohort life tables" or "Generation life table." Because many years must pass to accumulate the information needed to construct a cohort life table, such tables are rare. Due to difference in mortality patterns between men and women at different ages, life tables generally are constructed separately for each sex. The life table is a very useful tool for computing estimates of the mortality component of population change. This is done by the use of specific figures from the entire array which comprises the life table. The information in this array of figures is of different types, each of which is called a life table function (Chapter 3).

Life table functions: Each column of figures in the array which comprises a life table has a precisely defined meaning. Each expresses some significant feature of the cohort which the life table portrays. Since all the numbers in the life table relate to the original cohort, it is convenient to deal with a birth cohort of standard size, usually 100,000 or 10,000, or even 1,000. This is called the radix of the life table (Chapter 3).

Migration: The movement of people from one area to another involving a change of residence and not merely transitory travel. When the movement is between countries it is called international or foreign migration; when it is within a country it is called internal migration. Internal migrants are called out-migrants with reference to the area from which they depart and in-migrants with reference to the area to which they come. The numerical difference between in-migration and out-migration is called net migration and represents the net change in the population of an area resulting directly from migration (Chapter 1).

Natural increases: Excess of births over deaths. When deaths exceed births, there is what may be called a negative natural increase.

Net reproduction rate: Average number of girl babies that would be born to each woman in a cohort of women subjected to the age-specific birth and death rates prevailing at a given time (Chapter 4).

Parity-Specific birth rate: Birth rate relating the number of births of specified birth order to the number of women who have borne one child less than the number indicated by the specified birth order (Chapter 4).

Supplemental Course for Case Studies in Surveys and Censuses

Radix: The size of the birth cohort of a life table. For convenience, it is most commonly set at 100,000, 10,000 or 1,000 (Chapter 3).

Rate of population change: A relative measures of population change as the change in population during a period divided by the population at the beginning of the period (Chapter 1).

Registered birth: A birth which has been officially recorded in some form of civil register and which is included in the birth statistics. Statistics of registered births are sometimes compiled by area of occurrence of the birth and sometimes by area of residence of the mother. The two are not necessarily the same. Also, same births are registered in a time period after they occur and may be included in the totals for the period of registration rather than those for the period of birth. Sometimes, there are births which are not registered Chapter 1 and 4).

Registered death: A death which has been officially recorded in some form of civil register and which is included in the death statistics. As is the case in birth registration, registered deaths may be tabulated by place of occurrence, place of residence, period of occurence or period of registration (Chapter 1).

Sex ratio: The number of males per 100 females in a population. The sex ratio may be computed for the total population, for specific age groups, for persons born during a specified period, for persons dying during a specified period, and for other subgroups of the total population (Chapter 2).

Specific death rate: Death rate computed for a specific segment of the population (Chapter 3).

Stationary population: A population "closed" to migration having the same number of births as deaths over a given period of time, usually one year; for example a population with a natural increase of zero--the life table population (Chapter 3).

Survival ratio: The proportion of a cohort which survives from one age to an older age. When taken from a life table it is called a "life table survival rate" (Chapter 3).

Survivors: Those members of a cohort at one date who are still alive after the passage of a specified period of time. For certain demographic computations it is useful to distinguish different classes of survivors, such as survivors of births or survivors of migrants (Chapter 3).

Under-enumeration: In completeness of coverage in a census or survey. It is usually expressed as a percentage of what should have been the complete count rather than as a percentage of the number of persons enumerated (Chapter 2).

Under-registration: Incompleteness of registration of vital events (Chapter 1).

NOTES AND REFERENCES

1. Theoretically, something less than the total number of infant deaths should be subtracted. However, the small error introduced in the population under 1 year of age in each year corrects itself in subsequent years, so that this shortcut from the theoretically "best" procedure greatly simplifies the estimate without introducing significant errors in the results unless a separate figures for the population under 1 year old is to be published. Note that the simplified procedure would not be suitable for arriving at an estimate of the population under 1 year of age for evaluation of the completeness of enumeration of the population of that age in a census.

2. As with all indirect indicators, however, care must be taken to make sure that changes reflect true changes in the item one is seeking to measures rather than changes in the use of the item selected as an indicator.
3. For example, age specifies or age-parity specific birth rates or number of married women might be used.
4. The U.S. Bureau of the Census has published descriptions of some procedure for preparing such estimates in *Current Population Reports: Population Estimates*, Series P-25. No. 321 of that series (30 November 1965) provides a detailed description of one recommended method.

TEN

TECHNIQUES OF MAPPING IN POPULATION DISTRIBUTION

A case study of Ghosi Tahsil, Azamgarh

The techniques of mapping and interpretation of the spatial distribution of population in an area form an integral part of population geography. The statistical distribution of population is more meaningful to population geographers, when placed within a spatial context. Each item within the distribution, has two properties; its value and its location which may be either a point or a unit. Together, these properties produce the pattern of areal variation which constitute a spatial distribution of population.

OBJECTIVE

This chapter is mainly concerned with the techniques of mapping population distribution as simply as possible. How do population geographers use statistical techniques and construct quantitative maps and diagrams? Each of these maps diagrams is adaptable to a fairly wide range of population data, but each has its own characteristics as well as merits and demerits. The allied purpose of this chapter is to introduce some of the more statistical aspects of the spatial distribution of rural population in a region. The object is to portray a visual interpretation of population distribution on a map. Statistical indices may provide more precise and penetrating information. To provide a basis for comparison each technique will be used to illustrate the distribution of rural population on the basis of 1971 census in Ghosi Tahsil, Azamgarh.

Several attempts have been made to simplify and clarify the complexity of population distribution. As compared to linear distributions, areal distributions are less easy to analyse, because of the irregular size of administrative or geographical units, migration of population, and spatial variations in the physical and cultural habitat. There are also fundamental problems of associated with population mapping which attempts a visual representation of data. Subjectivity enters into the techniques of mapping which selecting such methods, as simple dots, multiple dots, choropleths, isopleths, as well as the value, size and location of dots and class intervals such as shading categories and isopleth intervals. It is significant to emphasize that the use of the following techniques loss both positive and negative aspects. The positive aspect is that different view point of population distribution can be obtained; the negative point relate to the generalization of data.

QUANTITATIVE DOT TECHNIQUE

An immense variety of quantitative symbols.[1] can be used to show the distribution on population; however, the most convenient technique of illustrating the distribution of population is by means of uniform dots,[2] each with an identical value placed at the main site of the settlement or as near as possible to the centre of satellite regarding population of distribution are available. Obviously the smaller the administrative unit (at the village level) the more accurate is the map.

The first step is to examine the total number of persons and then to select a quantitative scale to be represented by each dot. The success of the map depends largely on the selection of this value. The value of the dot for population distribution should neither be so low that there will be difficulty in inserting all the dots in the village where the number of persons are very high making the dots coalesce as a result, nor so high that there will be large number of empty villages or the sparsely populated villages may not be represented at all. Very often there may be problems in placing the dots in the units with very high or very low figures. In some cases, the dots may be so numerous as to coalesce. Some cartographers, in fact, claim that this result should be aimed at; the contrast between the dotless (white) and solid black regions with a gradual transition between them as the dots increase in frequency, is regarded as an ideal form of visual representation.

Other cartographers insist that the dots should be countable and, therefore, must not be allowed to merge. In practice dots are rarely counted; obviously the person in search of more precise information must return to the statistical source upon which the map is based. In case of a village with very low population on the other hand, even when the value attributed to the dot has been chosen with discretion, a single dot may have to represent the total value with the whole of a unit. The problem however is to put the dot clearly, and the map will cease to have any precise locational value.

If dots are to be placed evenly[3] and uniformly within each unit, as in the absence of more precise information, there must be the boundaries of the units and negative areas on the map; in practice these are often removed after the dots have been inserted. But straight rows of dots and dots parallel to the boundary of each unit should be avoided. The dots should be placed evenly by eye and some continuity attained with the dots in adjacent units. The actual size[4] of the dots presents a further problem. Their size must depend on the scale of the base map and on the number of dots to be inserted, but the dots must be neither so big that a coarse generalized effect is produced, nor so small that a blur is produced in areas of dense value. The various types of pens of planograph may be used to make dots of uniform size.[5]

Figure 10.1 exhibits the distribution of rural population. The distribution of rural population has been shown by uniform dots, each do representing 500 persons. Instead of using a located dot with a precise absolute number of population, it may be shown by a centi-dot map[6] or percentage dot map each dot representing 1 per cent the total rural population involved in the particular distribution. The map, which bears 100 dots, is known as a centi-dot or percentage do map. It not only facilitates arithmetical comparisons but also affords ready information concerning fractional but also afford ready information concerning fractional distributions and proportions. The map is also known as mille-dot map.[7] The distributional map, which contains 1000 uniform dots, is called mille-dot map, on which each dot representing 0.1 per cent of the total rural population. This may also be shown by a colour dot map.[8] If several types of distribution of rural population (religion, caste, language etc.) are to be shown on one map, the dots of different colour may be used. Colour must be chosen to provide contrasts.

The advantage of colour is that the data relating to areas can be reproduced and recounted, and can be repolotted by other cartographic techniques. The technique of distributional maps is well suited to that region, where the population is distributed unevenly and sporadically, a fact which might well be concealed by some form of choropleth or isopleth map.

Its disadvantage is that a dot will rarely represent a round number, the technique is also time consuming. The work involved is different especially, when micro-level maps (at the village level) are desired.

The advantage of a colour map is that the number of coloured dots or the proportion of the colours vary with changes in distribution producing similar changing patterns and emphasizing traditional zones. Prothero has drawn attention to the problems of mapping population distribution and made suggested that, "a dot distribution map would seem to be the first essential in any attempt to delineate population."[9]

The dot map requires a number of careful considerations such as the enumeration area, the dot value, the dot size and the dot location.

The x-axis Y-axis histograms (Figure 10.1) have also been shown at an interval of four kilometres distance to reveal the fact that as the distances increase from west to east and north to south population and the number of villages decrease.

MULTIPLE DOT OR PROPORTIONAL DOT TECHNIQUE

The total rural population of each enumerated village may be represented by a symbol of a dot of proportional size or by a multiple dot.[10] It may also be shown by proportional circles[11] squares, etc. The multiple dots are particularly suitable for showing the distribution of population by villages to demonstrate the varying nature of the levels of human adaptation of the land, economic significance of varying population resources, or the effect of usar infected or infertile soil, flood affected areas or irrigation, transport and communication facilities etc. The multiple dots provide the quantitative population of settlements as well as locational information of settlements of various size, if they are drawn to scale. The area of two dimensional figures such as circles, squares are also made proportional to the total rural population of villages they represent. So, multiple dots are widely used to show the spatial variations of rural population distribution of a data set.[12] A multiple dot map is very useful in comparison with a uniform dot in order to depict the distribution of population by size of settlements. It requires a map showing the actual position of hamlets or villages on a large scale.

Multiple dots, proportional in size to the population of different settlements or regions, may be grouped in their approximate geographical position for purposes of comparison of population and land areas. The disadvantages attached to this method are first, that the extreme range of population density to be found in many regions often leads to an overlap of symbols and causes difficulty in the drawing and in the interpretation of the map, and second that the eye has difficulty in equating the symbol to the area it represents and the method does not readily convey density of population. Proportional circles and squares may also be effectively employed to show the ethnic structure of the population.[13]

DRAWING OF DOTS OF VARIOUS SIZE

Multiple dots must be carefully selected on a suitable scale and drawn so that they are readily distinguishable, particularly when intended for reduction, each must be sufficiently large to reproduce clearly. A wide range of symbols is available on a procircle or circlemaster on a plastic sheet or printed on transparent self-adhering plastic sheets which can be applied directly to a map. A symbol is carefully placed in its exact position of the settlement on the map. Clarke concluded that efforts should be made to improve this kind of map by including only one type of symbol per map, by using standard sizes shown in a carefully constructed key, by avoiding overlapping symbols and unless absolutely necessary including no place-names which may destroy the pattern.[14]

Figure 10.2 the rural population of all the villages have been located on their respective site of settlement by multiple dots, which are proportionate to the population of the village as indicated in the key of the map; while the urban population has been depicted by a located sphere. The mean centre and standard distance have also been calculated and shown in the map (Fig.10.2).

The Nearest Neighbour analysis also considers the location of individual villages within a pattern in relation to others, which ultimately helps to understand the distribution of rural population in relation to the distance of each village.[15] Frequently, only settlements of similar size or class are considered as the nearest neighbour. Fig. 10.3A shows the nearest neighbour pattern of the relative location of settlements with population over 1000. To discuss the distribution of the nearest neighbour pattern of relative location of settlements numerically, the following formula[16] may be used:-

$$R_n = \frac{D}{0.5\left(1\sqrt{A/N}\right)}$$

where, R_n is the description of the distribution, D is the mean distance between the nearest neighbours, A is the area under study (in the same unit as D) and N is the number of villages.

The value of R_n will occur within the rage from O to 2.15. If all the villages were clustered together at only one location Rn would be zero (O). If all the villages were regularly distributed throughout the area, Rn would be 2.15, and if the villages were randomly distributed, Rn would be 1.00. Barnes and Robinson.[17] devised a linear distance map for revealing variation in density of relatively dispersed population. The average distance between villages equals 1.11 /density, density being taken as the nuclear of villages per square kilometre. Mather corrected the constant to 1.07. The method is to locate the villages and measure the distance of each settlement and its nearest neighbour and tabulate these distances as nearest neighbour; then calculate the mean distance between the villages and their nearest neighbours to know the observed mean distance. Measure the total area of the study region and calculate the Rn value by substituting the formula.

DENSITY OF POPULATION

The concept of population density analyses the distribution of rural population and assessed over population, underpopulation and optimum population by comparing population densities though statistical methods. It is impossible to discuss the distribution of population without indicating that there are a greater number of people in some places, leading to relatively higher densities and fewer in others leading to lower densities.[18]

Density can be measured in relation to total, arable, net cultivated, food-cropped or inhabited area [19] or an area weighted according to its land-use, which gives their different geographical values. The numerator may be either the total population or a category, such as rural, agricultural, or working population. Although these various types of density have some utility for comparison in time within one country, they cannot be easily used for international comparisons. But none is of undisputed absolute value and above all none escapes from criticism.[20]

Hence, population pressure upon the total area of nyaypanchayat has been taken into consideration, because there is a very low percentage of area under waste and barren land in 1971. In order to identify the actual pressure of population, the distribution of population in different panchayats are contained in the table 10.1 is analysed.

The spatial pattern of density (Fig.10.3B) is shown by spatial three-dimensional histograms [21]. From the topological view point it is assured that panchayats are equal in area. A striking visual impression of the real variations in the density of population can then be achieved by raising a column on a three dimensional axis on a suitable scale at an appropriate angle, from the plane surface to give an attractive and "factory-chimney" picture. The drawing of three-dimensional histograms is a time-consuming and laborious process requiring an artistic mind, but it can be speeded up by using a graph paper under a tracing paper. This technique has the advantage of depicting the actual density of each of the panchayats as well as giving a clear and attractive idea of spatial variation of the density of population.

CHOROPLETH TECHNIQUE

It is necessary to decide according to the scale of the map, whether the available data would most appropriately be portrayed with reference to a point or to an area. Thus, equal dot or multiple dot techniques appear to refer to given point locations, while choropleth techniques refer visually to area (Greek, "Choros" = "an area"). If the isopleth is the chief tool of the climatologist, the choropleth may be said to be the important tool of population geographers in his statistical treatment of population distribution. Hence, choropleth techniques receive more attention here and are dealt with in more detail than other quantitative techniques.

The choropleth depicts the average population per square kilometre over some administrative region for which statistics are available. Wright.[22] used the term choropleth to denote an areal symbol applied to an administrative subdivision such as an indication of the density of population in a panchayat in Ghosi Tahsil, Azamgarh. Raisz.[23] emphasizes that the term choropleth need not be limited to administrative divisions, but a map divided into squares for which a density could be calculated and then shaded would also be a choropleth map.

The principle of the choropleth map is a very simple one, in which straightforward techniques of shading are used to build up a pattern of spatial variation in population distribution. The procedure can be illustrated by using nyaypanchayat as a unit in the area under study.

The first step in the construction of a choropleth map is the calculation of the average density for each panchayat. The calculation of density is a laborious process, but it can be speeded up with the help of a calculator.

The next problem is the selection of a suitable scale of population density; it is possible to obtain different impressions from the same statistics. This may be in arithmetical progression (Fig.10.3C and Fig.10.6) or in terms of octile groupings of a eight-category map (Fig. 10.4) or in the form of mean deviation (Fig.10.5) standard deviation (Fig.10.7) geometrical progression or at irregular intervals. The last is justifiable if it reveals significant features of distribution which would be lost by any regular scale. 24. A dispersion diagram (Fig. 10.4) will help to show where significant groupings occur (quartile, sextile, octile, decile or percentile). For deciding the number of categories to be established, the general rule used is that the number of classes must not exceed five times the logarithm of the observation.[25]

Thc third stage is the drawing of the choropleth map. The boundaries of the panchayats, which form the basis of the density values are first drawn by a pencil. A code number of the letter or figure (A,B,C,D, etc. or 1,2,3,4, etc.) is inserted in each panchayat. When completed, the final drawing is made, outlining each group by a thin line and ignoring all other boundaries, for as a rule, their presence spoils the density impression of the shading. Occasionally, however, it may be essential for the map to show specific densities for each panchayat; in that case the boundaries of each panchayat may be retained. Tints of shading must be carefully chosen to distinguish the various density ranges on a choropleth map. To achieve a graphic effect, the density of the shading should be intensified with the increases in density of population. Care should be taken to provide sufficient shading contrast; a balance must be maintained between dark and light tints. The lowest density is commonly represented by blank areas. This is not altogether satisfactory, for it does give an impression of no density at all rather than of low density.

The main object, here, is to achieve a grading from lighter tones to represent densities at the lower end of the range to darker tones for higher densities of population.

But, there is a new technique (Fig. 10.3-C) of showing absolute population as well as density of population both together, using circles drawn in proportion to the population of the panchayats and shading according to the density.[26] per square kilometre. This technique of mapping has the advantage of portraying the condition of concentration of population nyaypanchayat-wise, both absolutely and a per square kilometre basis. In the case of two circles with the same shading, the larger circle represents more absolute population while on the two circles of the same size, the thicker shading shows more persons per square kilometre. Some information is lost by grouping density into classes and the use of shaded circle requires considerable drafting skill if they are to be easily read, but every map has its limitations as a representation of reality.

There is an interesting and novel technique of showing density of population (according to need into 4, 6, 8, 10 or 100 groups) by using quartile, sextile, octile, decile or percentile densities respectively. Here, (Fig.10.4) the densities of all panchayats have been arranged in descending order of magnitude and grouped into eight density ranges on the basis of octiles and hatched according to the ranges in which they fall. These values are calculated (after ranking) with the help of the following formulae:-

$$DO^1 = \frac{(N+1)1}{8} \qquad DO^2 = \frac{(N+1)2}{8}$$

where, DO^1 is the density of first octile, DO^2 is the density of the second octile, N is the number of panchayats. The density dispersion diagram shows the deviation of density of each panchayat from the median. The histogram, based on octile values, shows the surplus and dificit population of the area under study.

This technique of mapping has the advantage of demarcating the demographic regions, having equal number of panchayats on the basis of density relating to the median. It is easy to calculate and the value of octile is easily followed. It also waives abnormal or extreme density. This technique has some disadvantages also. In the case of an individual series of 50 panchayats, the density of population of each panchayats is first required to be placed in an arrayed order. It becomes a complex problem if, the series consists of a large number of units. In the case of the individual density of each panchyat, there is still another practical difficulty. Some times the density is in between two densities say 443.5 persons per square kilometre (in case of the second octile between 442 and 444 persons per square kilometre of the 12th and 13th, respectively). This density (443.5) is not to be found in the original density of the panchayats, and the density is finally required to be adjusted by interpolation.

COMPARATIVE DENSITY

Map (Fig. 10.5) shows the comparative density.[27]. It is interesting to compare the density of nyaypanchayats to the average density of the area under study to understand the concepts of underpopulation, overpopulation or optimum population. The visual impression of the distribution of population is better illustrated by expressing differences in terms of deviation in percentage. It is calculated by the formula.[28]

$$C.D. = \frac{P \times 100\%}{S}$$

where, C.D. = comparative density, P = density of panchayats,
S = density of tahsil.

All the panchayats have been grouped into eight categories at interval of 25 per cent and hatched according to the ranges in which they fall.

The same results may be obtained by maps on the basis of the same data showing density on the scale of shading related to mean density of the area.

This technique of categorization for shading removes the difficulty of making any type of selection. It saves a lot of time and energy while demarcating the demographic division. It is simple to calculate comparative density in terms of percentages; population geographers find it easy to make various types of comparisions as well as further statistical treatment of the data.

RELATIVE DENSITY

Figure 10.6 exhibits the relative density of rural population which is prepared and calculated by the Prothero method.[29] It requires a dot map. Relative rural density is obtained here by superimposing a grid of two kilometres over the dot map (Fig.10.1) each dot representing 500 persons and each square in the grid represents four square kilometres of area. To obtain the relative density of rural population per square kilometre the dots in each square grid can then be counted and the result (population = total dots obtained and multiplied by 500) is divided by 4 and the map shaded accordingly.

This technique of mapping changes the pattern of density and intensifies the density of the panchayats where larger villages are located, whereas on the grid, where smaller villages are situated, the relative density is lower. This technique has the disadvantage that very low densities are found in peripheral places whereas higher densities are found up to 2000 persons per square kilometre, where larger villages are found; virtually uninhabited or negative areas are also marked out by X on the map (Fig.6). If the grid is very small, the original dot distribution map will be approximately produced. If it is very large, then the picture will be too generalized. It reveals the fact that relative densities are variable enough on a square grid of 2 kilometre distance. The X axis and Y axis histograms show the distribution of population at a distance of 2 kilometre, which clearly reflects the uneven distribution of population. It is also a time consuming technique.

POPULATION CONCENTRATION

Population geographers are naturally interested in the unevenness or concentration of population, the degree of uniformity or randomness, and the degree of clustering. The degree of concentration is the greatest where a population is assembled at one point, and least where it is evenly distributed.[30] To assess the concentration of population, various statistical techniques may be used in which standard score, or Z-score [31], Lorenz curve[32], Chi-square (X^2)[33] and Nearest Neighbour analysis are important.

Figure 10.7 exhibits the spatial concentration of population by using the standard score technique. Standard score, a statistical technique of measuring population concentration which requires further processing of the original density, is relatively simple. It involves the calculation of the standard deviation σ and subsequently the standardization of the original density by using the formula $\frac{X - \bar{X}}{\sigma}$, where, X is the original density of the panchayat; X is the arithmetic mean density of the region and σ is the standard deviation of density. The standardized density, thus produced has zero mean (Z - Score) and unit S.D. (standard deviation) and the standard scores being "pure" numbers facilitate direct comparisons among local panchayats and among variables. Effective use of this technique, however, depends to a large extent upon the normal frequency distribution. In normal distributions the variables are distributed about the mean in such a way that approximately 68.26% of the frequencies will fall under that part of the curve with $\pm 1\sigma$ of the mean and it was, therefore, considered useful to divide this central part of the distribution into cell intervals of $\pm$ 0.5 standard deviation.

After conducting a test by the above-mentioned formula, it is found that there are considerable variations in the degree of concentration of population amongst various panchayats. All the panchayats have been grouped into seven categories on the basis of Z-score or standard score and hatched according to the ranges in which they fall.

This technique of mapping has the advantage of showing the area of abundance and the area of deficit population. It also facilitates direct comparisons among units and among variables. It also indicates the uneven distribution of population. This technique alters the pattern of density of population.

Another technique of measuring population concentration is by using the Lorenz curve (Fig. 10.7). The Lorenz curve also shows the degree of concentration of population. In order to draw the Lorenz curve panchayats are arrayed in order of decreasing density and then population and areas of panchayats are totalled for each density class. Here, at an interval of 5 panchayats the cumulative percentage of area (Y-axis) is plotted against cumulative percentage of population (X-axis). It uses a square graph with X-axis and Y-axis on a percentage scale. If the density of the objects distributed over the area is uniform, then the result will be a straight line running from O at an angle of 45° across the graph. A variation of lesser or greater degree in the density will be reflected in the degree of concavity of the curve.

GENERALIZATION OF THE DISTRIBUTION OF RURAL POPULATION

Two techniques describe the modified distribution of rural population. The first method is the idea of a running mean (J.P.Cole, 1965) and the other method is to calculate potential (C.D. Haris, 1954) of a distribution that can be applied on any suitable map representing rural population by uniform dots. Here, the first technique is taken into consideration.

Figure 10.8A shows the distribution of rural population on hypothetical grounds. Since a circle is even more compact than a square, it has a slight advancement over a square while adopting the running mean technique on a two-dimensional surface. A circle of suitable radius may be used. If the radius is very small the original dot distribution map will be approximately produced. If it is very large, then the picture will be too generalized. Here, the radius of the circle used is 4 kilometres to test the technique. The centre of this circle is placed successively over each intersection of the lines of superimposed grid of 4 kilometres on a uniform dot map. The dots failing within this circle on each occasion are counted, calculated and recorded. On the basis of these values various circles are drawn over each intersection of the lines of the grid.

The isopleth map [34] (Figure 10.8B and 10.8C) also shows the spatial distribution of population in the area under study. The isopleth map is drawn by the lines joining the places of equal density of population, with or without tinting. These lines are either drawn through points with identical density of population, or are interpolated proportionally between them. When an isopleth is used for a density of population, the problem is rather more difficult. The four main variables determining the techniques in which such isopleths may be drawn are the following:-

a. The selected value intervals: the interval of density of population should be carefully selected;

b. The shapes and sizes of the units for which statistics are available;

c. The situation of the plotting points (which may or may not be central) within each unit. The location of the central point of a statistical unit is a difficult matter, particularly when its (panchayat) shape is irregular or elongated. Interpolation is usually done by assuming a uniform increase of value between two points and so placing the isopleth these difficulties. The superimposition of a grid (Fig. 10.3) over a dot map point of each grid-cell. The grid may be of squares (as used by J.Ross Mackay and P.W.Porter), or hexagonal, involving isometric graph paper. The hexagon is the closest approximation to a circle (Fig.10.8), wherein the border is a uniform distance from the central point, which will allow an area to be covered completely with these non-overlapping units. Moreover, the central points of adjacent hexagons from equilateral triangles, avoiding problems of interpolation inherent in square grids, where identical values or densities are involved.

d. The actual techniques of interpolation.

The isopleth map (Fig. 10.8B) shows the generalised distribution of rural population in 1971. The running mean technique is applied to obtain the density of rural population. Here, the radius of the circle used is 4 kilometres. Now the centre of the circle is placed successively over each intersection of the lines of superimposed grid of 4 kilometres on a dot map Fig.10.1. The dots falling within the circle on each occasions are counted, calculated and recorded its population (total dots falling within each circle are multiplied by 500 to achieve the total population, as each dot, represents 500 persons), which will be divided by 50 (the area of the circle used) to obtain the density.

Selected isopleths (at an interval of 100 persons per square kilometre) are inserted on the basis of these densities. The final isopleth map is drawn to give a good picture of the distribution in the area.

The isopleth map (Fig. 10.8C) also depicts the modified distribution of rural population, 1971. Prothero is technique is applied to achieve the information regarding density of rural population. Now, count the number of dots successively of each square grid of 2 kilometres falling within it over the dot map. Calculate its population

(population M total dots falling within each square grid are multiplied by 500 each dot represents 500 persons) and divide the result by 4 (the area of square grid used) to obtain the density of rural population. Isopleths are inserted at intervals of 500 persons per square kilometre on the basis of these densities. The final isopleth may be drawn to give a good idea of the distribution of rural population in Ghosi Tahsil, Azamgarh, U.P.

Table 10.1 **The Distribution of Population in Different Panchayats**

Panchayat	Rank	Density Km^2	Area in Km^2	Population
Sarvan Gharibpur	1	1139	10.22	11,631
Madhuban	2	1011	12.04	12,178
Baragaon	3	886	15.06	13,342
Ghosi	4	874	15.51	13,552
Fatehpur Mandaon	5	838	8.53	7,148
Jajauli-Dostpur	6	777	10.01	7,776
Gontha-Tikari	7	745	16.30	12,148
Chummanar	8	722	21.00	15,168
Dhanauli-Lohra	9	717	20.52	14,713
Bhikharipur	10	683	13.41	9,157
Sultanpur	11	669	11.64	7,788
Nemdand	12	629	10.43	6,562
Kuranga-Bana	13	624	17.11	10,678
Kamlapur Sipah	14	614	11.67	7,161
Badraon	15	602	15.20	9,153
Kamal Sagar	16	601	19.05	11,453
Gauhar pur	17	599	16.44	9,852
Koeriapar	18	570	18.06	10,287
Surajpur	19	553	19.66	10,883
Manikpur - Haraunwa	20	546	12.47	6,814
Parasupur Sonjharia	21	545	7.66	4,172
Fatehpur Tal Narja	22	539	17.71	9,544
Dargah-Bairia	23	539	19.52	10,516
Mirpur M. Dariabad	24	535	15.67	8,386
Rasoolpur	25	535	28.54	12,425
Korauli	26	529	13.40	7,095
Hariyaon-Jaganpur	27	516	10.20	5,311
Akolhi	28	515	12.55	6,471
Maurbojh	29	506	19.49	9,855
Kalyanpur	30	505	18.28	9,225
Sipah-Shuklauli	31	501	24.35	12,207
Sondsar-Chandpur	32	501	14.35	7,192
Katihari Buzurg	30	498	17.77	8,852
Kasara-Makasudan	34	488	35.15	17,146
Usari-Sardha	35	487	11.38	5,538

Nadaval	36	470	14.80	6,957
Sohar-Paranpur	37	462	30.17	13,929
Alinagar-Dan iyal	38	444	26.27	11,669
Sahroj-Kachhi	39	442	21.09	9,315
Bhelabandh	40	437	16.76	7,330
Lairo-Donwar	41	433	16.66	7,218
Majhwara	42	410	23.55	9,665
Nevada Mundadand	43	402	15.01	6,029
Pakari Buzurg	44	343	28.96	9,930
Mal kauli	45	338	15.01	5,068
Maryadpur	46	337	29.45	9,936
Mungesar	47	335	20.71	6,939
Bhairopur	48	335	22.06	7,382
Dubari-Laxmipur	49	331	61.47	20,343
Ghaziapur	50	223	35.02	7,796
Total	50	528	937.43	480,885

REFERENCES

1. Williams, R.L. *Statistical Symbols for Maps- Their Design and Relative Value,* New Haven 1959.
2. Winterbotham, H.St.J.L. " Dots and Distribution", *Geography,* 19, 1934, 211-213.
3. Balchin, W.G.V. and Lewis, W.V. " The construction of Distribution maps ", *"Geography"*, 30, 1945, 91.
4. Mackay, J.R. (1949) " Dotting the Dot Map ": An Analysis of Dot Size, Number and Visual Tone Density, " Surveying and Mapping ", Washington, Vol.9.
5. Byron, W.G. (1956) " Dotting the Dot Map with Steel Drill Stamps " *Professional Geographers*, 8, No. 4 (1956), 5-7.
6. Mackay, J.R. (1953), " Percentage Dot Maps ", *Economic geography*", 29, 1953 263-266.
7. Dahlberg, R.E. " Towards the Improvement of the Dot Maps ", *International Year book of Cartography,* 7, 1967,157-166.
8. Jenks, G.F. " Pointillism as a Cartographic Technique ", *Professional Geographers,* 5, 1953, 46.
9. Prothera, R.M. " Problems of Population Mapping in an Under- developed Territory ", *Nigerian Geographical Journal*, 3, 1960.
10. Geer, Sten de. " A Map of Distribution of Population in Sweden, Method of Preparation and General Results ", *Geographical Review,* 12, 1922,72-83.
11. Toyne, P. and Newby, P.T. *"Techniques of human Geography,* Glassgow, 1971, 93.
12. Coulter, W. " A Dot Map of Distribution of Population in Japan ", *Geographical Review,* 16, 1926, 283-284
13. Trewartha, G.T. and Zelinsky, W. " Population Distribution and changes in Korea 1925-1949, *Geographical Review,* 45, (1955), 1-26.
14. Clarke, J.I. " Statistical Map Reading ", Geography, 44, 1959, 96-104.
15. Clark, P.J. and Evans, F.C. " Distance to Nearest Neighbour as a Measure of Spatial relationship in Population ", Ecology, 35, 1954,445-453.

16. Toyne, P. Newby, P.T. " *Techniques in Human Geography* ", Glassgow, 1971,119.
17. Barnes, J.A. and Robinson, A.H. A New Method for Representation of dispersed Rural Settlements ", *Geographical Review,* 30, 1940, 134.
18. Trewartha, G.T. " A case for population Geography ", *Annals of the Association of American Geographers.* Vol.43, 71-97.
19. Wright, J.K. " Some Measures of Distribution ", *Annals of the Association of American Geographers.* Vol. 27, 177.
20. Garnier, J. Beaujeu " *Geography of Population* ", translated by S.H.Beaver, Longman, London, 33.
21. Cole, J.P. and King, C.A.M. " *Quantitative Geography Techniques and Their Theories in Geography* ", London, Willey, 1968.
22. Wright, J.K. " The Terminology of Certain Map Symbols ", *Geographical Review,* 34, (1944)
23. Raisz, E. " *General Cartography* " 1st Edition, New York, 246.
24. Schultz, G.M. " An Experiment in selecting Scale Values for Statistical Distribution Map ", *"Surveying and Mapping"*, Washington,D.C., Vol.21, 224-230.
25. Toyne, P. and Newby, P.T. " *Techniques in Human Geography* ", Glassgow, 86.
26. Smith, D.M. " Patterns in Human Geography ", New York, 1975.
27. Haffman, A. " India, Main Population Concentration ", *Geographical Journal*, 3, 1948, 89-100.
28. Monkhouse, F.J. and Wilkinson, H.R. " Maps and Diagrams, their Compilation and Construction, London, Methuen and Co. Ltd., 1971.
29. Prothero, R.M. " Problems of Population Mapping in an Underdeveloped Territory ", *Nigerian Geographical Journal*, 3, 1960.1
30. Clarke, J.I. " *Population Geography* ", Oxford, Pergamen Press, 1972.
31. Symes, D.G., Thomas, E.G. and Dean, R.R. " The Yorkshire and Humberside Planning region: An Atlas of Population Change, 1951-1966, Department of Geography, University of Hull, Hull, Miscellaneous Series No. 8., 1968.
32. Cole, J.P. and King, C.A.M. " *Quantitative Geography : Techniques and Their Theories in Geography* ", Wiley Sons Ltd., London, 1968.
33. Davis, P. " Science in Geography ", Vol. 3, 30.
34. Mackay, J.R. " Some Problems and Techniques in Isopleth Mapping, *"Economic Geography"*, 27, 1951.

Fig. 10.1

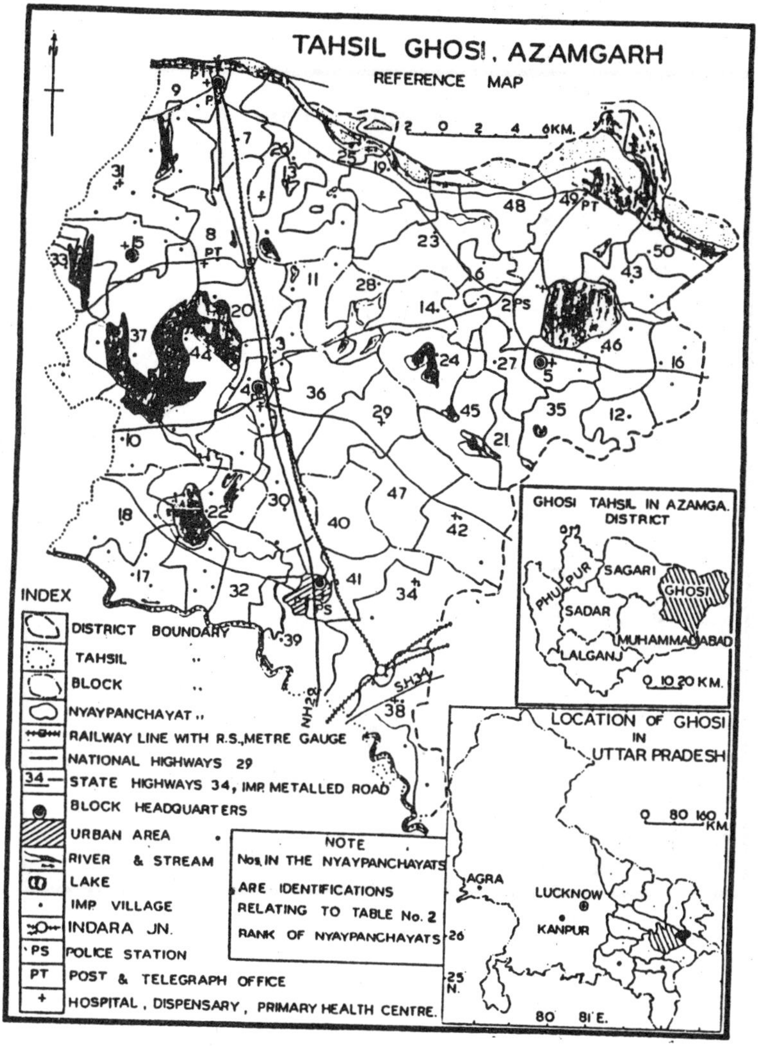
TAHSIL GHOSI, AZAMGARH
REFERENCE MAP
INDEX
DISTRICT BOUNDARY
TAHSIL
BLOCK
NYAYPANCHAYAT
RAILWAY LINE WITH R.S., METRE GAUGE
NATIONAL HIGHWAYS 29
STATE HIGHWAYS 34, IMP. METALLED ROAD
BLOCK HEADQUARTERS
URBAN AREA
RIVER & STREAM
LAKE
IMP. VILLAGE
INDARA JN.
POLICE STATION
POST & TELEGRAPH OFFICE
HOSPITAL, DISPENSARY, PRIMARY HEALTH CENTRE.
NOTE
Nos. IN THE NYAYPANCHAYATS ARE IDENTIFICATIONS RELATING TO TABLE No. 2 RANK OF NYAYPANCHAYATS
GHOSI TAHSIL IN AZAMGA. DISTRICT
PHULPUR
SAGARI
GHOSI
SADAR
MUHAMMADABAD
LALGANJ
LOCATION OF GHOSI IN UTTAR PRADESH
AGRA
LUCKNOW
KANPUR

Fig. 10.2

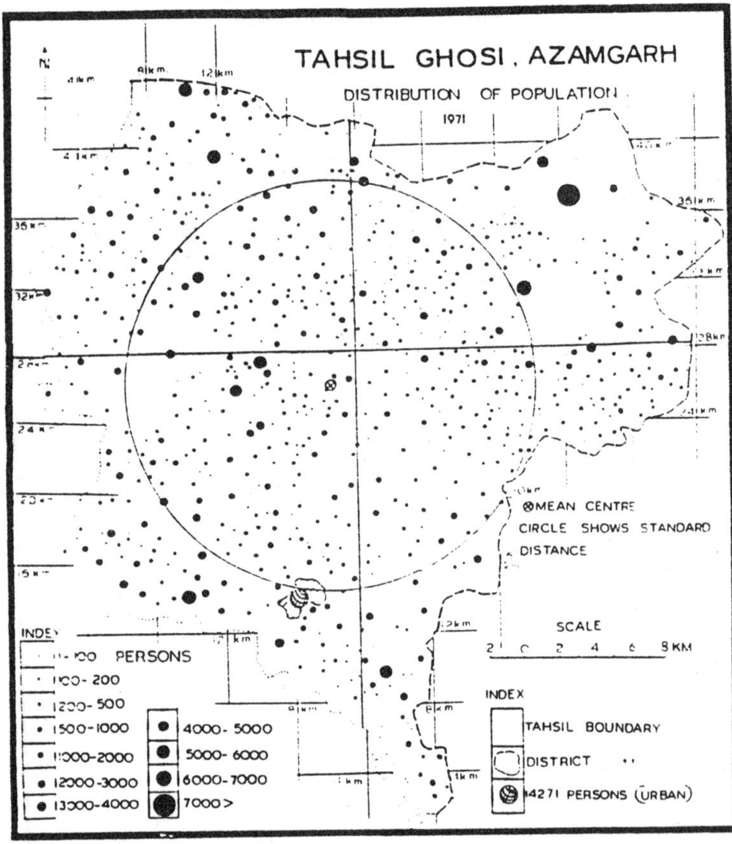
TAHSIL GHOSI, AZAMGARH
DISTRIBUTION OF POPULATION
1971
MEAN CENTRE
CIRCLE SHOWS STANDARD DISTANCE
SCALE
2 0 2 4 6 8 KM
INDEX
PERSONS
4000-5000
5000-6000
6000-7000
7000>
INDEX
TAHSIL BOUNDARY
DISTRICT
14271 PERSONS (URBAN)

Fig. 10.3

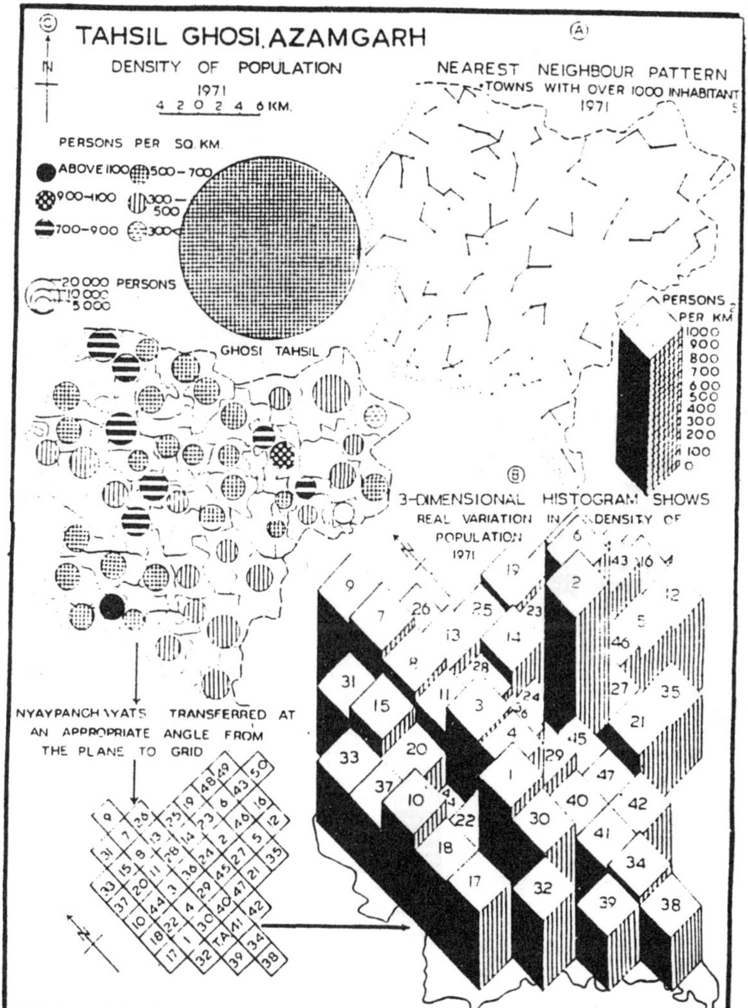
TAHSIL GHOSI, AZAMGARH
DENSITY OF POPULATION
1971
4 2 0 2 4 6 KM.
PERSONS PER SQ. KM.
ABOVE 1100
500 – 700
900 – 1100
300 – 500
700 – 900
300
20 000 PERSONS
10 000
5 000
GHOSI TAHSIL
NEAREST NEIGHBOUR PATTERN
TOWNS WITH OVER 1000 INHABITANT
1971
PERSONS PER KM²
1000
900
800
700
600
500
400
300
200
100
0
3-DIMENSIONAL HISTOGRAM SHOWS REAL VARIATION IN DENSITY OF POPULATION
1971
NYAYPANCHAYATS TRANSFERRED AT AN APPROPRIATE ANGLE FROM THE PLANE TO GRID

Fig. 10.4

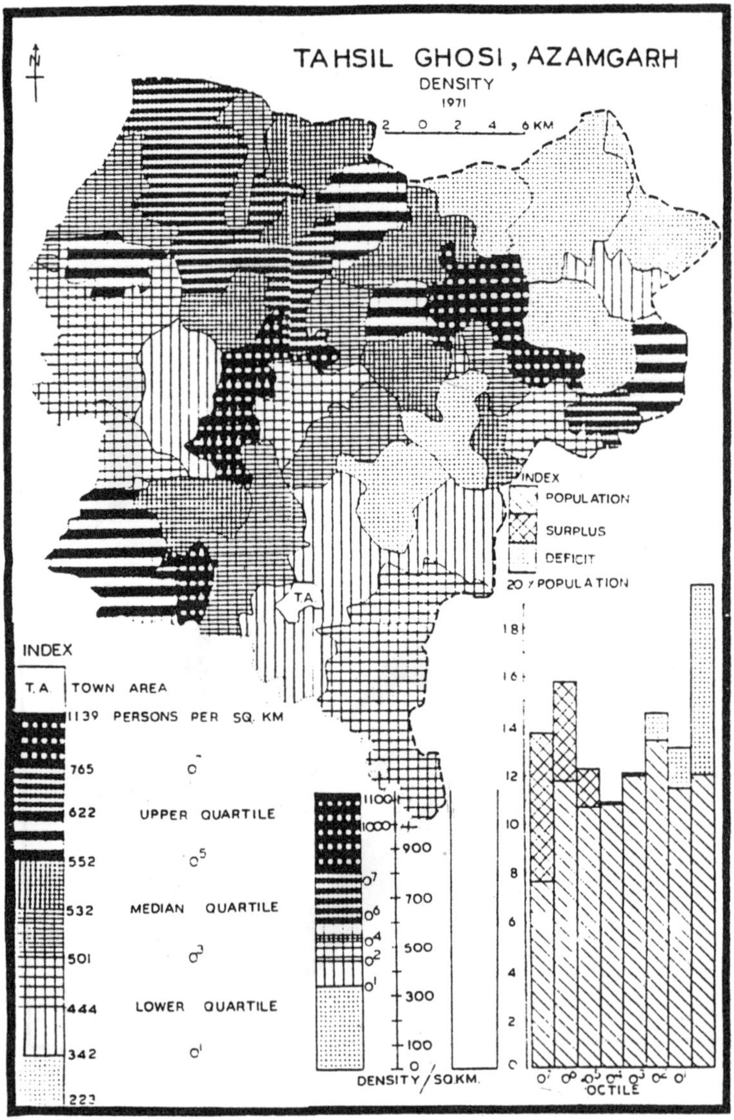
TAHSIL GHOSI, AZAMGARH
DENSITY
1971
2 0 2 4 6 KM
T.A.
INDEX
T.A. TOWN AREA
1139 PERSONS PER SQ. KM
765
622 UPPER QUARTILE
552
532 MEDIAN QUARTILE
501
444 LOWER QUARTILE
342
223
DENSITY / SQ.KM.
INDEX
POPULATION
SURPLUS
DEFICIT
POPULATION
OCTILE

Fig. 10.5

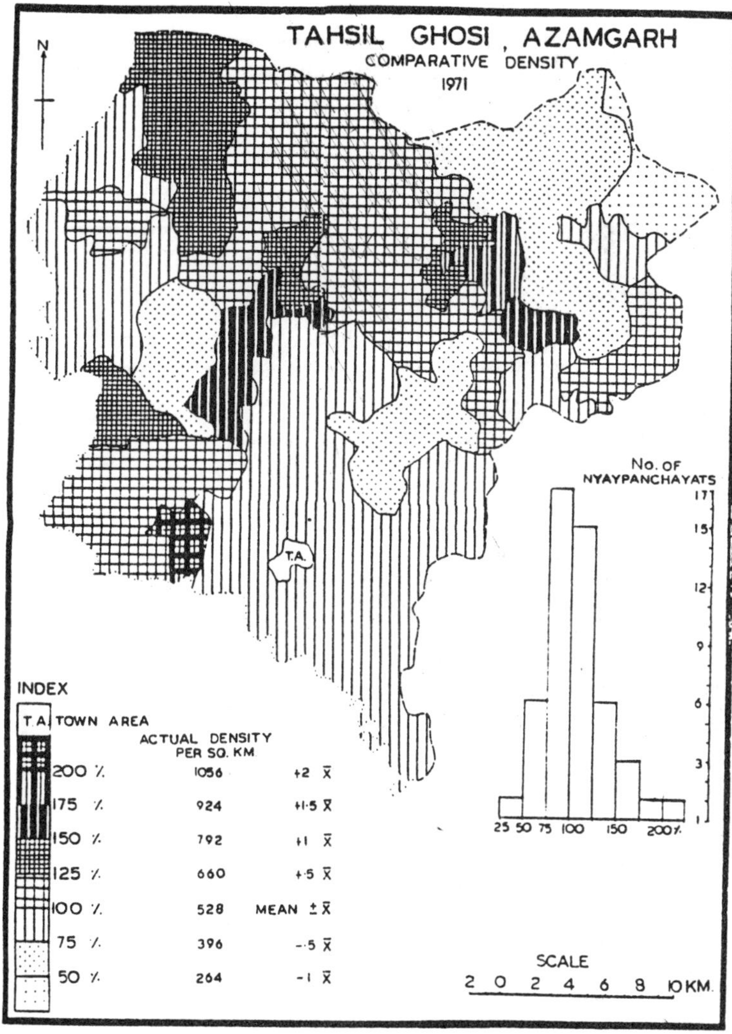
TAHSIL GHOSI, AZAMGARH
COMPARATIVE DENSITY
1971
N
T.A.
No. OF NYAYPANCHAYATS
17
15
12
9
6
3
1
25 50 75 100 150 200%
INDEX
T.A. TOWN AREA
ACTUAL DENSITY PER SQ. KM
200 % 1056 +2 X̄
175 % 924 +1·5 X̄
150 % 792 +1 X̄
125 % 660 +·5 X̄
100 % 528 MEAN ± X̄
75 % 396 -·5 X̄
50 % 264 -1 X̄
SCALE
2 0 2 4 6 8 10 KM.

Fig. 10.6

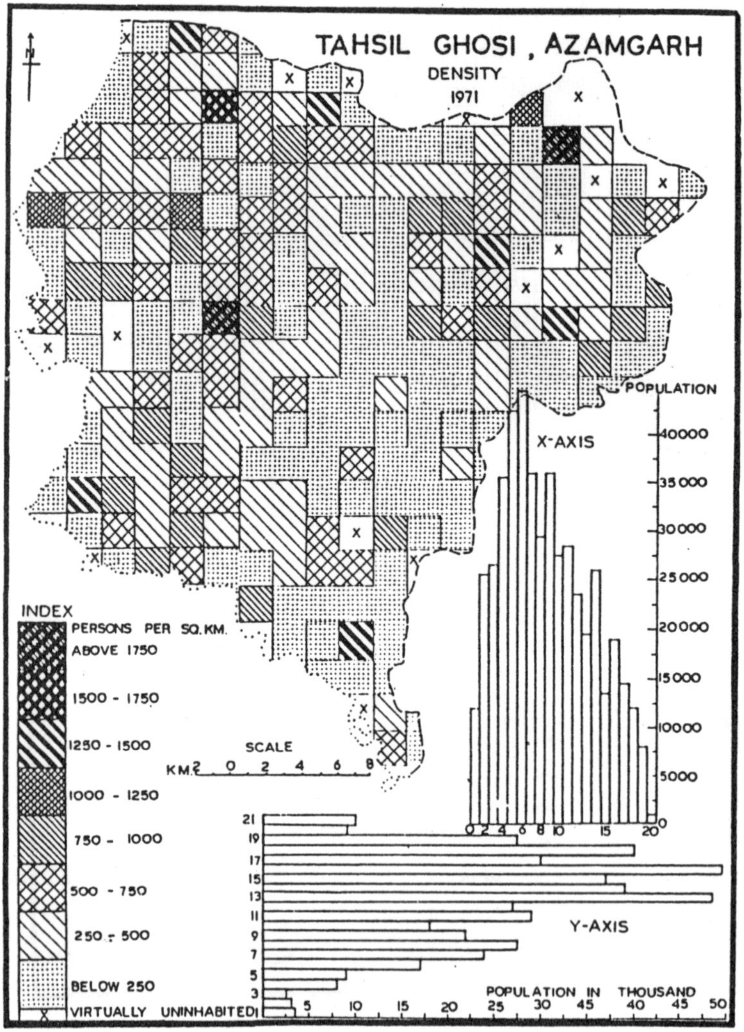
TAHSIL GHOSI, AZAMGARH
DENSITY
1971
INDEX
PERSONS PER SQ.KM.
ABOVE 1750
1500 - 1750
1250 - 1500
1000 - 1250
750 - 1000
500 - 750
250 - 500
BELOW 250
VIRTUALLY UNINHABITED
SCALE
KM 2 0 2 4 6 8
POPULATION
X-AXIS
40000
35000
30000
25000
20000
15000
10000
5000
0
0 2 4 6 8 10 15 20
Y-AXIS
POPULATION IN THOUSAND
21 19 17 15 13 11 9 7 5 3 1
5 10 15 20 25 30 45 40 45 50

Fig. 10.7

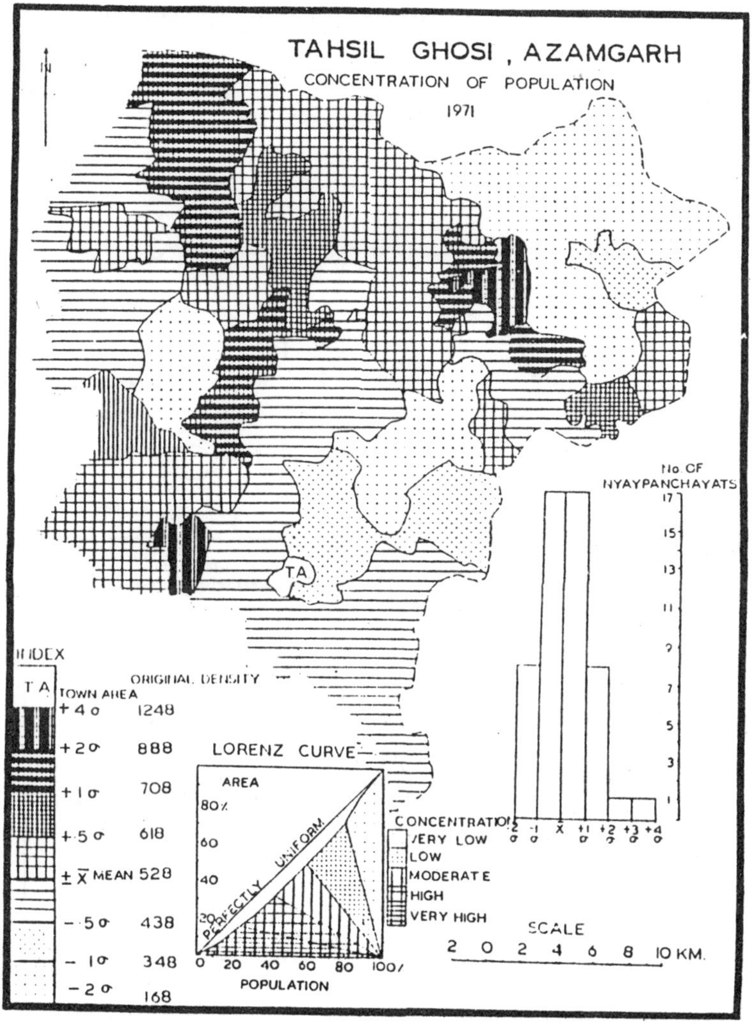
TAHSIL GHOSI, AZAMGARH
CONCENTRATION OF POPULATION
1971
N
INDEX
ORIGINAL DENSITY
TA TOWN AREA
+4 σ 1248
+2 σ 888
+1 σ 708
+.5 σ 618
± X̄ MEAN 528
-.5 σ 438
-1 σ 348
-2 σ 168
LORENZ CURVE
AREA
80%
60
40
20
PERFECTLY UNIFORM
0 20 40 60 80 100%
POPULATION
CONCENTRATION
VERY LOW
LOW
MODERATE
HIGH
VERY HIGH
No. OF NYAYPANCHAYATS
17
15
13
11
9
7
5
3
1
-2 σ -1 σ X̄ +1 σ +2 σ +3 σ +4 σ
SCALE
2 0 2 4 6 8 10 KM.

Fig. 10.8

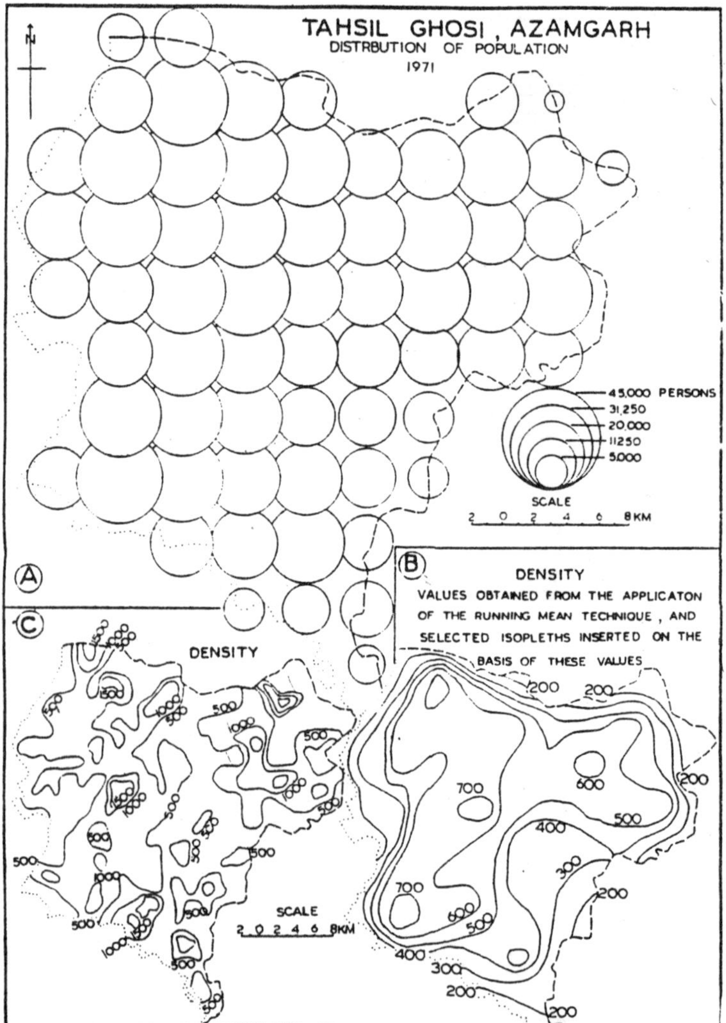
TAHSIL GHOSI, AZAMGARH
DISTRBUTION OF POPULATION
1971
N
45,000 PERSONS
31,250
20,000
11250
5,000
SCALE
2 0 2 4 6 8 KM
A
B
DENSITY
VALUES OBTAINED FROM THE APPLICATON OF THE RUNNING MEAN TECHNIQUE, AND SELECTED ISOPLETHS INSERTED ON THE BASIS OF THESE VALUES
C
DENSITY
SCALE
2 0 2 4 6 8KM
R.M.PROTHERO TECHNIQUE ON THE GRID OF 2KM.

ELEVEN

TECHNIQUES OF SYMBOLIZING POPULATION DATA

An entire map is a symbol and it is therefore not quite correct to designate certain components of a map as symbols. As such the population data on a map are selected and symbolized in order to depict facts or to make clear a series of relationships. One of the major functions of population geographers is to understand the relationships among symbols, their relative effectiveness, and their relative suitability for the purpose for which the map is constructed. Symbols show a kind of code by which population geographers can present the most effective fact in the limited space available.

Map symbols may be classified into two broad categories, qualitative and quantitative. Each of these may be further subclassified into three sub-categories, that is, point, line and areal symbol. Population geographers have to familiarise these symbols with the fact that all population data are associated with place. John K. Wright[1] has pointed out that when geographical or place quantities are reduced to dimensional terms, every place is either a point (location only), a line (one dimensional) or a volume (three dimensional). These are the kinds of symbols of population data the population geographer is called upon to represent on a map.

POINT SYMBOL

Point symbols such as dots, circles, squares, spheres, cubes or any other such varieties may represent any phenomena having territorial extension or simple location. A dot may represent the population of a village as well as its site, a circle, the population of a town, while a sphere, the population of a city. Thus, a point symbol may show either just type as in the case of a capital city or both type and amount, as in the case of a capital city or both type and amount, as in the case of a graduated circle representing the occupational structure of a city or a region. The point symbol is not satisfactory enough to show a ratio or a relationship. The representation of population facts by a point symbol merely requires that the symbol design be characteristic enough to be seen and understood by the map reader. The representation of population data by a point symbol may be accomplished either by repeating a uniform symbol (uniform dot) so that the aggregate number represents a total, or by varying the size (multiple dots) of each symbol in proportion to the total population of each village or by proportionate circles or squares, or by cubes or spheres showing the total population of cities.

LINE SYMBOL

Line symbols are of many kinds, but the most important one is traffic flow which may be used to show the migration of population, where permanent seasonal or daily. An arrow alone may show the movement but a line of varying width may show differences in the number of population. Another kind of line symbol is the line (isopleth showing the density of population) along which the same value of population density exists from place to place on a map.

AREA SYMBOL

Area symbols are also used to represent both qualitative and quantitative data pertaining to population. Population geographers may need to present quantitative and qualitative data such as religions, dominant occupations, racial composition, sex and age structure. Qualitative area symbolization should be accomplished by variation in pattern (Table 11.2). Whereas quantitative variation should generally utilize value changes (Table 11.3). The range from dark to light automatically gives the impression of varying amount, with the darker standing for the greater amount [2]. Thus, a darker area symbol looks more significant to population geographers. Of course, such emphasis could be used to advantage if population geographers felt the need to faces attention on one or more of the various qualitative element in mapping. Quantitative information may be combined with the qualitative to represent details of distribution (Table 11.4). This may be performed, in two ways: (a) by showing the ratio or a proportion of the whole or in derived value such as densities, for example arithmetical, physiological, agricultural, economic, nutritional densities, death rate, birth rate, sex-ratio, etc. (Table 11.5) and (b) by symbolizing totals and showing the percentage thereof or in absolute value. (Table 11.6) exhibits the ratio between two components. It should be noted that the presentation gives no indication of the total numbers involved. The total number of workers may be included in the presentation by using pie-diagrams in which the area of the circle represents the total number of workers and each circle may be subdivided to show the occupational distribution of the (Table 11.7) workers.

TABLE 11.1 **Total Population of Urban Areas in Azamgarh District, 1971**

Urban centres	Population
MauNath Bhanjan	64058
Azamgarh	40963
Mubarakpur	21253
Kopaganj	14271
Muhammadabad	8322

TABLE 11.2 **Sex-Ratio in Ghosi Tahsil, Azamgarh**

Panchayat	General	Higher Caste	Scheduled Caste	Literate Caste	Illiterate	Working	Non-Working
Dhanauli Lohra	921	929	893	301	1183	170	1610
Gontha Tikari	971	967	981	296	1326	310	1552
Korauli	1031	1031	1031	251	1408	200	1837
Kuranga Bana	1006	987	1065	158	1446	147	1848
Rasoolpur	990	964	1089	189	1282	143	1730
Surajpur	968	919	1113	390	1192	281	1632
Dargah Bairia	980	972	1001	240	1244	209	1731
Jajauli Dostpur	996	981	1051	262	1370	181	1657
Bhairopur	1001	990	1051	168	1268	110	1899
Dubari Luxmipur	968	949	1063	203	1216	203	1761
Ghaziapur	932	898	1081	213	1190	96	1809
Nevada Mundadand	1002	990	1066	143	1322	339	1690

Kamal Sagar	1035	1033	1045	420	1053	283	1610
Maryadpur	1009	1015	976	342	1311	243	1568
Nemdand	985	950	1075	275	1323	183	1719
Fatehpur Mandaon	1053	1040	1124	445	1423	195	1723
Madhuban	959	947	1014	334	1436	281	1542
Mirpur M.Dariabad	1102	1083	1155	234	1534	223	1783
Malkauli	1016	1017	1013	305	1345	63	1923
Hariyaon Jaganpur	1028	1025	1036	224	1317	276	1672
Usari Sardha	1096	1079	1172	236	1481	145	1967
Paraspur Sonjaria	1044	1047	1038	319	1569	220	2099
Majhawara	991	992	988	253	1309	122	1770
Mnngesar	1017	962	1186	274	1471	286	1776
Maurbojh	1033	1016	1088	242	1379	387	1602
Kalyanpur	945	930	1035	263	1165	253	1644
Ghosi	964	972	924	477	1210	176	1720
Baragaon	963	952	1020	476	1191	239	1588
Nadval	1041	1046	1016	315	1309	234	1797
Kamlapur Sipah	1014	980	1164	302	1472	136	1773
Akohli	917	869	1108	200	1152	191	1621
Sohar Paranpur	1016	995	1166	174	1288	296	1691
Katihari Buzurg	1043	1010	1152	222	1368	268	1676
Badraon	1011	967	1134	310	1287	475	1416
Sipah Shuklauli	1031	1013	1081	272	1358	502	1521
Chummanar	989	966	1080	226	1393	432	1524
Manikpur Haruwani	1045	999	1228	183	1339	62	1982
Pakari Buzurg	1001	1002	998	182	1236	111	1868
Bhikharipur	993	936	1260	282	1225	108	1793
Sultanpur	1055	1029	1116	183	1070	105	1946
Fatehpur Tal Narja	988	975	1118	628	1114	354	1609
Koeriapar	987	963	1094	467	1092	417	1547
Gauharpur	987	981	1015	205	1230	437	1574
Sarvan Garibpur	984	995	929	409	1275	586	1387
Sondsar Chandpur	1012	981	1102	203	1329	364	1590
Bhelabandh	921	911	943	236	1193	266	1572
Lairodonwar	933	907	1007	378	1229	273	1567
Sahroj- Kachhi	957	934	1051	326	1142	247	1619
Kasara Maksudan	909	904	930	200	1067	348	1468
Alinagar daniyal	967	967	967	164	1215	381	1527
Total	989	973	1050	297	1277	267	1663
Standard Deviation (Sd)	43	46	79	101	121	123	153
Kopaganj Town area	965	965	965	490	1365	369	1536

TABLE 11.3 **Active Population According to the Census Hand Book of Azamgarh District, 1971.**

Development Blocks	Working Population			Percentage of working population to total population	Percentage age of male to total male population	Percent- working female to total female popultion
	Person	Male	Female			
Atrauli	25,051	20,753	4,298	30.30	49.15	10.62
Koelsa	25,703	21,504	4,199	29.21	48.06	9.71
Ahiraula	27,318	23,519	3,799	28.54	48.82	7.99
Pawai	26,137	22,779	3,358	28.38	49.20	7.33
Phulpur	23,824	20,937	2,887	26.85	48.13	6.83
Marteenganj	22,253	18,679	3,574	27.12	47.55	8.36
Mahrajganj	27,325	24,304	3,021	29.69	51.19	6.78
Haraiya	28,518	24,684	3,834	29.69	50.60	8.11
Bilariyaganj	32,080	27,093	2,987	25.13	42.31	7.84
Azamatgarh	28,966	25,222	3,744	26.33	46.10	7.16
Tahbarpur	23,562	20,244	3,318	27.31	46.88	7.70
Palhani	25,689	22,380	3,309	28.68	48.54	7.61
Rani ki Sarai	21,253	18,728	2,525	27.63	48.17	6.64
Mirzapur	23,595	20698	2,897	27.40	48.37	6.69
Mohammadpur	20,048	17,486	2,562	26.22	47.17	6.50
Thekma	24,749	20,536	4,213	27.27	47.22	8.92
Lalganj	27,504	22,819	4,685	25.48	44.25	8.31
Mehnagar	28,577	24,006	4,571	26.82	46.46	8.33
Tarwa	29,791	24,085	5,706	27.54	46.03	10.21
Doharighat	27,245	22,750	4,495	29.10	48.09	9.71
Fatehpur Mandaon	31,582	25,964	5,618	28.73	47.22	10.19
Ghosi	25,061	20,316	4,745	30.13	48.46	11.50
Badraon	28,458	22,111	6,347	30.60	47.95	13.54
Kopaganj	35,166	25,554	9,612	34.75	49.52	19.39
Sathiaon	28,082	22,957	5,125	30.74	49.36	11.43
Mohammadabad	26,804	22,223	4,581	28.63	47.18	9.85
Jahanaganj	22,409	18,539	3,870	27.50	45.97	9.40
Ranipur	29,566	23,957	5,609	30.08	48.63	11.44
Pardaha	23,761	19,960	3,801	30.02	49.05	9.89

TABLE 11.4 **Industrial Categories of Urban Çentres According to the Census Handbook of Azamgarh District, 1971.**

Industrial categories	Maunath Bhanjan	Azamgarh M.B. M.B.	Mubarakpur T.A.	Kopaganj T.A.	Mohammadabad T.A.
Total population (working)	24,389	10,372	6,939	4,867	2,180
I	541	506	182	106	328
II	682	279	164	218	450
III	54	5	4	3	-
IV	38	76	3	-	1
VA	15,204	1,114	5,074	3,439	391
VB	1,947	949	455	138	213
VI	235	298	35	26	6
VII	2,701	2,261	589	687	387
VIII	372	389	57	28	10
IX	2,615	4,495	376	222	394

TABLE 11.5 **Density of Population According to the Census Handbook of Azamgarh District, 1971.**

Blocks	Physiological Density	Economic Density	Arithmetic Density	Caloric Density	Agricultural Density
Atraulia	514	674	524	567	183
Koelsa	552	763	549	607	203
Ahiraula	505	632	597	530	166
Pawai	486	585	438	482	147
Phoolpur	460	588	476	422	140
Marteenganj	362	466	352	476	117
Maharajganj	384	509	377	404	138
Harraiya	364	474	365	375	132
Bilariaganj	577	747	632	592	168
Azmatgarh	504	640	528	516	147
Tahbarpur	493	611	492	458	153
Palhania	687	850	699	639	196
Rani Ki Sarai	556	700	522	511	166
Mirzapur	560	683	511	526	165
Mohammadpur	436	502	405	394	120
Thekma	424	552	399	442	137
Lalganj	391	590	432	401	132
Mehnagar	394	568	414	413	138
Tarwa	435	561	413	433	136
Doharighat	469	734	560	486	183
Fatehpur Mandaon	458	773	438	480	192
Ghosi	455	711	548	464	169
Badraon	476	647	533	504	177
Kopaganj	513	654	525	519	186
Sathiaon	504	694	560	513	160
Mohammadpur	521	690	577	533	159
Jahanaganj	415	558	448	427	129
Ranipur	390	531	429	395	139
Pardaha	457	604	430	467	144
Total	464	619	472	474	153

TABLE 11.6 **Percentage of Working Population to Total Population in Development Blocks according to the Crnsus Handbook, Azamgarh District, 1971.**

Development Blocks	Total population	Total workers	Percentage of working population to total popul-ation
Atrauli	82,687	25,051	30.30
Koelsa	88,004	25,703	29.21
Ahiraula	95,724	27,318	28.54
Pawai	92,092	26,137	28.38
Phoolpur	88,732	23,824	26.85
Marteenganj	82,049	22,253	27.12
Maharajganj	92,033	27,325	29.69
Harraiya	96,054	28,518	29.69
Bilariyaganj	1,27,646	32,080	25.13
Azamatgarh	1,09,999	28,966	26.33
Tahbarpur	86,284	23,562	27.31
Palhani	89,581	25,689	28.68
Rani Ki Sarai	76,913	21,253	27.63
Mirzapur	86,110	23,595	27.40
Mohammadpur	76,464	20,048	26.22
Thekma	90,744	24,749	27.27
Lalganj	1,07,954	27,504	25.48
Mehnagar	1,06,552	28,577	26.82
Tarwa	1,08,190	29,791	27.54
Doharighat	93,616	27,245	29.10
Fatehpur Mandaon	1,09,920	31,582	28.73
Ghosi	83,167	25,061	30.13
Badraon	92,998	28,458	30.60
Kopaganj	1,01,184	35,166	34.75
Sathiaon	91,348	28,082	30.74
Mohammadbad	93,637	26,804	28.63
Jahanaganj	81,493	22,409	27.50
Ranipur	98,303	29,566	30.08
Pardaha	79,139	23,761	30.02

TABLE 11.7 **Occupational Distribution of Workers According to the Census Handbook of Azamgarh District,1971.**

Development Block	Working population			Percentage in primary occupation	Percentage in secondary occupation	Percent age in tertiary occupation
	Primary	Secondary	Tertiary			
Atrauli	22,510	1,149	1,319	89.86	4.59	5.55
Koelsa	23,402	929	1,371	91.05	3.62	5.33
Ahiraula	25,279	595	1,439	92.55	2.18	5.27
Pawai	23,817	859	1,461	91.12	3.29	5.59
Phulpur	21,113	750	1,961	88.62	3.15	8.23
Marteenganj	20,653	486	1,112	92.81	2.19	5.00
Maharajganj	25,228	721	1,369	92.35	2.64	5.01
Harraiya	26,904	435	1,117	94.34	1.53	4.13
Bilaariyaganj	29,023	1,103	1,942	90.82	3.13	6.05
Azamatgarh	25,366	1,359	2,234	87.59	4.70	7.72
Tahbarpur	21,651	522	1,380	91.91	2.23	5.86
Palhani	20,807	1,919	3,653	81.02	4.76	14.22
Rani Ki Sarai	18,421	927	1,903	86.67	4.37	8.96
Mohammadpur	18,328	670	1,046	91.43	3.35	5.22
Thekma	22,602	891	1,255	91.33	3.60	5.07
Lalganj	24,168	1,161	2,166	87.89	4.23	7.88
Mehnagar	25,928	1,119	1,528	90.73	3.92	5.35
Tarwa	26,518	1,367	1,899	89.03	4.59	6.38
Doharighat	23,459	1,076	2,679	86.22	3.95	9.83
Fatehpur Mandaon	27,458	1,300	2,811	86.98	4.12	8.90
Ghosi	19,919	3,115	2,008	79.53	12.46	8.01
Badraon	25,637	951	1,865	90.10	3.35	6.55
Kopaganj	28,732	4,235	2,198	81.70	12.05	6.25
Sathiaon	21,225	4,960	1,888	75.61	17.67	6.72
Mohammadbad	21,587	3,348	1,861	80.56	12.50	6.94
Jahanganj	19,047	1,870	1,485	85.02	8.36	6.62
Ranipur	25,789	1,779	1,990	87.25	6.02	6.73
Pardaha	19,055	2,854	1,847	80.20	12.02	7.78

All quantitative maps may be classified into two groups.

1. Maps which express a single category of data or those which show the absolute form.

2. Maps which exhibit the derived values, such as density, percentages, central tendency, etc. These maps indicate the comparison of two kinds of data, that the population. Here the divisor is a measure of the area and the dividends a summation of data (e.g. total population) for a statistical unit of some kind. Thus, 82,687 persons in an arable area of 122.77 square kilometres is a physiological density of 674 persons per square kilometre. The data for physiological density maps are made relative to the arable area for which the population data are available. The special value that results is a kind of physiological density index, showing numbers per unit area, and it requires some calculation.

Population density is a method of analysing the distribution of population; overpopulation, underpopulation and optimum population can be assessed by comparing population densities through statistical methods. It is impossible to discuss the distribution of population without indicating that there are more people in some places, leading to relatively higher densities and fewer in others leading to lower densities.[3].

Density can be measured in relation to total, arable, net cultivated, food cropped, or inhabited area [4] or an area weighted according to its land-use, which gives their different geographical value. The numerator may be either the total population or a category, such as rural, agricultural or working population.[5]. Although these various types of densities have some utility for comparison in time within one country they can be easily used for international comparisons too. But none of these measures is of undisputed absolute value and above all, none escapes from criticism.[6].

Arithmetic density is used by most of the geographers in the world because the data required by the following ratio are the most readily obtainable.

$$Arithmatic\ Density = \frac{Total\ Population}{Total\ Area}$$

Such a ratio is unsatisfactory because it exhibits the quantitative relationship between two elements which in themselves are highly constant. The numerator or total population indicates men of greatly contrasting societies, cultures and stages of economic development whose demands upon the physical earth stand in great contrast. The denominator of the ratio indicating units of the area fails to take into consideration the variable capacities of different environments for supporting human life and satisfying human needs. Because of its unsatisfactory result, population geographers employ some more accurate indices of population pressure on the resource base when the data are available, for example, physiological density. Physiological density is expressed by the following formula:-

$$Physiological\ density = \frac{Total\ population}{Total\ arable\ land}$$

This ratio is a somewhat more refined idea of density. However, while it eliminates from the denominator barren areas and other areas not suitable for agriculture on the one hand, it errs in eliminating all productive non-available land, such as forests natural pasture, scenic land, mining land, etc. on the other. It also has the drawback of continuing to evaluate all arable land as having the same productivity, and rating population as having the same capacities without considering their cultural background or stage of economic development. Some attempts have been made to calculate agricultural production by means of various statistical methods such as the carrying capacity in terms of calories or potential production unit (P.P.U.)[7] etc. But the calculation of potential production unit (P.P.U.) is extraordinarily difficult. It is difficult enough to compare actual yield not only because of the variety of crops, but still more because of the extensive use of land for grass and fodder from which the production of food is direct through animal products. An attempt was made by M.G. Kendall to compare the crop productivity among the countries of England by studying mathematically the yields of ten widely grown crops. But if a method could be found to evaluate statistically the agricultural productivity of different environments, types of farming and so on it would be possible to weigh the denominator in the physiological density ratio so as to get a more realistic comparison of population density in different physical and cultural environments.

The relation of the number of agricultural people to cultivated area or agricultural density in predominantly agricultural societies, such as India or other developing countries in the world is frequently found to be more useful than other types of densities. Agricultural density is expressed by the following ration:

$$Agricultural\ density = \frac{Total\ agricultural\ population}{Total\ cultivated\ land}$$

This ratio, however, represents no advance over other kinds of density ratios in differentiating between different qualities of environment or people. Even the more specialized density ratio still fall short of being able to express the man-land ratio in its real sense, or what is called the general economic density of population. The calculation of general economic density has been proposed by Garnier, using as a basis the net cultivable area in relation either to total population or to the number of rural inhabitants.[8] But Trewartha suggested that for the calculation of economic density, in the numerator not only the numbers of people should be included but also their socio-economic qualities, including stages of technological advancement, the denominator should denote not only total area, or even cultivated area, but rather the sum total of the natural resources equipment, so that economic density expresses the capacity of a region's natural environment to support human life at a particular stage of development.

In primitive, rural or developing societies (e.g. India) the carrying capacity of land may be possible to arrive at. But in highly complex, dynamic or developed societies such as Japan and U.K. a satisfactory means for measuring population pressure on the total resource base has never been accomplished. The means for supporting population often depends as much or even more, upon items imported from outside as upon those produced in Japan or in Great Britain. A spatial gap is thereby created between the place of production and the place of consumption. Therefore, the internal carrying capacity of domestic resources become relatively less important as societies advance in technology and regional specialization.[9] Singh[10] suggested nutritional density for the region having a strong agricultural dominance by the following ratio:

$$Nutritional\,density = \frac{Total\,rural\,population}{Total\,food - cropped\,area}$$

But the main purpose of the consumption of food is to supply the body with energy. Energy for the body comes from food, and, in the absence of food, energy can be produced only by the breakdown of body tissues. Food energy is expressed as heat energy. The unit of measurement used has been the Calorie or kilocalorie (this is one thousand times the small calorie used in physics)[11]. Energy for all bodily functions, including the maintenance of temperature and the continuous action of the heart and lungs. Energy is also needed for breakdown, repair and the building of tissues. There are metabolic processes. The rate at which these functions are carried out while the body is at rest is the basal metabolic rate (B.M.R.) These varies with sex, age, body-size activity and diseases such as goitre and many others.

The average human burns energy at his B.M.R. only when at complete rest. All ordinary movements require additional energy. An average day may envolve the following energy expenditure.[12]

Example 1:	**Activity**	**Calories**
Sleep	8 hours of rest in bed, at a B.M.R. of 1 Calorie per minute i.e 8x60x1	= 480
Light work	8 hours of day, say, herding cattle, at 2.5 Calories per minutes i.e. 8 x 60 x 2.5	= 1200
Others	8 hours of sitting and minor activities at 2 Calories per minute i.e. 8x60x2	= 960
	Total	2,640

If instead of 8 hours of light work, the person in this example did 5 hours of herding and 3 hours of heavy work e.g. hoeing hard ground at 4 Calories per minutes then his output of energy would be:

Example 2:	**Activity**	**Calories**
Sleep	as in above case	480
Light works	5 hours as in above case i.e. 5 x 60 x 2.5	750
Hard works	3 hours, as in above case i.e. minute i.e. 3 x 60 x 4	720
Other works	as in above case	960
	Total	2910

Now suppose what happens to the individuals undertaking the activities mentioned in the first example, if he gets exactly 2640 calories in his food, his weight will be steady and he will be functioning normally. However, if he then undertakes the activities in the second example, and eats no extra-food, his weight will gradually reduce because he will have to burn up his fuel reserve - which forms part of his own body. He would fairly soon, however, begin to limit his activities in order to stop this process. He would, therefore, probably work less hard at hoeing, so that instead of burning 4 calories per unit, he might use only, say 3.2 Calories, he would also tend to be tired at the end of the day, and might well increase his period of complete rest (at 1 Calorie per minute) by reducing the period of minor activities. He would, therefore, have reduced his Calories requirements to 2646 as follows:-

Example 3	**Activity**	**Calories**
Sleep	10 hours as above i.e. 10 X 60 X 1	600
Light work	5 hours as above i.e. 5 X 6 X 2.5	750

Hard work	3 hours of less hard work at 3.2 Calories per minute i.e. 3 X 60 X 3.2	576
Others	6 hours as above i.e. 6 X 60 X2	720
	Total	2646

This is just an example, but in most instances when people increases output of energy, including work, they feel more hungry and they increase their consumption of their staple food, be it rice, wheat, maize, barley or any thing else.

The following are important factors in the analysis of Calorie intake:-

1. Body size : A small person needs less energy than a tall person

2. Basal metabolic rate : It has already been mentioned that the B.M.R.varies and that it can be affected by factors including diseases of the thyroid gland.

3. Activity : The more physical work or play performed the more energy required.

4. Pregnancy: A woman requires extra energy to develop and to carry the additional weight of the foetus.

5. Lactation: The lactating mother needs additional energy to produce energy containing milk for the suckling baby.

6. Age: Infants and children need more energy for growth and activity than old persons, in whom the need for energy is reduced because there is a decline in activity and because the B.M.R. is usually lower.

7. Climate: In a warm climate, such as in India less energy is necessary to keep the body at its normal temperature than in a cold climate.

8. Carbohydrate: The main source of energy for most Indians is derived from carbohydrates present in the food.

9. Fats: In Indian diets fats usually provide calories (i.e. 8% to 10% of the total calories) than carbohydrates. In the most developed countries the proportional intake of fat is much higher (e.g. U.S.A. an average of 40--45% of the energy derives form fat). The term fat is used to denote all fats and oils that are edible and occur in human diets. It is of two types i.e. fat from land and water animals origin such as meat-fat, butter, fish, etc. and fat from vegetable origin. The fats caught public attention because excess intake of fats creates arteriosclerosis, coronary heart disease, and degenerative disease, etc. especially among affluent Indians, who are consuming westernized diet. It yields about a calorie per gram, more than twice as much energy as carbohydrates and proteins do (about 4 calories per gram) and can, therefore, reduce the bulk of the diet. Fats are essential for the nutrition of individual cells and tissues of the body. Thus specific types of fat are essential to health. Fats deposited in the human body beneath the skin as an insulation against cold, etc. serves as a reserve fuel and forms supporting tissues for many organs.

PROTEINS

These are necessary for the growth and repair of the body. The greater portions of the body substance is protein (after water). Proteins consumed in the diet undergoes a series of chemical changes in the gastrointestinal tract to form aminoacids. Proteins such as albumin in egg and casein in milk contain all the essential aminoacids in good proportions and are superior to other types of protein e.g. zein in maize, lysine in wheat, etc. The requirement of proteins varies from age to age, and sex to sex. For example, children needs more proteins than adults or the old for the growth of the body. A pregnant woman needs an additional supply of protein to build up the foetus inside her. Similarly a lactating woman needs extra proteins, because the milk she is secreting contains protein.

A joint Food and Agriculture Organisation (FAO) and World Health Organisation. Expert committee (FAO/1973) recommended a daily requirement of 0.55 grammes of milk or egg protein per kilogramme of body weigh for an adult male. A diet low in meat, fish or dairy products tends to be unattractive, but in developing countries like India where most people are poor such diets are the rule.

MINERALS

Minerals have a number of functions in a body. The principal minerals present in the body are calcium, phosphorus (to give rigidity to the whole body) potassium, sodium, chlorine, sulphur, copper, magnesium, manganese, iron, iodine and fluorine. Milk and fish are a good source of calcium. The following are the recommended levels of calcium intake based on suggestions by W.H.O. and F.A.O.

Category	Daily in take in milligrams
Adult	400-500
Children	400-700
Pregnant and lactating Woman	1000-1200

But on the above statement the calculation of nutrient is really extraordinarily difficult because, the daily requirement of nutrients for the human body such as carbohydrates, fats, proteins, minerals and vitamins etc. varies according to age, sex and activities (Tables 11.9).

Here, the author used the term carrying capacity or availability of food on the basis of the production of food crops and calculated it in terms of calorics to investigate the position of population and food supply per head per day at the block level for the area under study (Table 11.8).

TABLE 11.8 **Carrying Capacity of Azamgarh District**

Blocks	Total S.N.U. Per Annum	Per Head Per Annum (S.N.U.)	Per Head Per day (Calories)
Atraulia	1,24,222.42	1.50232	3.605.57
Koelsa	1,25.032.12	1.42076	3,409.81
Ahiraula	1,42,814.82	1.49195	3,580.67
Pawai	1,63,537.18	1.77580	4,261.93
Phulpur	1,42,727.20	1.60852	3,860.45
Marteenganj	1,20,651.79	1.47049	3,529.16
Maharajganj	1,79,116.69	1.94622	4,670.93
Harraiya	2,07,974.56	2.16518	5,196.44
Bilariganj	1,57,274.95	1.23212	1,957.08
Azamatgarh	1,75,447.89	1.59499	3,827.99
Tahbarpur	1,59,659.61	1.85039	4,440.95
Palhani	1,26,722.80	1.41462	3,395.08
Rani Ki Sarai	1,31,601.79	1.71105	4,106.51
Mirzapur	1,59,692.18	1.85452	4,450.83
Mohammadpur	1,70,061.82	2.22408	5,337.78
Thekma	1,57,472.76	1.73535	4,164.84
Lalganj	1,84,873.99	1.71253	4,110.06
Mehnagar	1,79,803.45	1.68747	4,049.93
Tarwa	1,80,383.86	1.66729	4,001.49
Doharighat	2,04,503.61	2.18449	5,242.79
Fatehpur Madaon	2,23,129.32	2.02993	4,871.82
Ghosi	1,60,416.37	1.92885	4,629.23
Badraon	1,72,179.16	1.85413	4,443.43
Kopaganj	1,84,570.74	1.82411	4,377.86
Sathiaon	1,63,596.55	1.79092	4,298.20
Mohammadabad	1,66,423.16	1.77732	4,265.57
Jahanaganj	1,25,831.18	1.54407	3,705.78
Ranipur	2,10,189.76	2.13818	5,131.64
Pardaha	1,36,366.81	1.72313	4,135.51

TABLE 11.9 **Daily Allowances of Nutrients for Indians**

	Man(55kg) (sedentary work)	Woman(47kg) (sedentary work)	Adolscents		Children
			Boys(13-15 years)	Girls(13-15 years)	(one year)
Energy (cal)	2400	1900	1200	2500	2200
Protein (gm)	55	45	17	55	50
Calcium (gm)	0.4-0.5	0.4-0.5	0.6-0.7	0.6-0.7	0.4-0.5
Iron (gm)	20	30	25	35	15-20
Vit.A (retinol) (micro gm)	750	750	750	750	250
Vit.B Carotene (micro gm)	3000	3000	3000	3000	1000
Thiamine (mg)	1.2	1.0	1.3	1.1	0.6
Riboflawin (mg)	1.3	1.0	1.4	1.2	0.7
Nicotinic acid (mg)	16	13	17	14	5
Ascorbic acid (mg)	50	50	30-50	30-50	30-50
Folic acid (micro gm)	100	100	50-100	50-100	50-100
Vitamin(Blw) (micro gm)	1	1	0.5-1.0	0.5-1.0	0.5-1.0
Vitamin B (I.U.)	200	200	200	200	200

Source: Recommended by the Nutrition expert Group in 1968. *Nutritive value of Indian Foods, C.Gopalan, B.V.Ramasastry and S.C. Balasubramaniam, National Institute of Nutrition, Indian Council of Medical Research, Hyderabad-7, 1980,p.27.*

The nutrient composition varies also according to the foodstuffs and their preparation (Table 11.10).

TABLE: 11.10 Food Composition: All the Values Given are per 100 grams of Edible Portion

Name of food stuff	Extra-ction rate %	Edibke porti on (%)	Mois-ture (gm)	Pro-tein (gm)	Fat (gm)	Minerals (gm)	Fibre (gm)	Carbo-hydra- (gm)	Energy (Keal)	Calcium (mg)	Phospho-rus (mg)	Iron (mg)	Carnotene (Mg)	Thiamine (mg)	Ribofla-vin (mg)	Niacin (mg)	Vitamin C (mg)
Bajra Pennisetum typhoideum	90	84	12.4	11.6	5.0	2.3	1.2	67.5	361	42	296	5	132	0.33	0.25	2.3	0
Barley (Hordeum vulgare)	70	100	12.5	11.5	1.3	1.2	3.9	69.6	336	26	215	3	10	0.47	0.20	5.4	0
Jowar (Sorghum vulgare)	90%	100	11.9	10.4	1.9	1.6	1.6	72.6	349	25	222	5.6	47	0.37	0.13	3.1	0
Maize dry (Zea mays)	89	100	14.9	11.1	3.6	1.5	2.7	66.2	342	10	348	2.0	90	0.42	0.10	1.8	0
Maize tender (Zea mays)	89	37	67.1	4.7	0.9	0.8	1.9	24.6	125	9	121	1.1	32	0.11	0.17	0.6	6
Rice raw milled	66.67	100	13.7	6.8	0.5	0.6	0.2	78.2	345	10	160	3.1	0	0.06	0.06	1.9	0
Sawn and Kodo millet (manduwa, kakun, kutki)	95	100	11.9	6.2	2.2	4.4	9.8	65.5	307	20	280	2.9	0	..	..	4.2	0
Wheat (Triticum aestivum)	90	100	12.2	12.1	1.7	2.7	1.9	69.4	341	48	355	11.5	29	0.49	0.29	4.3	0
Bengal gram (whole) (Cicer arietinum)	100	100	9.8	17.1	5.3	3.0	3.9	60.9	360	202	312	10.2	189	0.30	0.15	2.9	3
Cowpea (Vigna catjung)	95	90	13.4	24.1	1.0	3.2	3.8	54.5	323	77	414	5.9	12	0.51	0.20	1.3	0
Khesari dal (Lathyrus sativus)	-	100	10.0	28.2	0.6	2.3	2.3	56.6	345	90	317	6.3	120	0.39	0.17	2.9	0
Lentil (lens esculanta)	0	100	12.4	25.1	0.7	2.1	0.7	59.0	343	69	293	4.8	270	0.45	0.20	2.6	0
Peas dry (Pisum sativum)	-	100	16.0	19.7	1.1	2.2	4.5	56.5	315	75	298	5.1	39	0.47	0.19	3.4	0
Peas roasted (Pisum sativum)	-	100	10.1	22.9	1.4	2.4	4.4	58.8	340	81	345	6.4	18	0.47	0.21	3.5	0
Pigeon pea	-	100	13.4	22.3	1.7	3.5	1.5	57.6	335	73	304	5.8	132	0.45	0.19	2.9	0
Moth bean (Phaseolus aconitifolius) (urad, moong, moth) masoor)	-	100	10.8	23.6	1.1	3.5	4.5	56??	??	202	230	9.5	9	0.45	0.09	1.5	2

Name of food stuff	Extraction rate %	Edibke portion (%)	Moisture (gm)	Protein (gm)	Fat (gm)	Minerals (gm)	Fibre (gm)	Carbohydrate (gm)	Energy (Keal)	Calcium (mg)	Phosphorus (mg)	Iron (mg)	Carnotene (Mg)	Thiamine (mg)	Riboflavin (mg)	Niacin (mg)	Vitamin C (mg)
Potato (Solamun tuberosum)	-	85	74.7	1.6	0.1	0.6	0.4	22.6	97	10	40	0.7	24	0.10	0.01	1.2	17
Sweet potato (ipomaea bataes)	-	97	68.5	1.2	0.3	1.0	0.8	28.2	120	46	50	0.8	6	0.08	0.04	0.7	24
Ground nut	-	73	3.0	25.3	40.1	2.4	3.1	26.1	567	90	350	2.8	37	0.90	0.13	19.9	0
Linseed seed	-	99	6.5	20.3	37.1	2.4	4.8	28.9	530	170	370	2.7	30	0.23	0.07	1.0	0
Mustard seeds	-	-	8.5	20.0	39.7	4.2	1.8	23.8	541	490	700	17.9	162	0.65	0.26	4.0	0
Mango ripe (Mangifera Indica)	-	74	81.0	0.6	0.4	0.4	0.7	16.9	74	14	16	1.3	2743	0.08	0.09	0.9	16
Guava	-	100	81.7	0.9	0.3	0.7	5.2	11.2	5%	10	28	1.4	0	0.03	0.03	0.4	212
Papaya ripe	-	75	90.8	0.6	0.1	0.5	0.8	7.2	32	17	13	0.5	666	0.04	0.25	0.2	57
Rohu (Labeo rohita)	-	78	76.7	16.6	1.4	0.9	-	4.4	97	650	175	1.0	-	0.05	0.07	0.7	22
Tengra (fresh) (Mystus vittatus)	-	-	70.0	19.2	6.2	2.1	-	2.3	144	270	170	2.0	-	-	-	-	18
Buffalo meat	-	-	78.7	19.4	0.9	1.0	-	-	86	3	189	-	-	-	-	-	-
Egg hen	-	-	73.7	13.3	13.3	1.0	-	-	173	60	220	2.1	600*	0.10	0.40	0.1	0
Goat meat	-	-	74.2	21.4	3.6	1.1	-	-	118	12	193	-	-	-	-	-	-
Mutton muscle	-	-	71.5	18.5	13.3	1.3	-	-	194	150	150	2.5	0**	0.18	0.14	6.8	-
Leaver goat	-	-	76.3	20.0	3.0	1.3	-	-	107	17	279	-	-	-	-	-	-

*Contain also 1200 I.U. of Vitamine A.

Similarly, the daily requirement of calories varies directly with the body surface (i.e sex, age, body size, disease, etc.) and there is a basic requirement to keep the body alive. The requirement goes up with movement and work to high flevels with heavy manual work as shown in the following example.

The daily requirement of (calories for Indians

Man (55 kg)	Sedentary work	2,400
	Moderate work	2,800
	Heavy work	3,900
Women (47 kg)	Sedentary work	1,900
	Moderate work	2,200
	Heavy work	3,000
	Pregnant	+300
	Lactating	+700
Children	1-3 years	1,200
	4-6 years	1,500
	7-9 years	1,800
	10-12 years	2,100
Adolescent boys	13-15 years	2,500
	16-18 years	3,000
Girls	13-18 years	2,200

An idea of the average daily requirement of diet or calories can be had from the following example.

The average diet and its approximate nutrient value in India

Foods	Amount (gm)	Nutrient	Amount
Cereals	540	Protein	57 gram
Pulses	12	Fat	24 gram
Leafy vegetables	7	Carbohydrates	490 gram
Roots and tubers	7	Calcium	360 gram
Other vegetables	85	Iron	24 mg
Milk	80	Thiamine 0.7 mg	
Meat, Fish and eggs	5	Roboflavin	0.6 mg
Oil and fats	15	Vitamin A340ug(Microgram)	
Sugar and jaggery	13	Calories	2,400
Fruit	5		

Thus the average daily requirement of a human body without considering the age, sex and activity etc. is 2,400 calories (cal. or Kcal.) in the Indian situation. This is equivalent approximately to 8,76,000 calories per annum without considering the wastage in cooking and the diet thrown away unconsumed. This amount is known as a Standard Nutrition Unit (SNU) for India. But Stamp considered Standard Nutrition Unit as one million calories[15] a year for Great Britain. The S.N.U. considers only energy. Singh and Pandey [16] and U.P. Singh[17] considered it as 7,75,791 calories per annum (2,124 calories per day) which is lower than that of an Indian average requirement.

PROPORTIONAL SYMBOLS

Proportional symbols (squares, circles, cubes, spheres, etc. are used very effectively in population geography to show and compare urban population in a given area, under study, which can be located specifically at a point or at the site of the city. The exact location of the city can usually be found from a large-scale map, and then the size of the proportional symbol can be calculated in proportion to the total population of the city which it represents. A scale of symbols can be constructed. The relative importance of the various urban areas in Azamgarh District shows the relative importance of the city in terms of total population.

Quite apart from city location, proportional symbols can be placed on a map within the administrative region to which they refer. Proportional circles may be used together with wheels to show not only the total number of workers at a development block level but also workers engaged in primary, secondary and tertiary occupations.

In the case of proportional symbols the problem arises of choosing a scale for symbols so that small populations may be distinguished. The disadvantage attached to this method is that it leads to an overlap symbols and causes difficulty in the drawing and in the interpretation of the map especially in the most crowded areas.

PROPORTIONAL CIRCLES

To calculate the radii of proportional circles, we must work through the following procedure:-

1. Decide upon the maximum size of the circle that can be used to represent the largest number of population in the series. This must obviously depend upon the scale of the map, and the number of units on the map. It is clearly desirable to maintain the separate identity of each centre and the circles should neither overlap nor touch each other. But in some cases, where the size and shape of the unit are irregular it may be impossible to avoid some degree of overlapping without reducing the size of the smaller circles to an impracticable level. This is especially true if the range of the quantities is

large.

2. Calculate the square root of each of the population of the unit listed.

A range of other proportional symbols exists including squares, segments of circles, cubes, and spheres. Each of these is proportional either in total working population or volume to the quantity which it represents and each be located on a map in the same way as a proportionate circle.

The advantage of the circle lies in its fairly simple construction, and its neat appearance on a finished map. It is particularly suitable for use with data relating to points or units since it focuses attention on the location of each point. Because of its shape, it may be used to show urban population in conjunction with uniform dot symbols showing rural population in one map.

The only major disadvantage of the proportional circle is that it is more difficult to estimate differences in area by comparing the sizes of circles, than it is of some other types of symbol used. [18] The proportional circle is one of the oldest of the quantitative point symbols used for statistical representation. Towards the beginning of the nineteenth century it was used in graph illustrating the then new census materials. So far as it is known, the earliest age of graduated circles on maps was in the third decade of that century to show the relative population of the cities and towns of Ireland[19] Since that time, it has been near the top of any list of quantitative point symbol in the frequency of its use, and its ease of construction and interpretation makes it to be widely utilized.

The proportional circles are used for presenting amounts when the total of statistical units are of more interest than details of location. Thus, they are useful (i) when the units represented exist in close proximity but are large in aggregate number, such as the population of a city, or (ii) representing aggregate amount for relatively large territories. In the latter instance, the territory is considered only as a location even though it has areal extent. It shows both location and amount.

DIVIDED PROPORTIONAL CIRCLES (Pie graphs)

In many cases the quantities represented by proportional circles can be subdivided into a number of component parts. Population totals may be divided into workers, non-workers, males-females, rural-urban, industrial categories, etc. Such data can be illustrated by dividing each circle into a number of sectors, each occupying an appropriate share of the total area of the circle.

The first stage in construction of a pie graph is to draw proportional circles to represent the total active population of each block or unit according to a suitable scale. The next step is to subdivide each circle into sectors which by their size represent the percentage of the total contained within each such group. Clearly a 90° sector occupying a quarter of the circle would represent 25% of the total population of the unit, 180° sector 50% and so on. For any given percentage, we can calculate the interior angle of the sector by multiplying 3.6. Taking the sector for 30% in secondary industry.

$$30\% \times 3.6 = 108^{\circ}$$

The north line from the centre (0°)is usually used as a starting point for the division of circles, and sectors are marked progressively in a clockwise direction. It is as well to check before stating that the angles calculated add up to 360°, and small adjustments may have to be made to allow for the effects of rounding off to the nearest whole number.

In some cases it may be desirable to begin with the largest sectors and work downward in size, but this is not essential. In fact, the order is not critical, provided that it is the same for each circle. Once marked in, different sectors should be distinguished by a suitable scheme or shading.

Pie-graphs obviously share the advantages of simple proportional circles. Their chief advantage lies in their suitability for use as map symbols, relating either to points or to areas. Frequently, however, they are used as statistical diagrams in their own right, illustrating data which need not be considered within a spatial context. In some cases the data may often be presented as effectively, and yet more simply, by using divided proportional bars.

POPULATION DISPERSION GRAPH

Dispersion is a term which is very commonly used in the study of quantitative geography. Its dictionary meaning includes fluctuation, scatter, variation, variability, diversity, deviation or spread. The common uses in geography, however, are dispersion, scatter and deviation. Disperson can be ascertained either in the absolute or in the relative form while deviation is studied in its relative form.

A dispersion graph can be used to show the variation in relation to medium population of a series of inhabited villages and a scatter graph can be used to investigate the correlation between the two different sets of geographical data, such as population and area, population and double cropped area, population and rainfall, population and irrigation facilities, while a deviational graph can be used in relation to a mean in relative forms or in percentages.

A dispersion diagram is an important tool in the analysis of population distribution by size grouping of settlements. The median, quartile, decile and other percentile value derived from the diagrams have greater significance in some cases than mean values or coefficients derived from mean values in arriving at a more rational estimation of population distribution and of classifying population regime.

CONSTRUCTION OF A DIAGRAM

A diagram may be constructed from the total number of persons inhabiting various sizes of villages of a unit (such as development block) simply by plotting dots of suitable size, each of which represents the total number of population of an inhabited village against a vertical scale uniformaly graduated so that the base is one and the top is equivalent to the maximum number of population of the village. In certain instances it may be necessary to transform data by plotting it on a logarithmic graph paper. This differs from the normal graph paper in that the scale increases at a geometric rather than at an arithmetic rate. The scale on normal graph paper is usually divided into inches and tenth of an inch or centimetre while on a logarithmic paper the scale increases at a constant rate of 10, and is divided into 'cycle', the difference between the beginning and end of each cycle being ten times greater than the previous cycle. Thus, if the first cycle on a logarithmic paper runs from 1 to 10, the second will run from 10 to 100, the third from 100 to 1000, and the fourth from 1000 to 10000 and so on.

The circumstances in which a logarithmic graph paper may be used are the following:

A. When the data is very large, a logarithmic scale tends to 'compress' the values because the cycles successively increase by a factor of 10.

B. When there are more data at one end of the range of a distribution than at the other because the scale is increasing progressively, the upper end is relatively more compressed" than the lower end.

A population dispersion diagram shows the population of individual inhabited villages of Ghosi tahsil at the development block level. The data are derived from the Census Hand Book of Azamgarh District 1971 to construct the dispersion diagram (right hand side). The diagram is shaded and prepared from the same data (left had dispersion diagram). The interquartile ranges have been distinctively shaded, while the median and the quartile values are indicated by means of columns shaded for the purpose of comparison. A logarithmic graph paper is used on the ordinate axis to show the population of each inhabited village of Ghosi Tahsil, Azamgarh.

It is advisable to construct a dispersion diagram on the basis of the data pertaining to population of more than 50 units.

A dispersion diagram is suitable for micro-regional analysis of population. Population dispersion diagrams are easy to construct. They show at a glance the dispersion of the total number of population of each inhabited village for any unit. They give an indication of the size of inhabited villages and the actual variability without the necessity of making lengthy statistical calculations. The median value as well as the total number of population of inhabited villages have many advantages over the mean value since the latter may give a false impression.

Population dispersion diagrams have only a limited value of greater importance, because the vertical scale is graduated from one to the highest population of an inhabited village. The total number of persons of an inhabited village are then plotted to give the individual population dispersion for each unit.

SCATTER GRAPH OR DIAGRAM

Scatter graphs are used to investigate the relationship between two different sets of geographical data. It differs from a dispersion graph because both variables are scaled along both axes, while in a dispersion graph only one variable (the total population of inhabited villages) is scaled along only the vertical axis (y-axis). In a scatter graph it is customary to scale the independent variable or casual factor or area along the horizontal axis (x axis) while the dependent variable or resultant factor or population is scaled variables.

It is important that there should be some logical reason for expecting a relationship between the two variables concerned. If, this is not the case, any relationship discovered may be purely coincidental. In fact, there is usually a cause and effect association between the two sets of values plotted 20 (Table 11.12). Thus a scatter diagram shows the graphical correlation of population and the area on a different scale using simple, semi-log and log-log graph paper, which produce different patterns and reveal the fact that there is a close relationship between population and area.

TABLE 11.12 **Statement Showing Method of Calculation for Spearman's Rank Correlation Co-efficient ($P = Rh_o$)**

Panchayat	Population Rank	Area Rank	d	d^2
Dubari Luxmipur	1	1	0	0
Kasara	2	2	0	0
Ghaziapur	3	31	28	784
Sohan- Paranpur	4	5	1	1
Maryadpur	5	19	14	196
Pakari Buzurg	6	20	14	196
Rasoolpur	7	8	1	1
Alinagar	8	12	4	16

Sipah Suklauli	9	9	0	0
Majhwara	10	23	13	169
Bhairopur	11	34	23	529
Sahroj Kachhi	12	25	13	169
Chummanar	13	3	10	100
Mungesar	14	42	28	784
Dhanauli	15	4	11	121
Surajpur	16	15	1	1
Dargah	17	17	0	0
Maubojh	18	21	3	9
Kamal Sagar	19	14	5	25
Kalyanpur	20	26	6	36
Koeriapar	21	18	3	9
Katihari Buzurg	22	29	7	49
Fatehpur Tal Narj	23	24	1	1
Kuranga- Bana	24	16	8	64
Bhelabandh	25	35	10	100
Lairo onwar	26	36	10	100
Gauharpur	27	22	5	25
Tikari Gontha	28	11	17	289
Mirpur Daniyal	29	30	1	1
Ghosi	30	6	24	576
Badraon	31	28	3	9
Baragaon	32	7	25	625
Malkauli	33	49	16	256
Nevda Mundadand	34	46	12	144
Nadwal	35	41	6	36
Sondsar Chanpur	36	37	1	1
Bhikharipur	37	27	10	100
Korauli	38	40	2	4
Akolhi	39	45	6	36
Manikpur Harauwa	40	43	3	9
Madhuban	41	10	31	961
Kamalapur	42	38	4	16
Sultanpur	43	32	11	121
Usai Sardaha	44	47	3	9
Nemadand	45	44	1	1
Hariyaon Jaganpur	46	48	2	4
Sarvan Garibpur	47	13	34	1156
Jajauli Dostpur	48	33	15	225
Fatehpur Mandaon	49	39	100	100
Paraspur Sonjharia	50	50	0	0

Spearman's Rank correlation co-efficient, R = $\frac{1-6\sum d^2}{N-N} = 1-\frac{6(8164)}{124950} = 1-\frac{(489984)}{1249950}$

$= \frac{1-6(8164)}{125000-50} = 1-0.3920288$

$=0.6079712$

POPULATION AND SPACE ASSOCIATION

The investigation of the real world situation and the theoretical ideas suggest that there is close relationship between population and the area in Ghosi tahsil, Azamgarh district. The problem can be restated by the hypothesis that the population (dependent variable) is dependent upon the space (independent variable). As the area of panchayats increases, the number of population also increase. This simple statement is illustrated by a scatter diagram with the dependent variable on the vertical axis (y-axis) and the independent variable on the horizontal axis (x-axis) on different scales. (Table 11.11)

TABLE 11.11 METHOD OF CACULATION OF PEARSON'S PRODUCT MOMENT CORRELATION

Panchayat	Population Y	Y-Y	Area in (sq. km) X	X-X	(X-X)X(Y-Y)
Dubari Luxmipur	20,343	10,725.3	61.47	42.72	4,58,184.81
Kasara	17,146	7,528.3	35.15	16.40	1,23,464.12
Chummanar	15,168	5,550.3	21.00	2.25	1,24,088.18
Dhanauli Rampur	14,713	5,095.3	20.52	1.77	9,018.68
Sohar-Paranpur	13,929	4,311.3	30.17	11.42	49,235.05
Ghosi	13,552	3,934.3	15.51	-3.24	-12,747.13
Baragaon	13,342	3,724.3	15.06	-3.6	-13,742.66
Rasoolpur	12,425	2,807.3	28.55	9.80	27,511.54
Sipah	12,207	2,589.3	24.35	5.60	14,500.08
Madhuban	12,178	2,560.3	12.04	-6.71	-17,179.61
Tikari-Gontha	12,148	2,530.3	16.30	-2.45	-6,199.24
Alinagar Daniyal	11,669	2,051.3	26.27	7.52	15,425.78
Sarvan Garibpur	11,631	2,013.3	10.22	-8.53	-17,173.44
Kamal Sagar	11,453	1,835.3	19.05	0.30	550.59
Surajpur	10,883	1,265.3	19.67	0.92	1,164.08
Kurangabana	10,678	1,060.3	17.11	-1.64	-1,738.89
Dargah	10,516	898.3	19.52	0.77	691.69
Koeriyapar	10,287	669.3	18.06	-0.69	-461.82
Maryadpur	9,936	318.3	29.45	10.70	3,405.81
Pakari Buzurg	9,930	312.3	28.96	10.21	3,188.58
Maurbojh	9,855	237.3	19.49	0.74	175.60
Gauharpur	9,852	234.3	16.44	-2.31	-541.23
Majhwara	9,665	47.3	23.54	4.79	225.57
Fatehpur Tal Narja	9,544	-73.7	17.71	-1.04	76.65
Sahroj Kachhi	9,315	-302.7	21.09	2.34	-708.32
Kalyanpur	9,225	-392.7	18.28	-0.47	184.57
Bhikharipur	9,157	-460.7	13.41	-5.34	2,460.14
Badraon	9,153	-464.7	15.20	-3.55	1,649.69
Katihari Buzurg	8,852	-765.7	17.77	-0.98	750.39
Mirpur Daniyal	8,386	-1,231.7	15.67	-3.08	3,793.64
Ghaziapur	7,796	-1,821.7	15.02	16.27	-39,639.05
Sultanpur	7,788	-1,829.7	11.64	-7.11	13,009.17
Jajauli Dostpur	7,796	-1,841.7	10.00	-8.75	16,114.88
Bhairopur	7,382	2,235.7	22.06	3.31	-7,400.17
Bhelabandh	7,330	-2,287.7	16.76	-1.99	4,552.52
Lairo Donwar	7,218	-2,399.7	16.66	-2.09	5,015.37
Sondsar Chandpur	7,192	-2,425.7	14.36	-4.39	10,648.82

Kamlapur Sipah	7,161	-2,456.7	11.67	-7.08	17,393.44
Fatehpur Madaon	7,148	-2,469.7	8.53	-10.22	25,240.33
Korauli	7,095	-2,522.7	13.4	-5.35	13,496.45
Nadwal	6,957	-2,660.7	14.80	-3.95	10,509.77
Mungesar	6,939	-2,678.7	20.71	1.96	-5,250.25
Manikpur Harauwa	6,814	-2,803.7	12.47	-6.28	17,607.24
Nemdand	6,562	-3,055.7	10.43	-8.32	19,312.02
Akolhi	6,471	-3,146.7	12.55	-6.20	19,509.54
Nevada Mundadand	6,029	-3,588.7	15.01	-3.74	13,421.74
Usari- Sardha	5,538	-4,079.7	11.38	-7.37	30,067.39
Hariyaon Jaganpur	5,311	-4,304.7	10.29	-8.46	36,434.68
Malkauli	5,068	-4,549.7	15.02	-3.73	16,970.38
Paraspur Sonjhatria	4,172	-5,445.7	7.66	-11.09	60,392.81
Total	4,80,885	1,24,497.8	937.43	299.63	10,53,570.75

This correlation between population and space can be analysed by a number of statistical indices.21. In order to investigate the distribution and magnitude of one variable with the other, comparisons may be made, so that their correspondence could be estimated. In order to hypothesize the association between population and space 50 panchayats have been considered and has been calculated on Karl Pearson's Production Moment Correlation.22

$$r\,2 = \frac{Covariance\ of\ x\ \text{and}\ y}{\sigma x\,.\,\sigma y}$$

$$= \frac{\frac{1}{N}\sum(x-\bar{x})(y-\bar{y})}{\sigma x\,.\,\sigma y}$$

$$= \frac{940788.949}{50 \times 8.86 \times 3195.37} = 0.6646$$

where r = Karl Pearsonian correlation coefficient, Sigma (Σ) = The summation sign

Σ(x - x) (y - y) = sum of all values of covarience of independent variables (area i.e. x) and dependent variables (population i.e. y).

σx = Standard deviation of x variable i.e. area.

σy = Standard deviation of y variable i.e. population.

N = Number of units or nyayapanchayats.

X = Arithmetic mean of one series 'Xs'

y = Arithmetic mean of another series 'Ys'

It may also be calculated by the formula of Spearman's Rank correlation coefficient (P = Rho)[23]

$$P = \frac{1-6\sum d^2}{N(N^2-1)}$$

where P (Rho) = the rank correlation coefficient.

d = the rank differences of population and space.

N = the number of panchayats,

On the basis of the above formula after testing, it found that there is a positive correlation of high degree that is 0.61 between population and space in Ghosi Tahsil Azamgarh which is lower than that of Karl Pearson's Product Moment correlation by 0.05.

The correlation coefficient 24 provides a numerical index of the degree of relationship, but it may be preferable to draw the line which most closely approximates to the general trend of the panchayats plotted on a scatter-diagram. This is a regression line of 'best fit'. There are in fact two regression lines for x and y on for y on x. In the first instance, it is possible to predict the approximate value of y, gives a figure for x and vice-verse for the regression of x on y. The equation for y i.e. population (unknown on x i.e. area (known) is calculated by the following

$$(y-\overline{y} = r\frac{\sigma y}{\sigma x} \quad (x-\overline{x})..........(1)$$

for x i.e. area (unknown) and y i.e. population the expression is

$$(x-\overline{x}) = r\frac{\sigma x}{\sigma y} \quad (y-\overline{y})...........(2)$$

The regression equation of y (population) on x (Area) for the data referring to population and space for 50 panchayats in the areas under study becomes:-

$$y - 9617.7 = 0.6646 \frac{3195.39}{8.86} (x - 18.75)$$

$$= 0.6646 . 360 .65349 (x - 18.75)$$

$$= 238.029 (x - 18.75)$$

$$= 238.029 x - 4463 . 0437$$

$$y = 238.029 x - 4463.0437 + 9617.7$$

$$= 238.029 x + 5154 .6563$$

$$= 238 x + 5154.6$$

Taking arbitrary values

if x = 40 then y = 238 x 40 + 5154.6
= 9520 + 5154.6
= 14674.6

If x = 10 then y = 238 x 10 + 5154.6
= 2380 + 5154.6
= 7534.6

These values may be used to draw the regression line on the scatter diagram and in the same manner the regression line for y on x is obtained. The equation for the later is

$$X - 18.75 = 0.6646 \frac{8.86}{3195.39} (y - 9617.7)$$

$$= 0.0018427 y + 1.027465$$

POPULATION PYRAMIDS

Population pyramids are prepared to show and analyse the population growth and sex-age composition of the population of a region. These are primarily used to study both sex and age in a graphic form pyramids may be used to illustrate features other than sex and age structure. Compound pyramids may also be used to show the population growth for many years or to represent decennial totals of migrants into a region with the apex indicating the earliest, the base, and the latest returns. Each tier is then sub-divided to show ethnic structure, age structure, marital status, etc. of the migrant stream. It may be superimposed to show structural changes in the population of any given region over a period of time. Similarly, population pyramids representing population of two decades (1961-71) may be superimposed for comparative purposes or population pyramids representing rural workers and urban workers may be superimposed for comparison. It may be used for forecasting the population by superimposing present and projected sex and age pyramids for a particular reigon.[25]

CONSTRUCTION OF POPULATION PYRAMID

The construction of population pyramid is based either on absolute number or proportion data of population pertaining to sex and age composition. The data are plotted directly from absolute quinquennial totals or decennial totals given in the census returns, after a suitable vertical scale has been chosen. It is customary to construct a scale in the centre along a line showing zero while it is conventional to plot age along the vertical scale with the large base representing the youngest group, on the apex the oldest and to measure the numbers (absolute or percentage) of the population at each age along the horizontal axes, with males to the left of the centre or vertical scale and females to the right. If, a pyramid is based on percentage, the sum of the length of all the bars including both male and female is always the same, that is hundred per cent female separate. If a linear scale is used, all the population pyramids will be the same height, and the variation will be in their relative width. If the width of each tier in the pyramid is made proportional to its length, the relative height of pyramid will vary as well as their width. The pyramids are then orthomorphic and their shapes may be easily compared. Even so, the pyramids will vary enormously in size from that of a large town to a small rural community.

A population pyramid is more or less triangular in shape. The broad base of a population pyramid indicates that the majority consists of young people, while the sides gradually slope toward a point, representing the decrease brought about by deaths in each successive decennial or quinquennial age group. Although one-year, five year or quinquennial groups are used, ten-year groups are generally adequate and involve much less calculation and time. Hence, population pyramids are better to construct on decennial age groups, but a population pyramid based on quinquennial group provides the population geographers with as much information about sex and age composition as he is likely to need for most purposes. In any case detailed local information for one-year group is difficult to obtain, whereas decennial data are published in the Indian censuses. There are slight variations in the methods by which decennial data may be plotted in the form of a pyramid.[26]

THE ABSOLUTE METHOD

The construction of a population pyramid on the basis of absolute number of people helps to compare both the shape and the size of populations (Table 11.13). But it is better to compare the countries having more or less similar number of people on a similar scale, while it is difficult and disadvantageous to construct the pyramid on the basis of absolute numbers on similar scales, such as in the case of India and Italy. In this case, the use of a common scale means that Italy which has a smaller population looks too small creating difficulties in comparison and construction. Similarly, pyramids will vary enormously in size from a large city to a small village. But it is most useful to compare the age and sex composition of the same country of two different decades. (e.g. 1961-71).

THE COMPARABLE METHOD

If a population geographer wants to represent how a number of populations differ in sex and age composition without considering the size of the total population, he can make comparisons most effectively by constructing population pyramids on the basis of percentage or proportion of population data (Table 11.13). There are two possible ways of carrying out this method. Either each male age group may be shown as (1) percentage of the total male population and similarly each female age group may be expressed as a percentage of the total female population or (2) each male and each female group may be shown as a percentage of the total population. The second method is better because it has the advantage of giving a more realistic total view of sex and age variations.

TABLE 11.13 **Village Hengapur, Tahsil Sadar, District Azamgarh.**

Age years	Total Male	Popula- Percen- tage of total male	Female	Percen- tage of total female	Literate Male	Female	Total Population Percen- tage of total popula- tion	Percen- tage of total popula- tion
0-4	34	11.93	39	15.6	1	-	6.36	7.29
5-9	39	13.68	40	16.0	12	3	7.29	7.48
10-14	40	14.04	24	9.6	24	4	7.48	4.49
15-19	35	12.28	25	10.0	23	1	6.54	4.67
20-24	23	8.07	18	7.2	17	-	4.30	3.36
25-29	13	4.56	14	5.6	9	-	2.43	2.62
30-34	16	5.61	28	11.2	7	-	2.99	5.23
35-39	23	8.07	15	6.0	11	2	4.30	2.80
40-44	17	5.96	10	4.0	10	-	3.18	1.87
45-49	8	2.81	8	3.2	5	-	1.50	1.49
50-54	8	2.81	7	2.8	2	-	1.50	1.87
60-64	10	3.51	7	2.8	4	-	1.87	1.32
65-69	5	1.75	4	1.6	1	-	0.94	0.71
70 and above	6	2.11	1	0.4	-	-	1.12	0.18
TOTAL	285	100	250	100	131	10	53.3	46.7

In population pyramid based on percentage the areas of the pyramids are identical, but the population pyramids differ in shape. These difference in shape are clear to the eyes of the population geographers when the population pyramids are placed side by side, but they are much more striking when one pyramid is superimposed on one another.

COMPOUND POPULATION PYRAMID

Compound pyramids may be used to illustrate the marital status of males and females by (Table 11.14). It may be used to show the population growth also (Table 11.15). Tiers in the pyramid may be prepared to show the decennial growth of population with the apex indicating the earliest, and the base the latest returns. Each tier is then subdivided to show the regional variation in growth of population. These population pyramids are best constructed with a space left between each tier, across which lines are drawn to join the component or subdivisions.

TABLE 11.14 MARITAL STATUS ACCORDING TO SEX AND AGE
Village- Hengapur, Tahsil- Sadar, Distt.- Azamgarh.

Age in years	Married		Unmarried		Widowhood	
	Male	Female	Male	Female	Male	Female
0-4	4	- 30	39	-	-	
5-9	4	6	35	34	-	-
10-14	9	8	31	16	-	-
15-19	29	21	6	4	-	-
20-24	19	17	4	1	-	-
25-29	13	13	-	1	-	-
30-34	15	27	1	-	-	1
35-39	20	15	1	-	2	0

40-44	15	9	-	-	2	1
45-49	7	7	-	-	1	1
50-54	7	7	1	-	-	-
55-59	7	9	-	-	1	1
60-64	9	5	-	-	1	2
65-69	5	4	-	-	-	-
Above 70	5	-	-	-	1	1
TOTAL	168	148	109	95	8	7

Source: Surveyed conducted by Hanuman Prasad, Deptt. of Geography, D.A.V. Post Graduate College, Azamgarh in April, 1982.

TABLE 11.15 **POPULATION CHANGE IN AZAMGARH DISTRICT**

Census year	Popul-ation	Sadar	Ghosi	Sagri	Phulpur	Mohamm-adabad	Lalganj
1901	14,88,174	2,04,114	2,56,844	2,34,363	3,12,234	2,55,792	2,24,827
1911	14,92,818	2,46,762	2,45,265	2,30,599	3,05,644	2,40,737	2,23,811
1921	15,28,657	2,47,010	2,45,481	2,33,522	3,21,228	2,47,318	2,34,098
1931	24,71,577	2,60,565	2,63,708	2,35,301	3,17,374	2,58,409	2,36,220
1941	18,22,893	3,06,965	3,10,653	2,69,003	3,52,782	3,13,552	2,69,938
1951	21,02,423	3,47,726	3,58,923	3,11,549	4,00,170	3,69,240	3,14,815
1961	24,08,052	3,95,161	4,14,053	3,51,434	4,49,057	4,44,416	3,53,931
1971	28,57,484	4,56,315	4,95,156	4,25,732	5,29,288	5,37,553	4,13,440

Source: Surveyed by Hanuman Prasad, Deptt. of Geography, D.A.V. P.G. College, Azamgarh, in the month of April, 1982.

SUPERIMPOSED POPULATION PYRAMIDS

Age and sex pyramids may be superimposed to show structural changes in the population of an area over a period of time. Similarly, superimposed population pyramids representing population of different region may be superimposed for comparative purposes to show the actual population upon that of a hypothetical stationary population. The latter method has great value in the analysis of the rhythm of population growth, but care must be taken also that the data utilized' "applied to the same area, and changes in enumeration made in the interim period between the recording of the two sets of data employed must be considered.

The projection of population is also illustrated by superimposing present and projected sex and age pyramids for a particular region principally for planning purposes.

A population pyramid is a static picture whereas the population of an area is always changing. The percentage of population in various sex and age categories changes because of the continuous action of mortality, fertility and migration. The population pyramid freezes this motion at a particular moment in time.[27] From a slightly different perspective, the pyramid can be viewed as a picture of the biological history of a population -- the result of about hundred years of births, deaths and migration. The crests and troughs in the population pyramid show high birth and death rates respectively.

If in an area's birth rate drops or death rate increases or vice-versa the resulting crests and troughs of the population pyramid travel up through the age categories of the pyramid until all the people represented by bars (age group showing crest or trough) are dead, assuming there has been no migration. The analysis of these bulges and dents depends upon the historic knowledge (knowledge about the cause of the births and deaths) of the region to population geographers. A population with high birth and death rates is represented by a population pyramid, which has a broad base reflecting its high fertility while large steps between successively older age groups reject its high mortality. If such a population has not experienced any fluctuations in birth and death rates for a long time, the steps are rather large all the way upto sixty years of age.[28] This type of population pyramid is the chief characteristics of developing countries, such as India.

Thompson and Lewis [29] distinguished five types of population pyramids in the world:-

1. This type of population pyramid has a broad base and gently sloping sides. It is typical of all high birth and death rate countries before they have exercised control over either births or deaths. The median age is low, and the total dependency ratio's high. India's population pyramid for 1951 is of this kind.

2. This population pyramid has a broader base than that of the previous one and the sides bow in much more sharply as they slant from bottom to the top. This pyramid is typical of countries that are beginning to grow rapidly as a result of marked reduction in infant and child deaths and are yet reducing their fertility. In such countries populations are increasing rapidly, median ages are falling (really they are now the lowest in the world because of decreasing death rates of infants and young children), and youth - and total - dependency ratio's are the highest in the world. Ceylon and other countries such as the Philippines, Brazil and Mexico belong to this category.

3. This population pyramid resembles an old-fashioned beechive. It represents countries with low birth rates (a narrow base) and low death rates. Its shape could represent most of the populations of western Europe. The chief characteristic of this population pyramid is that the median age is the highest, its total dependency is the lowest of all the populations, and its largest component of dependency is in the older ages.

4. The bell-shaped population pyramid is a type recently produced by such countries as the U.S.A. and Canada. This shape represents a population which, after more than hundred years of declining birth rates and death rates, has reversed the trend in fertility while keeping the death rate low a population with a pyramidal shape of this type is growing, has a declining median age, and has increasingly high youth - and total dependency ratios. It is a transitional type.

REFERENCES

1. Wright, John k. " Crossbreeding Geographical Quantities ", *The Geographji-cal Review,* Vol.45, 1955, 52-65.
2. Robinson, Arthur H. "*Elements of Cartography* ", Wiley, 1966.
3. Trewartha, G.T. "*A Case for Population Geography* ", Vol.43, 1953, 71-97.
4. Wright, John K. " Some Measures of Distribution ", *A.A.A.G.,* Vol.27, 1937, 177.
5. For a discussion of different kinds of population density indices, see Dr. Imre Frenczi, the synthetic optimum of population, International Institute of Intellectual co-operation, League of Nations,1938.
6. Garnier, J.B. "*Geography of Population* ", Translated by S.H. Beaver, London, Longman, 1978.
7. Stamp, L. Dudley, "The Classification of land ", In *Applied Geography,* Harmondsworth, Penguin, England, 1964.
8. Garnier, J.B. " *Geography of Population* " Translated by S.H.Beaver, Longman, London, 1978.
9. Damco, G.J., Rose, H.M. and Schnell, G.A. *"Population Geography : A Reader",* Mcgraw Hill, New York, 1970.
10. Singh, J. " Optimum Carrying Capacity of Land, Caloric Density and Intensity of population pressure change in Punjab (1951-61)," *National Geographical Journal of India* 17, 1971, 31-49.

(b) Farmer, B.H. *"Available Food Supplies"* Population and Food Supply, Cambridge, 1969.

11. The unit of measurement used has been the Calorie (Large) or Kilo Calorie (This is one thousand times the small calorie used in Physics). The kilocalorie is defined as heat necessary to raise the temperature of one litre of distilled water from 14.5° C to 15.5° C. The calorie is defined as the heat necessary to raise the temperature of one gram of distilled water from 14.5° C to 15.5° C, while jule is defined as the heat necessary to raise the temperature of 0.24 gram of distilled water from 14.5° C to 15.5° C.
    (1 Calorie = 1 Kilocalorie (Kcal) = 1000 calorie (cal)
    =4200 joules (j). Now a days the joule is being introduced in the place of calorie. Kilocalorie is often used and written as Calorie (Cal).
12. Latham, M.C. *"Human Nutrition in Tropical Africa",* 1979.
13. Recommended by the Nutritional Expert Group in 1968 in " Nutritive value of Indian Foods " by C. Gopalan, B.V. Rama Shartri and S.C. Balasubramanium, National Institute of Nutrition. Indian Council of Medical Research, Hyderabad- 7 (A.P.), 1980, 27,Table 2.
14. M.C. Lantham "Human Nutrition in Tropical Africa 1979",
15. Stamp, L.D. *"The Classification of land in Applied Geography",* Penguin, 1964.
16. Singh, R.B. and Pandey, S. " Population Density in Pharenda Tahsil: A spatio-temporal Analysis ", *Uttar Bharat Bhoogol Patrika,* 1979,115-126.
17. Singh, U.P. " Optimum Carrying Capacity of Land Caloric Density and Population pressure in Salempur Tahsil ", *Uttar- Bharat Bhoogol Patrika,* XVI No.1, 41-48.
18. Dickinson, G.C., *"Statiscal Mapping and the Presentation of Statistics",* Arnold, 1963.
19. Robinson, A.H. " The Map of Henry Drury Harness ", *The Geographical Journal,* 121,1955, 440-450.
20. Davis, P. " Data Description and Presentation " in Science in Geography, Walton Street, oxford, Oxford University Press, 1974.

21. Robinson, A.H. " The Necessity of Weighting Values in Correlation Analysis of Areal Datye "*A.A.A.G.*, 46, 1956,223-226.
22. Monkhouse, F.J. and Wilkinson, H.R. "*Maps and Diagrams : Their Construction and Compilation*", Methuen, London, Appendix, 504-507.
23. Bhattacharya,A.B. "Statistical" Bharati Bhawan, Exhibition Road, Patna 1, 289.
24. Chadwick, J.G. "Correlation between Geographical Distribution: 'A statistical Technique", *Geography,* 1961, 46, 25-30.
25. See method illustrated in F.W. Notesian (1944) "*The Future Population of Europe and The Soviet Union, Geneva.*
26. Monkhouse, F.j. and Wilkinson, H.R. "*Maps and Diagrams: Their Compilation and Construction*", London, Methuan, 1971.
27. Thomson, Warren, S. and Lawis, David, t. "*Population Problems*", Tata McGraw Hill, 1976, 102.
28. Op. cit -. 107.
29. Op. cit - 113.

TWELVE

TECHNIQUES OF GROUPING POPULATION DATA AND THEIR REPRESENTATION

A QUANTITATIVE APPROACH

The distribution of population by size group of settlements can be best understood and appreciated, if the data are summarized statistically and are plotted graphically to show the characteristics of such a distribution as well as the frequencies of the occurrence of villages by size group of settlement. This not only make the interpretation of data easier but also facilitates comparisons with other distributions. In this way, the complexity of the information is considerably reduced, whilst its usefulness is increased. The whole process may be regarded as one of controlled generalization about a given numerical distribution.

A set of data pertaining to the population of the inhabited villages of Ghosi Tahsil is recorded in the census of 1971[1]. Suppose, we wish to investigate the way in which population sizes of inhabited villages vary from one village to another. In order to have an idea how the populations of various settlements are distributed a histogram can be constructed shown in Fig. 12.1A, 12.1B, 12.1C and 12.1D instead of the traditional classification of population by size group of settlements that is below 200, 200--500 persons and so on.

METHODOLOGY

The population data are first grouped into classes, so that it is known how many occurrences fall into each of a series of quantitatively different sets of villages. The number of occurrences are plotted against the appropriate classes and a histogram.2 is drawn into the 'building blocks' and the pattern which it represents is called the frequency distribution for that population of villages by size grouping of settlements. So far as the population of Ghosi Tahsil is concerned the population for individual inhabited villages are grouped into eight classes at intervals of 1000 inhabitants depending on their order of magnitude. The number of uninhabited villages are also shown by a black bar on the left side in the very beginning of the diagram. The oblique hatched bars show the total number of villages, while the superimposed dotted bars show the absolute total population by size grouping of settlements which are readily apparent. The way in which these population data by size group of settlements vary is shown by both the histogram and by the superimposed-histogram. The Salient features are listed in Table 12.1 and are shown in Fig.12.1A.

TABLE 12.1 **DISTRIBUTION OF POPULATION BY SIZE GROUP OF SETTLEMENTS IN GHOSI TAHSIL, AZAMGARH, 1971.**

Size Groups of settlements persons inhabited villages	No. of inhabited villages	Percentage of inhabited villages	Rural population	Percentage of rural poipulation
Below 1,000	616	81.70	2,17,519	45.23
1,001-2,000	94	12.47(94.1)	1,23,073	25.59(70.82)
2,001-3,000	29	12.47(98.01)	69,052	14.36(85.18)
3,001-4,000	6	0.80(98.81)	20,405	4.24(89.42)
4,001-5,000	3	0.40(99.21)	14,168	2.95(92.37)
5,001-6,000	4	0.53(99.74)	21,198	4.41(96.78)
6,001-7,000	1	0.13(99.87)	6,621	1.38(98.16)
7,001-8,000	0	0.00(99.87)	0	0.00(98.16)
8,001-9,000	1	0.13(100.00)	8,849	1.84(100.00)
Total	754	100.00	4,80,885	100.00(100.00)

Note: Calculative percentages are given in brackets.

Thus, in effect, we are converting the population of individual inhabited villages into a grouped form or by size group of settlements, and then illustrating it graphically on a sound and logical statistical ground instead of the traditional classification of settlements by size grouping of settlements, which has no statistical base.

There are many circumstances in which, for the sake of simplicity, clarity or practicality, information in grouped form is of greater value to population geographers than individual data.[3]. This is often the case when, in addition to describing the data statistically, we also wish to represent it graphically or in the form of a map. Simplicity results from the reduction of a large body of data to more easily manageable proportions. There may be greater clarity, because it is often easier to identify underlying trends when the emphasis is taken off individual values. Practicality is achieved, because it is impossible to differentiate between a large number of individual values when mapping.

The number of classes used can vary according to the characteristics of the data involved, provided that between them, they cover the whole range of values. Obviously the distribution of population by villages which have population ranging from only one person to 8849 persons normally requires more classes than those with few. If, too few classes are used, a good deal of detail may be lost, while there may be empty classes if the number chosen is too great. In general, there should be as many classes as possible without introducing empty classes. As a general guide the number of classes should not exceed five times the log of the number of observations in the distribution.

A set of figures relating to the distribution of rural population according to 132 individual inhabited villages of Kopaganj development block is listed in the census of 1971. Suppose, we wish to classify this data as a first step, say, to draw a histogram using the rule of thumb method mentioned above, the number of classes may be worked out from the formula.

$$N = 5 \times \text{Log. } 132$$

$$= 5 \times 2.12 \text{ (to 2 decimal place)}$$
$$= 10.60 \text{ say,}$$
$$= 10 \text{ (to nearest whole number).}$$

This may be regarded as the maximum number, of course and fewer classes can be used if it appears that a better result might be obtained. In table 12.1 and Fig. 12.1A the histogram contains one empty class. The construction of a histogram requires the use of a fixed interval, but this method is not always best suited to population data of 754 inhabited villages. Its advantage lies in its ease of calculation, but it is not sufficiently flexible to cope with strongly positive skewed distribution, when the majority of villages are concentrated within a fairly small part of the overall range.

VARIABLE INTERVALS

Class limit based on an interval which varies in some regular way are the most difficult to calculate. One method of introducing an interval of this sort involves the use of successive terms in a geometric progression as class boundaries. The first term in progression is multiplied by a chosen amount to give the next term, which in turn is multiplied by the same amount to give the next in sequence and so on. For example, the sequences such as 2,4,8,16,32, etc. and 2,6,18,54, etc. are in geometrical progression with multipliers or common ratio, of 2 and 3, respectively. The problem is to find a common ratio that will enable the requisite range of values to be covered in the desired number of classes. The following ratios will help in solving the problem. They are the logarithmic.5 square-root and cube-root ratios etc.

THE LOGARITHMIC RATIO

The logarithmic ratio is calculated in the following manner:-

a. Find the logarithm of the lowest value in the distribution and substract if from the logarithm of the highest value.

b. divide the result by the number of classes required;

c. starting with the logarithm of the lowest value, make a list by adding to it progressively the result of step 2, until the logarithm of the highest value is reached;

d. find the anti-logarithms of each of the terms in the list and use these as the class boundaries required. They should all be terms in geometric progression, although the common ratio is unlikely to be a whole number.

Let us take the example of the distribution of population by size grouping of settlements in Ghosi Tahsil in 1971. We may now work through the following procedure.

Log. 8849 = 3.94689 Assuming that for this example there are to be 10 classes so, 3.94689/10 = 0.394689

Assuming that for this example there are to be 10 classes

So, 3.94689/10 = 0.394689

= 0.395 (to 3 decimal place).

Class interval	Cummulative log to 3 decimal place	Anti-log to 1 decimal place	Nearest Round
Below 0.395	0.395	2.5	3
* 0.395	0.790	6.2	6
* 0.395	1.185	15.3	15
* 0.395	1.580	38.0	38
* 0.395	1.975	94.4	94
* 0.395	2.370	234.4	234
* 0.395	2.765	582.1	582
* 0.395	3.160	1,445.4	1445
* 0.395	3.555	3,589.2	3589
* 0.395	3.946	8,849.0	8849

Since we are using discrete data, we may define the class limit as shown in column 4, but with continuous data the figures shown in column 3 are more valid.

The method of defining class limits is well suited to the distributions, which exhibit a positive skew since classes are narrow at the lower end of the range, where the majority of values lie, but became broader towards the upper end, where there are relatively few values. This results in a more balanced allocation of values to classes, a characteristic which is often helpful in napping. Table 12.2 and Fig. 12.1 (d) illustrate the way in which the pattern of class frequencies has been altered by adopting a variable interval. The positive skewness is converted into negative skewness. It minimizes the positive skewness in the distribution. At the same time it is a time-consuming and laborious process.

TABLE 12.2 **Distribution of Population by Size Grouping of Settlements in Ghosi Tahsil, 1971**

Size grouping of settlements persons/inhabited village	Number of inhabited villages	Percentage of inhabited village	Rural population	Percentage of Rural population
Below 3	3	0.40	5	0.00
4-6	1	0.13(0.53)	6	0.00
7-15	11	1.46(1.99)	123	0.03(0.03)
16-38	28	3.71(5.70)	797	0.16(0.19)
39-94	64	8.49(14.19)	4,429	0.92(1.11)
95-234	143	18.96(33.15)	23,082	4.80(5.91)
235-582	227	30.11(63.26)	94,477	19.65(25.56)
583-1445	210	27.85(91.11)	1,78,647	37.15(62.71)
1446-3589	57	7.56(98.67)	1,24,515	25.89(88.60)
3590-8849	10	1.33(100.00)	54,802	11.40(100.0)
Total	754	100.00 (100.00)	4,80,885	100.00 (100.00)

Thus, this method also minimizes the positive skewness and exaggerates the negative skewness in the distribution of rural population by size group of settlements.

Changes of this nature in the distribution of population by size group of settlements may be referred to as 'data transformation'.

These are sometime used to convert skewed distributions approximately into normal ones for purposes of statistical analysis.[6].

In the above case a distribution with a positive skew has been converted into one with a negative skew, indicating that the strength of the transformation has been greater than required. A better result might be obtained by applying the same technique, but using square-roots instead of logarithms to establish the class boundaries.

SQUARE ROOT RATIO

This method would produce a different result based on the original data, thereby altering the frequency of inhabited villages and the number of persons in each size grouping of settlements. Square-roots have a rather weaker effect than logarithms, and we might, therefore, expect the new distribution of population by size group of settlements to be fairly symmetrical, resembling a normal distribution. So far as the distribution of population by size group of settlements in the area is concerned the data obtained by using square-roots is far from satisfactory as it minimizes the positive skewness in the distribution by size group of settlements.

TABLE 12.3 **Distribution of Population by Size Grouping of Settlements in Ghosi Tahsil, Azamgarh, 1971.**

Class Interval	frequency	frequency in %	Rural Population	Percentage of rural population
Below 10^2	111	14.72	5,747	1.19
10^2-20^2	273	36.21(50.93)	64,863	13.49(14.68)
20^2-30^2	209	27.72(78.65)	1,25,210	26.04(40.72)
30^2-40^2	103	13.66(92.31)	1,19,567	24.86(65.58)
40^2-50^2	33	4.38(96.69)	67,252	13.99(79.57)
50^2-60^2	15	1.99(98.68)	43,444	9.03(88.60)
60^2-70^2	3	0.40(99.08)	13,164	2.74(91.34)
70^2-80^2	5	0.66(99.74)	26,168	5.44(96.78)

80^2-90^2	1	0.13(99.87)	6,621	1.38(98.16)
Above 90^2	1	0.13(100.00)	8,849	1.84(100.00)
Total	754	100.00 (100.00)	4,80,885	100.00(100.00)

Note: Cummulative percentage are given in the brackets.

The square root method minimizes the positive skew, indicating that the strength of the transformation has been much less than required. A better result might be obtained by applying the same technique but by using cube-roots, instead of logarithm or square roots to fix the class boundary. This would produce a different transformation of original data pertaining to population distribution by size group of settlements, thereby altering the number of frequencies in each class interval. Cube-roots produce more satisfactory results than do the other methods. We might, therefore, expect the new distribution of population by size group of settlements to be fairly symmetrical about a central modal class of population, thus resembling a normal distribution as shown in Fig. 12.1C.

TABLE 12.4 **Distribution of Population by Size Group of Settlements**

Class Interval Persons	Frequency	Frequency in percentage	Rural population	Percentage of rural population
Below 3^3	28	3.71	411	0.08
3^3-5^3	113	14.99(18.70)	8,688	1.81(1.89)
5^3-7^3	202	26.79(45.49)	46,217	8.95(10.84)
7^3-9^3	197	26.13(71.62)	98,016	21.04(31.88)
9^3-11^3	137	18.17(89.79)	1,34,451	27.96(59.84)
11^3-13^3	41	5.44(95.23)	69,440	14.44(74.28)
13^3-15^3	24	3.18(98.41)	61,759	12.84(87.12)
15^3-17^3	6	0.80(99.87)	25,308	5.26(92.38)
17^3-19^3	5	0.66(99.87)	27,746	5.77(98.15)
Above 19^3	1	0.13(100.00)	8,849	1.85(100.00)
Total	754	100.00 (100.00)	4,80,885	100.00 (100.00)

* Cummulative percentage frequency (c.p.f.) is given in brackets.

The logarithmic scale is used on the y-axis to show the number of occurrences of inhabited villages and the number of persons residing in such size group of settlements instead of using simple graph paper, because it requires less space. It is also well suited to show the extreme distribution of population, for example the population ranging from one to 21,7519 persons.

In order to overcome this difficulty and to make for case convenience it is better to convert or transform the actual number of persons and occurrences of inhabited villages falling in each size group of settlements into percentages and ultimately into cumulative percentages. Then these are best plotted in Figure 12.2A, 12.2B, 12.2C and 12.2D the graph as shown in Figure 12.2A, 12.2B, 12.C and 12.2D. The distribution of population by size group of settlements may be plotted as a superimposed Ogive curve to show the relationship of inhabitants and inhabited villages by size group of settlements.

Population by size group of settlements on the basis of quartiles is an important tool in the study of population distribution in an area. These are calculated with the help of the following formulae.

$$P.L.Q. = \frac{(N + 1)\,1}{4}$$

$$P.M.Q. = \frac{(N + 1)\,1}{2}$$

$$P.U.Q. = \frac{(N + 1)\,3}{4}$$

where, P.L.O. = population of lower quartile village
P.M.Q = population of median village, and
P.U.Q. = population of upper quartile village.

The population of the lower, median and upper quartile village of various blocks of Ghosi Tahsil has been calculated with the help of above formulate and has been shown in the Table 12.5 and on the Fig.12.3B.

TABLE 12.5 Distribution of Population on the basis of Lower, Median and Upper Quartile Values in Ghosi Tahsil, Azamgarh, 1971.

NAME OF THE BLOCKS

Population Mandaon	Doharighat	Fatehpur	Ghosi	Badron	Kopaganj
Lower Quartile	168	160	145	181	191
Median	421	345	352	405	456
Upper Quartile	816	639	725	866	1049

Table 12.5 reveals the fact that Kopaganj block surpasses all the blocks of Ghosi Tahsil in the population of lower quartile, medium and upper quartile which indicates that there are higher sizes of villages in Kopaganj block compared with to other regions.

TABLE 12.6 **Distribution of Population by Size Grouping of Settlements in Ghosi Tahsil, Azamgarh, 1971 on the Basis of Quartiles.**

NAME OF THE BLOCKS

Class Interval	Doharighat	Fatehpur Mandaon	Ghosi	Badron	Kopaganj
Lower Quartile	2,742	3,674	2,806	3,541	3,591
	(2.93%)	(3.34%)	(3.37%)	(3.81%)	(3.55%)
Lower-Median	10,390	12,011	9,365	10,529	9,284
Quartile	(11.10%)	(10.93%)	(11.27%)	(11.32%)	(9.17%)
Median-Upper	22,310	21,267	18,334	22,516	24,549
Quartile	(23.83%)	(19.80%)	(22.04%)	(24.21%)	(24.26%)
Upper Quartile	58,174	72,468	52,662	56,412	63,760
	(62.14%)	(65.93%)	(63.32%)	(60.66%)	(63.02%)
Total	93,616	1,09,920	83,167	92,998	1,01,184
	(100%)	(100%)	(100%)	(100%)	(100%)

* Figures in Brackets are in percentage.

Table 12.6 and Fig.12.3C reveal the fact that 2.93% to 3.81% of the population live in 25% of villages below the lower quartile, 9.17% to 11.32% persons reside in 25% of the villages below the lower quartile, 9.17% to 11.32% persons reside in 25% of the villages between the lower quartile and mediam 19.80% to 24.26% persons dwell in 25% of the villages from the medium to upper quartile, while 60.66% to 65.93% of the inhabitants reside in 25% of inhabited villages above the upper quartile.

REFERENCES

1. Trewartha, G.T. " A Case for Population Geography ", *A.A.A.G.*, 43, 1953, 71-97.
2. Rana P.B.Singh " Clan Settlements in Saran Plain, (Middle Ganga Valley) A Study in Cultural Geography. N.G.S.I., B.H.U., Varanasi, 21.
3. Sinha, D.M., Census, 1971, " District Census Hand Book, Uttar Pradesh Series " 21, Azamgarh, 102-159.
4. Gregory, S. *"Statistical Methods and the Geographers"* , London, Longman, 1978.
5. Davis, Peter *"Science in Geography"* , Oxford, 1977.
6. Toyne, Peter and Newby, Peter t. *"Techniques in Human Geography"* Glassgow, University Press, 1971.
7. Gregory, S. "Transformation of Data" in *Statistical Methods and Geographers,* London, Longman, 1978.
8. Bhattacharya, A.B. "Cummulative Frequency Curve or the Ogive". It is normally pronounced as 'Ojive' in 'Statistical' Patna, 116.

Fig. 12.1

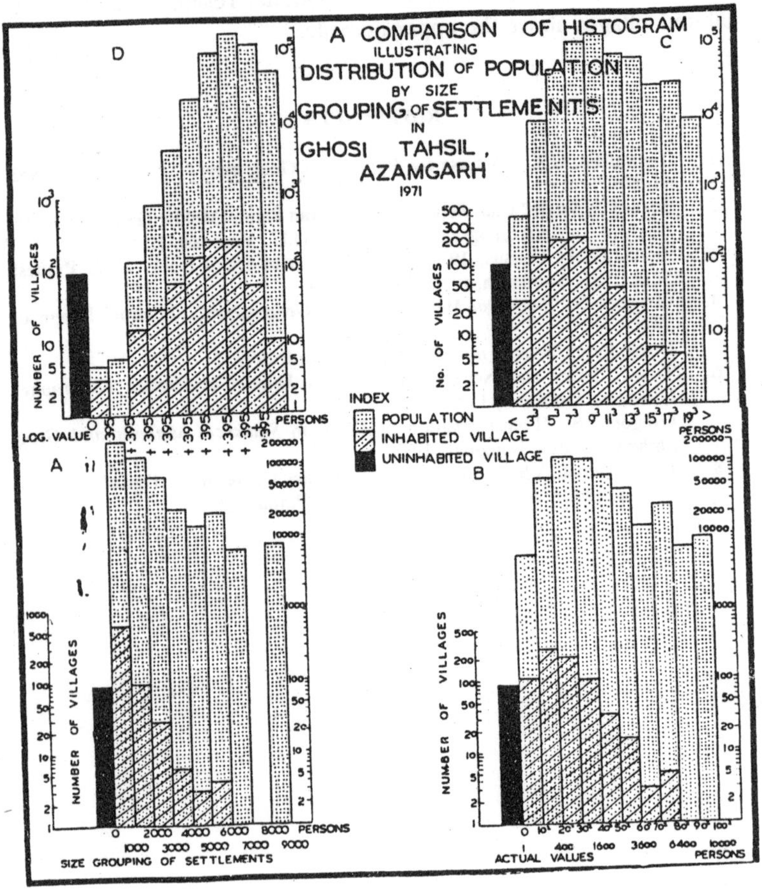
A COMPARISON OF HISTOGRAM
ILLUSTRATING
DISTRIBUTION OF POPULATION
BY SIZE
GROUPING OF SETTLEMENTS
IN
GHOSI TAHSIL,
AZAMGARH
1971
INDEX
POPULATION
INHABITED VILLAGE
UNINHABITED VILLAGE
D
C
A
B
NUMBER OF VILLAGES
No. OF VILLAGES
LOG. VALUE
PERSONS
SIZE GROUPING OF SETTLEMENTS
ACTUAL VALUES

Fig. 12.2

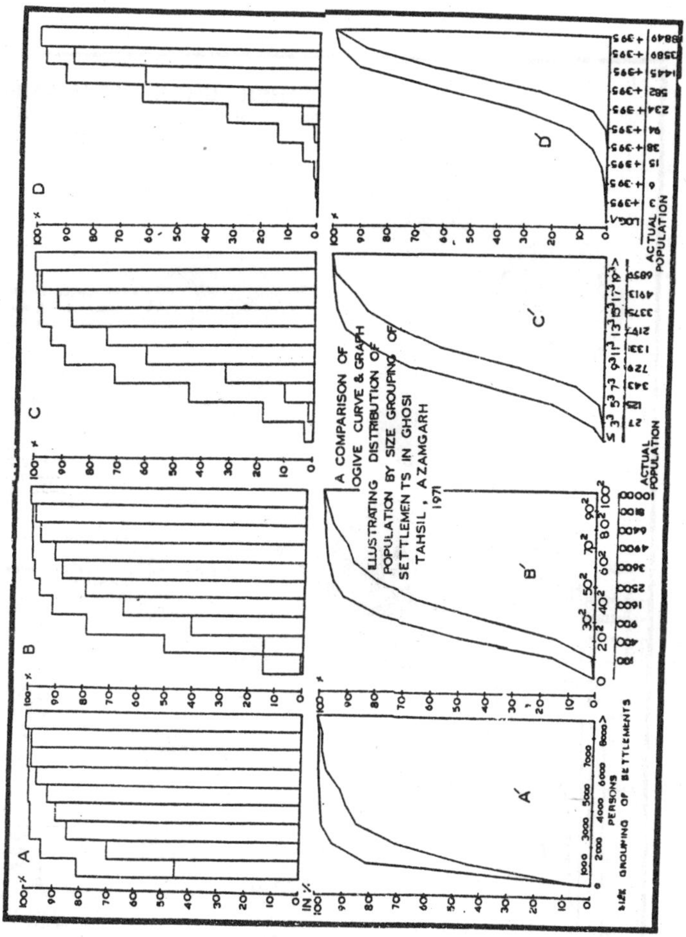
A COMPARISON OF OGIVE CURVE & GRAPH ILLUSTRATING DISTRIBUTION OF POPULATION BY SIZE GROUPING OF SETTLEMENTS IN GHOSI TAHSIL, AZAMGARH 1971
A
B
C
D
A′
B′
C′
D′
IN %
SIZE GROUPING OF SETTLEMENTS
PERSONS
ACTUAL POPULATION
ACTUAL POPULATION

Fig. 12.3

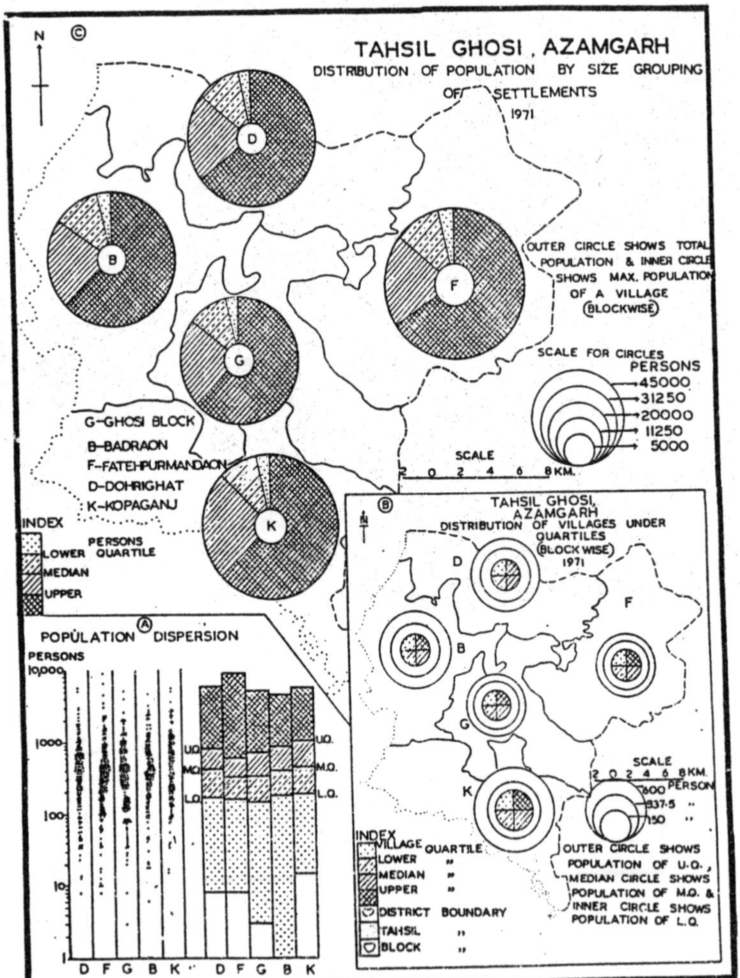
TAHSIL GHOSI, AZAMGARH
DISTRIBUTION OF POPULATION BY SIZE GROUPING OF SETTLEMENTS
1971
OUTER CIRCLE SHOWS TOTAL POPULATION & INNER CIRCLE SHOWS MAX. POPULATION OF A VILLAGE (BLOCKWISE)
SCALE FOR CIRCLES
PERSONS
45000
31250
20000
11250
5000
SCALE
2 0 2 4 6 8 KM.
G-GHOSI BLOCK
B-BADRAON
F-FATEHPURMANDAON
D-DOHRIGHAT
K-KOPAGANJ
INDEX
PERSONS QUARTILE
LOWER
MEDIAN
UPPER
POPULATION DISPERSION
PERSONS
10,000
1000
100
10
1
U.Q.
M.Q.
L.Q.
D F G B K D F G B K
TAHSIL GHOSI, AZAMGARH
DISTRIBUTION OF VILLAGES UNDER QUARTILES (BLOCK WISE)
1971
SCALE
2 0 2 4 6 8 KM.
600 PERSON
337.5
150
INDEX
VILLAGE QUARTILE
LOWER
MEDIAN
UPPER
DISTRICT BOUNDARY
TAHSIL
BLOCK
OUTER CIRCLE SHOWS POPULATION OF U.Q., MEDIAN CIRCLE SHOWS POPULATION OF M.Q. & INNER CIRCLE SHOWS POPULATION OF L.Q.

THIRTEEN

CENTRAL TENDENCY AND DISPERSION OF POPULATION

A number of centrographical methods are used to describe the central tendency or mean point.[1] in the spatial distribution of population; they cover range locations rather than values. Just as a distribution on a line has a mean, median and dispersion etc. that could be measured so does a two-dimensional distribution have a mean centre of population often referred to as mean point, centre of gravity, centroid or balancing point weight on a hypothetical rigid plane.[2].

The Mean Centre

Central tendency is the mean centre is in the spatial distribution of population over a period of time. Like the arithmetic mean of the numerical distribution, its main disadvantage is that it is greatly influenced by an extreme situation. It is a measure of central tendency within a spatial distribution, and is calculated in a similar way to the mean of a numerical distribution.[3]

Methodology

A more precise and graphical way of finding the mean centre of a dot distribution is to place a grid of squares over the distribution map from a fixed reference point, so that the mean centre, the intersection of x axis and y axis falls both to the 'North' and 'East' of the distribution. In fact the Y axis and x axis (both vertical and horizontal) must of course interest at right angles. Thus, it is a combination of the mean values of two separate numerical distributions scaled along different axis to locate the mean centre of a spatial distribution. To find out the mean centre of a spatial distribution the X axis and Y axis are treated as one-dimensional distributions. These require an application of the use of classes and grouped data. It is convenient, though not essential to have whole number class intervals and class mid-points. Here, an interval of four kilometres in distance is used for the calculation of the mean. The X axis (horizontal) is taken and the frequency of villages in each class is found. Thus, there are 19 villages in class I and 75 in class 2, and so on. Similar is the case with the Y axis (vertical or northing). There will be an approximate value of 18.307 kilometres on the x axis and 26.27 kilometres on the y axis and these points can now be located on the maps (Fig.13.1). This, however, could prove to be a fairly lengthy process with 754 inhabited villages. It may be better, therefore, to consider the data in grouped form using the existing grid lines as class boundaries. The results are shown in Table 13.1.

Table 13.1 enables approximate values for the coordinates of the mean centre to be worked out using the following formula.[3].

$$\overline{X} \cong = X_o + \sum \frac{fd}{N} \quad \text{and} \quad \overline{Y} \cong = Y_o + \sum \frac{fd}{N}$$

where X is the mean value on the x axis of the distribution, $\cong$ means "approximate equal to," X_0 is the mid-value of the chosen class, f is the frequency of villages in each class, d is the deviation from the chosen class, N is the total number of villages, Σ is the sum of all values and Y is the mean value on the y axis of the distribution.

TABLE 13.1 TABULATION OF DATA FOR CALCULATION OF MEAN CENTRE. NO. OF VILLAGES OBSERVED IN EACH GRID SQUARES.

EASTING

0 4 8 12 16 20 24 28 32 36 40 44

												No.of village in each row
44	-	4	7	12	1	-	-	-	-	-	-	24
40	-	10	19	9	14	9	3	2	2	1	-	69

36	5	21	13	13	17	18	19	23	12	8	1	150
32	5	10	7	16	18	28	22	7	6	4	-	123
28	6	3	8	23	20	11	22	23	22	13	-	151
24	-	10	14	14	12	6	12	13	5	-	-	86
20	3	14	8	16	12	10	6	1	-	-	-	70
16	-	3	10	10	11	6	3	-	-	-	-	43
12	-	-	-	1	15	1	-	-	-	-	-	27
8	-	-	-	-	-	6	1	-	-	-	-	7
4	-	-	-	-	-	1	3	-	-	-	-	4
0												
	19	75	86	114	120	106	91	69	47	26	1	

No. of villages in each column. X-Axis

TABLE 13.2

	EASTING					NORTHING				
Class interval in km.	Mid-Point X_o	f	cf	d	fd.	Y_o	f	cf	d	fd.
0-4	2	19	19	-4	-76	2	4	4	-6	-24
4-8	6	75	94	-3	-225	6	7	11	-5	-35
8-12	10	86	180	-2	-172	10	27	38	-4	-108
12-16	14	114	294	-1	-114	14	43	81	-3	-129
16-20	18	120	414	0	0	18	70	151	-2	-140
20-24	22	106	520	1	106	22	86	237	-1	-86
24-28	26	91	611	2	182	26	151	388	0	0
28-32	30	69	680	3	207	30	123	511	1	123
32-36	34	47	727	4	188	34	150	661	2	300

36-40	38	26	753	5	130	38	69	730	3	207
40-44	42	1	754	6	6	42	24	754	4	96

$$\sum f = 754 \qquad \sum fd = \frac{-587 \;\; +819}{232} \qquad\qquad \sum f = 754 \qquad \sum fd = \frac{-522 \;\; +726}{204}$$

$$X \cong 18 + \frac{232}{754} = 18 + 0.307 = 18.307\,km \qquad Y \cong 26 + \frac{204}{754} = 26 + 0.27 = 26.27\,km$$

THE MEDIAN CENTRE

The median centre of population or centre of convergence is the point where the whole population could be assembled with the minimum aggregate travel distance. Hart, Porter and Quinn [4] have suggested many devices for the median location. The median point differs from the median centre, in that it is the intersection of two orthogonal lines each dividing the position into two equal groups. Lines may be drawn parallel to them to divide the population into quarters in each direction, the point of intersection being termed quartiles. The median point is equally influenced by every individual in the distribution, and so is less influenced by extremes than that of the mean centre. The median point also remains unaffected by movements within the distribution and is more stable than the mean centre. It is, therefore, the best tool of centrality for a distribution and is more useful for comparing different distributions in the same area at the same time. Hart also suggests that it is probably preferable to the mean centre as a central point for plotting isopleths in areas of uneven distribution.

The mean centre and the median centre are very useful to the planners in locating the site of service centres,factories, towns, new schools, hospitals tubewells and other social amenities.
The median centre can be worked out by the following.[5]

$$Med. = L + \left(\frac{\frac{N}{2} - F}{fm} \right) C$$

where Med = median centre, L = lower limit of the class in which the median occurs, F = cumulative frequency below L, fm = frequency of the class in which the median occurs, N = total number of villages, C= class intervals in kilometres.

$$Median\ for\ x\ axis = \frac{\left(\frac{754}{2} - 294\right)^4}{120}$$

$$= 16.5 + \frac{(377 - 294)^4}{120}$$

$$= 16.5 + \frac{(83)^4}{120} \qquad = 16.5 + (0.69)4$$

$$= 16.5 + 2.77) \qquad = 19.27\ Km.$$

$$Median\ for\ y\ axis = 24.5 + \frac{\left(\frac{754}{2} - 237\right)4}{151}$$

$$= 24.5 + (0.927)4 \quad 24.5 + 3.708 \quad = 28.21\ km.$$

STANDARD DISTANCE AND POPULATION DISPERSION

A standard distance[6] is roughly equivalent to (SD) in a numerical distribution and measures the degree of dispersion of villages about the mean centre. Various attempts[7] have been made to study the population dispersion[8] which is complementary to the study of central tendency. The standard distance has been developed by Stewart and Warntz[9] as the dynamical radius of a population. Once the mean centre of the distribution has been found, it is possible to describe in various ways the distribution about this of the values from which the mean is calculated. Here, the standard distance for the rural distribution of population in Ghosi Tahsil is calculated by the following formula.[10]

$$\text{Standard distance (S.D.)} = \sqrt{\sum \frac{d^2}{N}}$$

Where d is the distance of a given point (X,Y) from the mean centre (X,Y). Once again it is easier to obtain an approximate result by using grouped data and substituting in the formula.

$$S.D. \cong = C\sqrt{\sum \frac{fxd^2}{N} - \frac{\left(\sum fxd^2\right)}{N} + \sum \frac{fyd^2}{N} - \frac{\left(\sum fyd\right)^2}{N}}$$

$$= 4\sqrt{\frac{3638}{754} - \frac{(232)^2}{754} + \frac{3232}{754} - \frac{(204)^2}{754}}$$

$$= 4\sqrt{4.8249 - 0.0946 + 4.2865 - 0.07}$$

$$= 4\sqrt{4.7303 + 4.2165} \quad = 4\sqrt{8.9468.}$$

$$= 4 \times 2.9911201 = 11.96448 = 11.96\ km.$$

TABLE 13.3 **Tabulation of Data for Calculation of Standard Distance**

	Easting				Northing			
C.I. in km.	fx	d	d^2	fxd^2	fy	d	d^2	fyd^2
0-4	19	-4	16	304	4	-6	36	144
4-8	75	-3	9	675	7	-5	25	175
8-12	86	-2	4	344	27	-4	16	432
12-16	114	-1	1	114	43	-3	9	387
16-20	120	0	0	0	70	-2	4	280
20-24	106	1	1	106	86	-1	1	86
24-28	91	2	4	36	151	0	0	0
28-32	69	3	9	621	123	1	1	123
32-36	47	4	16	752	150	2	4	600
36-40	26	5	25	650	69	3	9	621
40-44	1	6	36	36	24	4	16	384

$\Sigma f_x d^2 = 3638$ $\Sigma f_y d^2 = 3232$

A circle of radius equal to the standard distance (11.96 km) has been drawn about the mean centre of the distribution of villages in the area under study. Here, the mean centre of the distribution of rural population is located near the village Rampur Tiwari (Code No.519) in Nadval panchayat. A feature of standard distance is that this circle will contain approximately two-thirds (in fact 68.26%) of the total number of villages and about one-third of the villages will be left outside the circle provided that these are 'normally' distributed about their mean centre. Here, the percentage is lower with 425 out of 754 villages (56.37%) located within the circle marked. Indicates that the pattern of villages, which is clearly influenced by the layout of roads, railways and other cultural habitats and highly fertile soil of Tamasa Ghaghara Doab east and other natural environment, is not a normal spatial distribution.

A normal spatial distribution may be suggested as one in which there is a symmetrical decrease in the frequency of villages with increasing radial distance from a central nodal place. Three-dimensional spatial histograms may be used in a similar way (simple histogram) to investigate the properties of spatial distribution of rural population.

One approach would be to drew separate histograms for the horizontal and vertical of the villages in the pattern. In this case both of these would obviously exhibit a skewed distribution and the alternative is shown in Fig. 10.2 where a three-dimensional histogram is used to represent the distribution of rural population.

A normal spatial distribution illustrated in this way would appear as a central peak surrounded by columns becoming progressively lower towards the outer edge of the study area. However, in this case the distribution has more than one modal class, and is clearly skewed towards the bottom right. Histograms of this type are, of course, more difficult to construct than those used previously, and frequently an adequate impression of the distribution may be given simply by recording the total number of villages in each grid square. It is worth mentioning that in either case the result will be influenced by the number of classes grid squares used.

FINDINGS AND CONTRIBUTIONS

The original findings are the following.

1. The nature of distributional pattern of rural population has been tested through various statistical indices. The data have been taken from the 1971 census for statistical analysis. The findings of the result have been plotted in the form of maps and diagrams.

2. The multiple dot map reveals that there is homogenous distribution of population as the areas lies in the fertile and homogenous region of Tamasa Ghaghara Doab east, but on the micro scale heterogeniety can be marked out; lowlands and diara tracts have very uneven distribution of population.

3. The X-and Y-axis histogram reveal that there is uneven distribution of rural population. It also reveals that as the distance increases from the west to east and from north to south population decreases.

REFERENCES

1. Sviatlovsky, E.E. and Eells, W.C. " The centrographical Method and Regional Analysis ", *Geographical Review*, 27, 1937,240-254.
2. Porter, P.lW. " What is the point of Minimum Aggregate Travel", *Annals of the Association of American Geographers 53 no.2*, 1963,224-232.
3. Hart, J.F. " Central Tendency in Areal Distribution ", *Economic geography* 30,No.1,1954,48-59.
4. Cole, John P. and King, Cuchlaine, A.M. *"Quantitative Geography- Techniques and Theories in Geography"*, London, Willey, 1968.
5. Davis, Peter *"Science in Geography"*, Vol.3, Oxford,Oxford University Press,1874
6. Quinn, J.A. " The Hypothesis of Median Location ", *American Sociological Review,* 8, 1943, 148.
7. Bhattacharya, A.B. " Statistical ", Bharati Bhawan, 1970.
8. Bachi, R. " Standard Distance Measure And Related Methods for Spatial Analysis ", Reg. Sci. Assoc. Paper 10, 1963.
9. Warntz, W. and Neft, D. " Contribution to a Statistical Methodology for Areal Distribution ", *Journal of Regional Science* 2, 1960.
10. Prasad, Hanuman (1981), Population dispersion in Distribution of Population by Size grouping of settlements in Ghosi Tahsil, Azamgarh paper read at the 68th Session of Indian Science, Congress Association, B.H.U., Varanasi.

FOURTEEN

POPULATION GROWTH

The study of population growth and its cartographic representation is becoming increasingly important. This is primarily because the phobia of population explosion all over the world has taxed the administrators, planners, economists and so on. It has been a source of concern among geographers, demographers, sociologists, anthropologists and politicians on the one hand and social, educational, economic and political institutions on the other.[1] An Increasing population gives rise to basic problems pertaining to food, cloth and shelter. The growth of population is a hindrance to the path of progress. It creates the problem of unemployment and leads to a rise in expenditure increases. Population growth also affects adversely the cost of production in an area. Population is the view point of reference from which all other elements are observed[2]. The decline in the death rate, and the evolution of the birth rate are two variables the combination of which have had varied consequences, above all, for the rhythm of growth of population.[3]

The growth or decline of population in a district over a certain period amounts to the sum of natural increase which has taken place plus the net migration into the area during the period under study. Areas which experience a high natural increase in population may in actual fact face a decline in population because emigration is heavy, and vice-versa. The growth of population is, often, but not always related to economic circumstances. There is no natural-biological law of population growth, but the physical and social conditions of life which determine this growth of population vary from place to place and continue to do so as long as human society exists. Malthus (Essay on Principles of Population in 1978) original theory of the cycle of population growth stated this relationship. The growth of population, whether it is positive or negative, undoubtedly does reflect the history of man's response to the environmental possibilities in the area. Moreover further trends in population growth may only be estimated from the evidences provided by the past behaviour of population growth.

The dynamics of population growth vary considerably from one area to another. The growth may take the form of a steady, long continued increase, which fluctuate widely from one decade to another, or may exhibit an accelerated or a decelerated rate.

METHOD TO ANALYSE POPULATION GROWTH

In recent years the application of statistical techniques to population study has broadened and deepened the field of population geography. Four categories of population growth have been distinguished by S.D. Ddoge5 based on a careful analysis of patterns of growth of population for parts of New England. The categories were (i) continued growth, (ii) decline of 25% from a peak, (iii) decline of 25--50% from a peak, and (iv) decline of over 50% from a peak.

Three categories of population growth for Belgium were distinguished by H.M.Kendall.[6] based on patterns of growth of population. C.F. Kohn[7] in his work on population trends in the United States employed six categories. These growth categories of Kohn were (i) increase and subsequent decline, (ii)decline and subsequent increase (iii)accelerated decline, (iv)decelerated decline,(v) decelerated increase,and (vi) accelerated increase. These types of population growth are best shown by a series of maps, but they may be incorporated in one map with the aid of an ungraded shading system.

In a paper on population trends in India A. Geddes[8] demonstrated that variability in the growth of population has a distinctive regional significance. J.Beaujeu-Garnier[9] calculated the demographic development with great precision from the known birth rates and death rates and divided the countries of the world into three stages and subdivided them into six population growth types.

The growth categories were (l) The Primitive type, (ii) The Guatemalan type, (3) The Thailand type, (4)the Chile type, (5)the United States type, and (6) the West Germany type.

THE PRIMITIVE TYPE

The Primitive type is characterized by a high birth rate and a high death rate -- a true squandering of human life, for although births are very numerous, the infant mortality rate is of the order of 200 per thousand and more than half of the children die before reaching the age of fifteen. It includes the most isolated and backward peoples of the world, numbering probably no more than 100 million and the numbers remaining in primitive conditions are rapidly decreasing as medical science comes to their aid and reduces the death rate.

THE GUATEMALAN TYPE

In this type the birth rate remains very high whilst the death rate has already begun to decline, giving a natural increase between 20 and 30 per thousand. This trend shows the greatest increase in population in the near future, for the decline in the death rate has already begun and may still accelerate.

THE THAILAND TYPE

In this type the birth rate is still very high but the death rate has fallen more markedly; the natural growth rate is thus highest in the world,between 25 and 35 per thousand. In this region the population may well double in less than a quarter on a century. The world is thus faced with an alarming increase in population. Ro Tozan in 1754 described the custom of limiting the size of family in Japan. "It is essential to control family size, and abortion and infanticide became a common practice in all classes during the latter half of the Tokugawa era. It is a terrible fact that in a village consisting of ten houses every year over two babies are killed."[10]

THE CHILE TYPE

In this case,the birth rate has already fallen slowly and the death rate has been drastically reduced no. This type characterized by a natural growth rate between 15 and 20 per thousand. In this category the natural growth rate is equal to the present average for the whole world.

THE UNITED STATES TYPE

In this group the birth rate is already low and the death rate has been reduced to its minimum. It includes the developed countries of the world.

THE GERMANY TYPE

It is characterized by a negative population balance sheet in recent years, where the birth rate is the lowest in the world and the death rate relatively high. West Germany has recorded an annual loss of 3.1 per thousand, whilst the Democratic Republic has a negative balance of 1.6.

There are various methods for representing population growth, for example, simple line-graph, percentage increase graph, polygraph, deviational graph, compound line-graph and choropleth maps etc.

A SIMPLE LINE GRAPH

A simple line-graph shows only a single series of values connected by one line. It usually shows the absolute growth of population. The total population of a given areas are plotted as ordinates on a simple scale while the chronological values, usually, in decennial periods, are plotted as abscissae on an usually, in decennial periods, are plotted as abscissae on an arithmetic scale (Fig.14.1). After the points have been plotted they are usually joined by a continuous line.

LOGARITHMIC INCREASE GRAPH

In some cases where the data pertaining to population growth are large or when there are more data at one end of the range in population growth, the logarithmic scale may be used to show the absolute population growth. In this case, the population growth have been plotted as ordinates on a logarithmic scale and time value as abscissae on the arithmetic scale. (Fig.14.1).

PERCENTAGE INCREASE GRAPH

It may be used to show the growth of population in percentage, whether positive or negative, instead of absolute figures. This graph is known as the percentage increase graph, when the line graph shows the percentage of growth of population. In this case the percentage of growth of population have been plotted as ordinates and chronological values as abscissae on an arithmetic scale. The points are joined and the resulting lines are conventionally assumed to show the rate of population growth, which may be positive or negative.

POLYGRAPH OR MULTIPLE LINE GRAPH

A multiple line or polygraph includes several sets of values connected by distinctive lines, usually involving some direct comparison. Polygraphs may be used to show the growth of population in relation to food supply, birth rate, death rate and so on. The values of population growth and production of food may be plotted independently in one frame. The resulting line shows the relation between them. It is usually used to show the Malthusian, Neomalthusian, technocratic or demographic transition theory, etc. This composite graph is known as the polygraph when various simple line graphs or curves are drawn on the same frame to show the relationship between two sets of population data. Care must be taken to differentiate between any multiple lines which might cross it.

DEVIATIONAL GRAPH

Cyclical fluctuations and trends in the growth of population may be represented graphically by methods other than the chronological plotting of population growth. It is easier to make comparison if the deviations are expressed as percentages. Cumulative graphs are effective in showing cyclical fluctuations of population growth. For this type of graph decennial deviations from the mean decennial growth or from the base are obtained by substraction, and the accumulated deviations by adding them. The accumulated deviations are then plotted.

COMPOUND LINE GRAPH

A compound line graph usually known as the aggregate line graph or band graph exhibits trends of population growth in both the total and its constituents by a series of lines on the same frame, the area between two successive lines may be shaded distinctively, Fig.14.1 is a compound graph used to analyse the growth of total population and the growth of population of individual tahsils in Azamgarh District from 1901 to 1971.

METHODS OF CONSTRUCTION OF THE GRAPH

The abscissae are measured on a horizontal scale and and the ordinates on a vertical scale. The horizontal scale usually represents a series of equal time division (independent variable) while the vertical scale shows a series of quantitative (absolute population) or percentage values (dependent variable). In each of these line graphs, the line joining the points is referred to as a curve which shows the overall changes in population growth. The practice of joining points by smooth curves should therefore be avoided as far as possible. Curves, if necessary, can be smoothened by the employment of statistical methods, such as curve fitting or running mean methods.[11] but unless such methods are employed points should be joined by a series of short straight lines which shows one veritable picture of population growth. Some times comparisons of variability of population growth are facilited, if, the data of population growth are reduced to percentages. Direct comparisons of various census units may also be shown on one graph by plotting the mean growth of population as ordinates and various census units arranged either in order of magnitude or geographical situation as abscissae.

The series of figures to be graphed is examined and the maximum value noted, for on this and on the available size of paper depends the vertical scale to be adopted. The top of the vertical scale should just exceed the maximum value. The whole vertical range of values must be represented when zero is significant, even at the cost of a considerable empty space at the bottom of the graph since a false impression of relative variability in the trends of the lines may be given unless the whole range can be appreciated. A vertical line is ruled on either side of the horizontal scale line, and the equal intervals representing quantities are marked by neat ticks.

The plotting of these various graphs must be carried out on accurately ruled graph paper. It is preferable, however, on completing the plotting, to trace off the graph lines, the frame and the scale,. using tracing paper and a pen. This gives a cleaner finish and combines the accuracy of plotting which graph paper allows with the clarity of white paper un obscured by the close and unnecessary grid of the graph paper. Moreover, a graph paper is rarely of sufficient quality to take ink well, if it is ruled in faint colour lines. A more open grid of perhaps half-inch squares may occasionally be added to help the eye to follow the lines across to estimate the value involved.

The frame and grid of the graph paper must be ruled as lightly as possible, while the graph lines will be made considerable clearer. Several different varieties of lines can be used in drawing polygraphs. Care must be taken in scaling the values on the graph not to overload the figure strings of noughts should be avoided on the vertical scale by, for example, lettering millions, thousands, etc. at the top of the scale and numbering the units 1,2,3, and so on.

CHOROPLETH METHODS

Perhaps the most obvious method of portraying the growth or decline of population is to prepare a series of distributional maps by bars, graphs and choropleth methods in chronological orders showing the past and present distributions. Such a series gives a broad picture, but it is a difficult task to measure and compare the growth of population from one tahsil to another without recourse to a very close examination of the maps. To overcome this difficulty multicensal or intercensal growth of population can be shown directly usually in the form of the percentage growth in the increase or decrease of population, which has occurred between the two censuses. These changes are best plotted in the form of a choropleth map. Some further indication of absolute numerical growth may be given by superimposing proportional wheels or circles on the choropleth. The tahsils of Azamgarh district have been grouped into ranges according to percentage increase in population mainly during 1881 to 1971. The ranges are very high, high, medium, low and very low. Within the boundary of each tahsil a circle has been drawn proportionate to the total population of the tahsil in 1971. In each circle a sector in proportion to the addition during 1961--71, has been provided to give a visual depiction of the growth in individual tahsils. The remaining portion within the boundary of each tahsil has been hatched according to the ranges in which it falls.[12] (Fig.14.2).

Predictable models of population growth have considerable importance in relation to future physical and economic planning needs. Not only is there a need for forecasting future population totals but also how the growth will be geographically distributed. Hence, there is a growth literature concerned with regional model making.[13]

TABLE 14.1 **Growth of Population in Ghosi Tahsil, Azamgarh 1901-1971**

Year	Population	Growth in percentage	Mean decinnal growth = 10.18% Deviation in %	Accumulated deviation in %
1901	2,56,844	-	-	-
1911	2,45,265	-4.51	-14.69	-14.69
1921	2,45,481	0.09	-10.09	-24.78
1931	2,63,708	7.43	2.75	-27.53
1941	3,10,653	17.80	7.62	-19.91
1951	3,58,923	15.54	5.36	-14.55
1961	4,14,053	15.36	5.18	-9.37
1971	4,95,156	19.59	9.41	0.04

TABLE 14.2 NATURAL INCREASE OF POPULATION IN THE LOWER GANGA GHAGHAR DOAB

1891-1971

Year birth rate in percentage	Mean decennial death rate in percentage	Mean decennial increase in percentage	Decennial natural
]891	27.31	30.51	-3.20
1901	30.02	29.12	0.90
1911	34.00	30.21	3.79
1921	35.12	34.23	0.89
1931	30.56	26.00	4.56
1941	31.00	19.06	11.94
1951	22.46	16.48	5.98
1961	30.50	13.25	17.25
1971	30.55	13.90	16.65

TABLE 14.3 GROWTH OF POPULATION IN AZAMGARH DISTRICT DURING 1881-1891.

Tahsil	Population in 1891	Population in 1921	Net variation 1891-1921	Percentage variation 1891-1921
Azamgarh (Sardar)	2,78,611	2,89,488	10,877	3.90
Ghosi	1,25,886	1,39,916	14,030	11.14
Sagri	1,78,533	1,89,295	10,762	6.03
Lalganj (Deogaon)	2,39,425	2,64,851	25,426	8.14
Mohammadabad	3,27,017	3,59,746	32,729	10.00
Phulpur (Mahul)	3,12,146	3,44,723	32,577	10.44
TOTAL DISTT.	14,61,618	15,88,019	1,26,401	8.64

TABLE 14.4 **GROWTH OF POPULATION IN AZAMGARH DISTRICT DURING 1891-1921**

Tahsil	Population in 1891	Population in 1921	Net variation 1891-1921	Percentage variation 1891-1921
Azamgarh	2,89,488	2,47,010	-42,478	-14.67
Ghosi	1,39,916	2,45,481	105,565	75.44
Sagri	1,89,295	2,33,522	44,227	23.36
Lalganj	2,64,851	2,34,098	-30,753	-11.61
Mohammadabad	3,59,746	2,47,318	-112,428	-31.25
Phoolpur (Phulpur)	3,44,723	3,21,228	-23,495	-6.81
Total Distt.	15,88,019	15,28,657	-59,362	-3.74

TABLE 14.5 **GROWTH OF POPULATION IN AZAMGARH DISTRICT, DURING 1921-1971**

Tahsil	Population in 1921 1921-1971	Population in 1971	Net variation 1921-1971	Percentage variation in
Azamgarh	2,47,010	4,56,315	2,09,305	84.74
Ghosi	2,45,481	4,95,156	2,49,675	101.71
Sagri	2,33,522	4,25,732	1,92,210	82.31
Lalganj	2,34,098	4,13,440	1,79,342	76.61
Mohammadabad	2,47,318	5,37,553	2,90,235	117.35
Phulpur	3,21,228	5,29,288	2,08,060	64.77
Azamgarh Distt.	15,28,657	28,57,484	13,28,827	86.93

REFERENCES

1. Hans Raj " Fundamentals of Demography ", Delhi, Surjeet Publication, 1978.
2. Trewartha, G.T. " A Case for Population ", A.A.A.G.,43, 1953, 71-97.
3. Beaujeu, J.- Garnier " Geography of Population ", London, Longman, 1978.
4. Monkhouse, F.J. and Wilkinson, H.R. " Maps and Diagram ", London, 1971.
5. Dodge, S.D. " A study of Population Regions in England on a New Basis ", *A.A.A.G.*,25,1935, 197-210.
6. Kendall, H.M. " A Survey of Population Changes in Belgium ", A.A.A.G., 28, 1938, 152.
7. Kohn, C.F. " Population Trends in the United States since 1940 ", *Geographical Review,* 25, 1945, 98-106.
8. Geddes, A. " The Population of India : Variability of Change as a Regional Demographic Index ", *Geographical Review,* 32, 1942, 562-73.
9. Beaujeu, J.- Garnier " Geography of Population ", London, Longman, 1978.
10. Dempster, Prue *"Japan Advances- A Geographical Study",* London, Metheun and Co., 1969.
11. Davis, Peter " Science in Geography- Data Description and Presentation ", Oxford, 1977, 18-21.
12. Prasad, Hanuman " Growth of Population in Azamgarh District-" A study in Research Methodology", Paper presented at the first Annual conference of NAGI, organized by Punjab University, Chandigarh.
13. Isard, W. " Methods of Reginal Analysis ", In An Introduction to the *Regional Science,* New York, 1960, 493-568.
14. Misra, R.N. *"The Lower Ganga- Ghaghara- Doab, A study in Population and Settlement,* Agra,1977.

Fig. 14.1

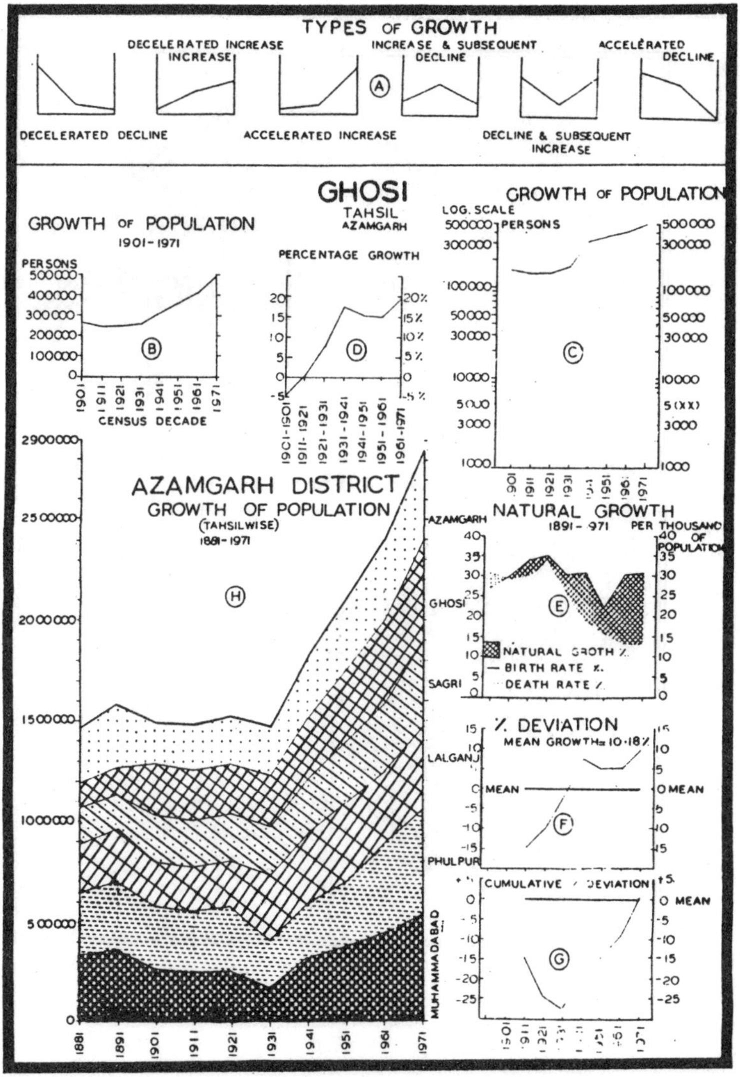

Fig. 14.2

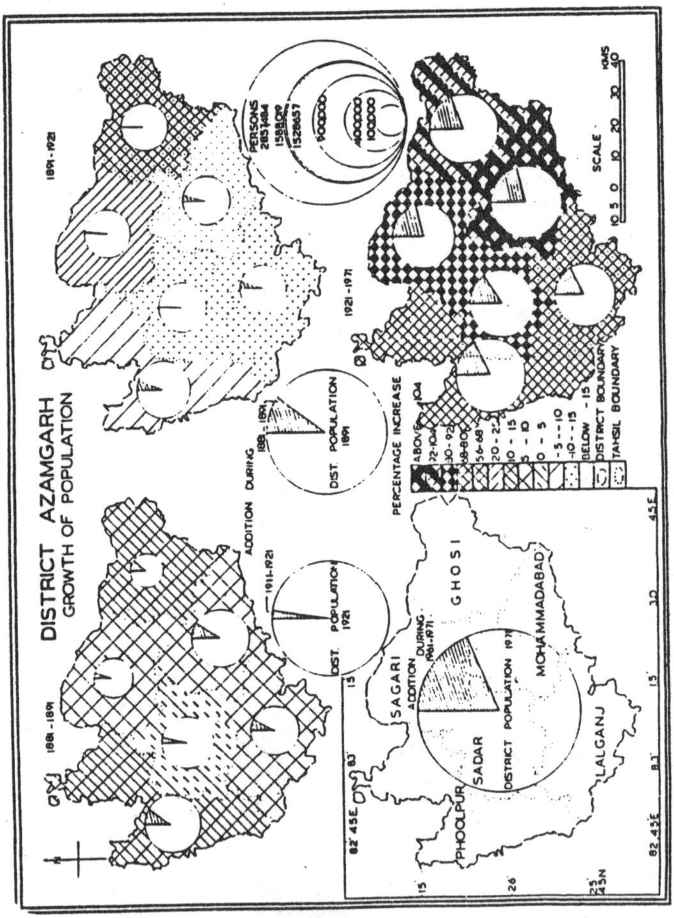
DISTRICT AZAMGARH
GROWTH OF POPULATION
1881-1891
1891-1921
1921-1971
ADDITION DURING
1911-1921
DIST. POPULATION 1921
DIST. POPULATION 1891
PERSONS
PERCENTAGE INCREASE
DISTRICT BOUNDARY
TAHSIL BOUNDARY
SCALE
GHOSI
SAGARI
SADAR
PHOOLPUR
LALGANJ
MOHAMMADABAD
DISTRICT POPULATION 1971

FIFTEEN

METHODS OF URBAN POTENTIAL MEASURE

A Case Study of Bihar

Bihar the heartland of the Indian Union, has benefited considerably by making use of untapped natural resources. Urban centres have sprang up rapidly as a result and can be found even in the marginal and forested lands of Bihar. For the growth of towns and increasing their potentiality transportation, agriculture, location of industries and energy resources have an important role to play.

In terms of population, the urban centres of Bihar have shown a marked increase from 1.10 million persons in 1901 to 8.69 million in 1981. The region, with an area of 174.038 sq.km. has 220 urban centres with 12.46 per cent of the total population in 1981 in comparison with 8.48 per cent in 1961 and 10.04 per cent in 1971. This is on account of various factors,such as natural growth, migration, increase in the areas of some old towns as well as the creation of new towns.

While in the North Bihar plain only 6 per cent of the population is urban, the ratio is 14 per cent in the South Bihar plain, and 20 per cent in the Chotanagpur plateau. Hence the North Bihar plain is more densely populated but it is less urbanized. At the district level variations are even more pronounced. In the State as a whole the district of Dhanbad ranks first with 50.70 per cent of the population as urban. Patna with 36.87 per cent and Singhbhum with 32.04 per cent rank second and third, respectively. So far as the percentage of urban population to total population of the district is concerned, the picture which emerge is the overwhelming rural character of the greater part of Bihar. The objective of the study is to highlight the methods of analysing the concept of population potentiality of Warntz (1960) for the urban population in Bihar and to suggest a new method for growth potentiality measurement.

Methods of Study

The concept of 'potential' as developed by Warntz (1960)[2] and the 'gravity model' developed by Reilley (1931)[3] appear in many forms in social science literature but here we are concerned with the distance formulation and the potentiality of urban centres in Bihar.

The potentiality at any point is defined as:

(Formula ???)

1 DdA or (Api / r) or \Pi
r r

where dA is small elements of the area, and

r is the distance from each area to the point concerned. Similarly, the point at which 1/r DdA minimized the integration defines the median centre.

In the second formula, A is the total number of small subareas involved, Pi is the population in each sub-area and r is the distance from the particular point to a representative point in each sub- area. Court (1966) [4] has also pointed out that usually simplifying assumptions are made in computing the contribution of an area's own population, that is 'self - potential' to the 'total potential' existing at the central point of an area.

TABLE 15.1 **URBAN POTENTIALITY FOR PATNA, 1981**

Points of measurement from Patna	Distance in kilo-metres	Per kilometre density of population
Dhanbad	218	4,894
Chaibasa	328	2,797
Ranchi	236	2,713

Munger	122	3,822
Gaya	83	4,093
Hazaribagh	168	1,975
Purnea	218	1,312
Bhagalpur	172	1,764
Arrah	125	2,061
Dumka	239	1,068
Giridih	180	1,365
Sasaram	127	1,811
Biharsharif	50	4,460
Muzaffarpur	59	3,216
Darbhanga	86	2,069
Chapra	83	2,041
Saharsa	136	1,242
Begusarai	97	1,584
Bettiah	130	1,112
Motihari	119	948
Katihar	320	420
Daltonganj	198	546
Hajipur	20	5,382
Samastipur	80	1,100
Sitamarhi	75	1,164
Aurangabad	115	746
Siwan	90	871
Nawada	90	812
Madhubani	110	657
Gopalganj	110	616
Patna Own	-	11,17,734
Total		11,76,398

With the help of this potential value "isopleths also be used with the effect in plotting potentials of population.5 The influence of any point or population can be expressed as its number of people divided by its distance to the spot at which its potential is being assessed. "It has cultural, social, economic and political significance."[6]

$$\frac{1}{r} DdA \quad \text{or} \quad \left(\sum_{i=1} Api/r \right) \quad \text{or} \quad \frac{P_i}{r}$$

In this way, the population potential for all the other 30 districts have been calculated and the result is given in Table 15.2. According to Table 15.2 the highest potential has been recorded for patna (1,176,398) while the lowest is for Gopalganj (120,864). The second lowest figure is for Dhanbad, the third for Singhbhum and the fourth, Ranch. This leads us to the conclusion that Siwan, Gopalganj,

Madhubani and Nawadah are least connected with the centre of civilization, that is Patna in terms of social, cultural, economic and political relations. The same condition prevails in Santal Parganas and Palamau where rugged terrain and forested land prohibits high population potential.

TABLE 15.2 **URBAN POTENTIALITY IN BIHAR, 1981**

District	Urban potential
Patna	11,76,398
Dhanbad	11,15,100
Singhbhum	9,52,573
Ranchi	6,89,781
Munger	5,25,327
Gaya	3,91,266
Hazaribagh	3,92,402
Bhagalpur	3,60,624
Purnea	3,30,207
Bhojpur	3,17,360
Santal Pargana	3,05,347
Giridih	3,17,225
Rohtas	2,74,875
Nalanda	3,04,269
Muzaffarpur	2,59,213
Darbhanga	2,41,205
Saran	2,35,808
Saharsa	2,33,152
Begusarai	2,27,384
West Champaran	1,88,289
East Champaran	1,54,113
Katihar	1,85,346
Palamau	1,51,286
Vaishali	2,32,208
Samastipur	1,61,280
Sitamarhi	1,35,488
Aurangabad	1,44,373
Siwan	1,22,543
Nawada	1,38,025
Madhubani	1,33,538
Gopalganj	1,20,864

Source : Calculated and compiled by the author from Census of India, 1981.

On the other hand, the districts of Patna, Dhanbad and Ranchi have a developed transport system and administrative centre, the growth of light engineering industries have not made only these districts economically significant but have also contributed towards high population potentials. In the surrounding area of Patna, the satellite urban centres of Hajipur, Dinapur, Phulwarisharif, Fatwah and Sonepur are rural service centres and all of them have added to the high population potential around Patna. The greatest potentiality added to Patna is away to the the fact that it is the State capital of Bihar.

The hexagonal arrangement of cities of Muzaffarpur, Darbhanga, Munger, Biharsharif, Gaya, Arrah and Chhapra around Patna[7] provide their services to the respective zone of influence. On account of this the urban population potential of Patna is highest among all the district headquarters of Bihar. An iso-potential map has been prepared with the help of districtwise population potential, which is useful in preparing development plans for urban places and their hinterland organisation.

GROWTH POTENTIAL

Table 15.3 show the growth potential of urban population in Bihar (1981). It has been estimated in terms of location coefficient, the percentage of urban population to total population in each district, per cent increase of urban population (1971--81), number of urban centres in a district and the percentage of urban population of the State. The aggregate value of all the above elements divided by five gives an average potentiality value for each district.

TABLE 15.3 SUMMARY OF URBAN CONCENTRATION AND POTENTIALITY IN BIHAR (1981)

District	LC Value for urban population	Number of urban centres	Percentage of urban population to total population	Percentage increase in urban population (1971-1981)	Percentage of urban population of the state	Urban potentiality index
Patna	1.98	12	36.87	64.30	12.85	26.60
Dhanbad	6.97	30	50.70	67.21	12.26	33.92
Singhbhum	1.37	22	32.09	43.41	10.55	21.88
Ranchi	0.70	10	20.93	79.36	7.36	23.67
Munger	1.78	12	14.07	30.89	5.36	12.83
Gaya	1.04	5	10.82	41.67	3.91	12.83
Hazaribagh	0.54	10	15.11	59.45	3.81	17.79

Bhagalpur	1.09	5	11.62	36.74	3.49	11.58
Purnea	0.72	9	7.96	68.32	3.29	17.85
Bhojpur	1.26	8	10.78	51.04	2.96	14.80
Santal pargana	0.36	12	6.88	39.03	2.93	12.24
Giridih	0.71	11	14.20	36.03	2.83	12.95
Rohtas	0.69	6	9.73	50.07	2.65	13.81
Nalanda	1.88	5	13.62	83.61	2.56	1.33
Muzaffarpur	1.20	1	8.06	50.16	2.18	2.52
Darbhanga	1.54	1	8.77	33.18	2.02	.30
Saran	1.29	4	8.17	72.18	1.95	17.51
Saharsa	0.57	7	5.72	58.66	1.94	14.77
Begusarai	1.61	4	10.55	45.22	1.77	12.63
West Champaran	0.55	4	7.35	23.37	1.66	7.38
Katihar	0.88	2	9.41	67.60	1.54	16.28
Palamau	0.17	6	5.64	53.20	1.24	11.25
East Chamaparan	0.57	5	4.65	67.09	1.30	15.72
Vaishali	1.06	3	6.48	38.64	1.24	10.08
Samastipur	0.60	4	4.16	54.16	1.01	12.78
Sitamarhi	0.66	5	4.52	74.77	1.00	17.19
Aurangabad	0.52	5	6.94	70.92	0.99	16.87
Siwan	0.71	3	4.41	51.19	0.90	12.04
Nawada	0.50	3	6.65	46.07	0.84	11.43
Madhubani	0.41	3	3.11	68.80	0.83	15.23
Gopalganj	0.67	3	4.98	131.29	0.78	28.14

In this way, the highest potentiality has been estimated for Dhanbad (33.42). Gopalganj ranks second (28.14), Patna third (26.60) Ranchi fourth (23.67). The lowest growth potential is 7.38 for West Champaran district and 9.30 for the Darbhanga district. These growth potentials have been subdivided into four categories on the basis of quartile and median. The first group above 23 or 17.65 includes the districts of Dhanbad, Gopalganj, Patna, Singhbhum, Ranchi, Hazaribagh, Purnea and Nalanda districts. The districts of the second group are Madhubani, Aurangabad, Sitamarhi, East Champaran, Katihar, Saran and Bhojpur. The districts below: Q_1 value(12.50) are Nawada, Vaishali, West Champaran, Begusarai, Darbhanga, Santal Pargana, Bhagalpur and Munger.

The locational coefficient value by itself can give the concentration index but the aggregate value of a number of components gives a better concentration index than the location coefficient itself. In the present study, the potentiality value has been carved out by dividing the concentration index which is the aggregate of a number of variables divided by the number of urban centres in a district. This can be expressed by the formula:

$$P_1 = \frac{\sum n^x + X_2 + X_3 x_3 \ldots + X_n}{\sum N}$$

Where P_1 denotes potentiality index,
X_1 and X_2 are different variables, and
N denotes the number of towns in a district. This formula gives districtwise average growth potential value of urban places in Bihar.

CONCLUSION

The urban potential of Warntz may be calculated by the urban population per kilometre in spatial dimension of a district in relation to different outlying nodes over the greater part of the region. But a new method has been given here which does not need spatial calculations to show the future growth trend of urban centres with the help of a past growth rate in a district.

The urban population potential is the sign of economic development and culture of an urban centre in comparison with the primate city of that region. Thus higher potentiality and higher commuter relationship increases the rate of rural population migration within the zone of influence of a particular urban centre. The percentage increase and concentration of population in a particular district depends upon the number and size of urban centres in the area.

REFERENCES

1. Mandal, R.B. " Growth of Urban Population in Bihar ", *The Geographical Knowledge,* 1972.
2. Warntz,W. and Neft, I. " Contributions to a Statistical Methodology for Areal Distribution ", *Journal Of Regional Science,* 2, 1960, 45-46.
3. Reilly, W.S. " The Law of Retail gravitation ", New York, 1930.
4. Court, A. *"Population Distribution and Self Potential"*, San Fernandes Valley, 1966, Mimeographed.
5. Stewart, J.Q. " Empirical Mathematical Rules Concerning the Distribution and Equilibrium of Population ", *Geographical Review,* 37, 1948, 41-85.
6. Monkhouse, F.J. and Wilkinson, H.R. " Maps and Diagrams ", London, Metheun, 1971.
7. Mandal, R.B. " The Geography of Rural Settlements in Bihar plain " Unpublished Ph.D. Thesis, Patna University, 1972.

Fig. 15.1

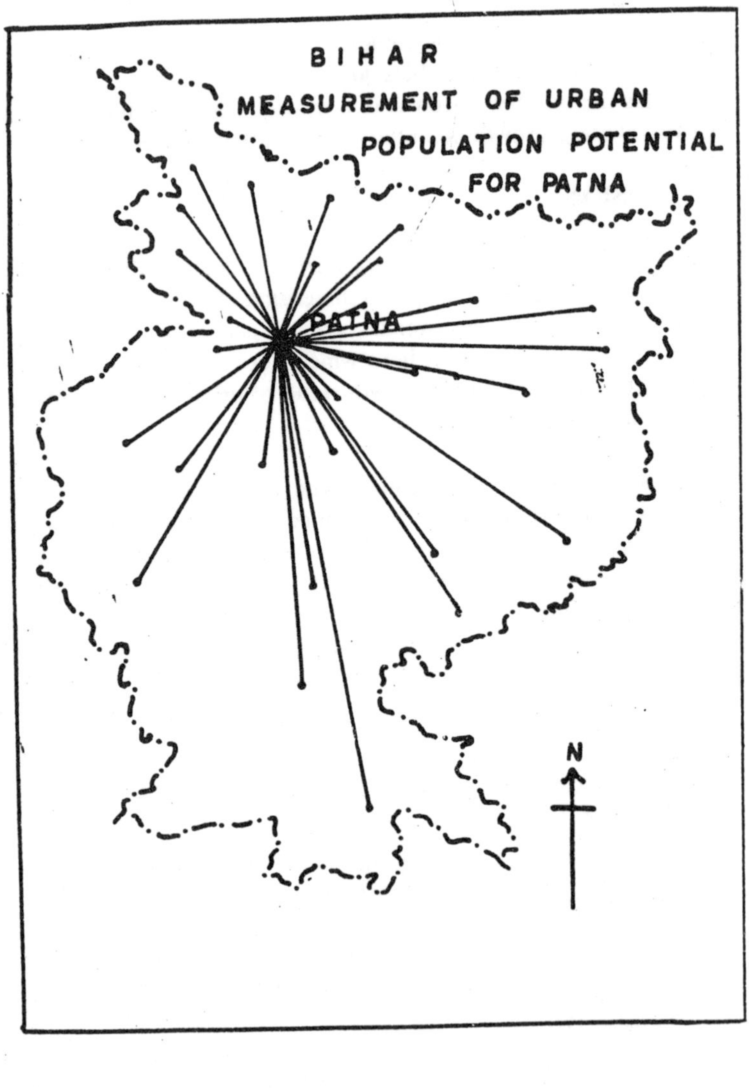
BIHAR
MEASUREMENT OF URBAN POPULATION POTENTIAL FOR PATNA
PATNA
N

Fig. 15.2

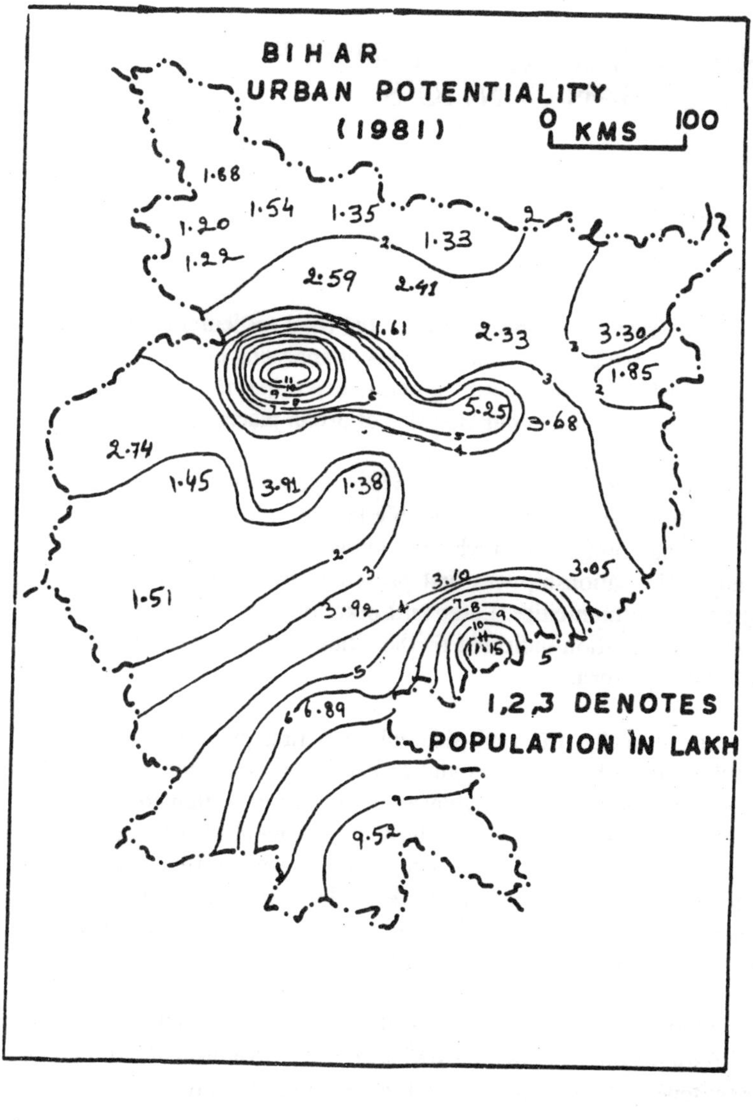
BIHAR
URBAN POTENTIALITY
(1981)
0 KMS 100
1,2,3 DENOTES
POPULATION IN LAKH

SIXTEEN

RANK-SIZE RELATIONSHIP OF URBAN CENTRES

Rank-size rule is the analysis of the total settlement network in a region. Hence it is a tool which aims at analysing national settlement system and helps in describing and interpreting the relationship between the rank and population size of urban places.

The distribution of urban areas according to their rank of population size, plotted on a double logarithmic graph paper, gives S shaped curvilinear trend which is known as the rank-size rule. This empirical relationship was first presented by Auerbach (1913)[1] in a study of German cities. Later on Lotka[2] observed that the law of urban concentration indicated by the cities of the United States fell in the same pattern.

Scientifically, the rank-size rule was first put forward by Zeipf (1941)[3] as a theoretical model to express the relationship between observed and empirical regularity in the size of settlement hierarchy, either urban or rural. This orderly development of urban places according to their rank and size is the basis of this relationship. However, the region on which this rule is applied must be a complete and self-sufficient one that is, not part of a large region or greatly overlapping another region.[4]

Under this rule, the number of urban centres should continue to increase as their population size decrease.[5] Obviously one should expect fewer city level centres and more small towns than major urban centres. According to Haggett this relationship may not be universally true because small towns are not everywhere more numerous than major urban centres.[6] A straight line rank-size curve for settlements in many countries and regions of the world[7] suggests that this is a normal condition,[8] even though we may not know the reasons why it should exist. Probably, this relationship will result solely from the balance of local variability and the organizational needs for a hierarchy of urban centres under a given set of demand and supply conditions.[9]

The rank-size rule was generalized by introducing a constant as the exponent for the rank and the formula is as follows.[10]

$$P_r = a\, r^{-b}$$

This may be rewritten as

$$P_r = \log a - b \log r$$

Where r is the rank of a city, P_r its population and a and b are constants, a can be interpreted as the expected population of the biggest city and b as the slope of the linear relationship between log r and log P_r.

The rank-size regularity as expressed by zeipf is as follows:

$$P_r = P_1 / rq$$

where q is an exponent which approximates to unity. This suggests that if the population of the largest city is divided by the rank of any city in the same region, the result with approximately be the population of the city whose rank number is used as a divisor.

This rank-size rule is a regular relationship which often exists between the absolute size of an urban centre (measured by its population, not area) and its rank (the centre with the largest population in the region ranking 1, the next largest 2, and so on to the smallest town). This relationship may be expressed by the simple formula:

$$P_n = P_n / n$$

where P_n is the population on the nth town in the list of urban centres and P_1 is the population of the region's largest urban centre, that is, the centre which ranks 1 in the list.

This empirical evidence has been questioned heavily by Rosing (1966)[11] and others who state that the rank-size rule is not very geographical.

Stewart (1947)[12] has admitted the significance of the rank-size rule. The theory of agricultural location by Von Thunen (1820),[13] Weber's theory of industrial location (1909),[14] Jefferson's law of Primate city (1939),[15] the central place theory of Christaller (1966)[16] and Losch (1954),[17] and Staller's allometric law of biology[18] are also highly influenced by the development of this regularity.

Christaller and Losch have put forward a functional size-class hierarchy of towns as a basis for the analysis of their spatial arrangement, function and size. The basic assumptions are that a rural area supports a town which in turn serves the rural area with small towns serving small areas and large towns serving large areas. Most of the theoretical and experimental work in central place studies revolves around assumptions of a fixed number of constants K (Christaller) and non-fixed K (Losch).[19] Berry and Garrison (1958)[20] have, however, presented location theories of urban places as one of the several alternative schemes to the rank-size rule.

FACTORS AFFECTING RANK- SIZE RULE

Factors such as administrative set-up, transportation linkages, industrial development and commercial spread have played a multiple-role in changing the rank-size relationship of urban places in Tanzania. As for example, the diamond mining and industrial centre of Mwadui has a strong centripetal force attracting people to collect natural resources. Similarly, all the port cities, such as Dar es Salaam, Tanga, Mtwara, Lindi and Zanzibar have strong forces of transport, commercial development, centre of break-o-bulk and favourable coastal-cum-administrative positions have highly helped these centres as leading ones in rank-size rule.

The population change in a centre within a certain time interval changes the rank of a centre. The rank of any centre is dependent upon the hierarchical arrangement of the nodality value--which may be population size or an index based on different functions available at a place. The latter may depend upon the provision of administrative and transport facilities and the development of commerce and industry. The dissimilar and unproportionate development of these facilities causes variation in the centripetal forces involved in the growth of urban places. Further, with their greater force of attraction, the large centres have developed at longer distances, while the smaller towns and villages have a close proximity to each other.

This concept of close proximity has, however, changed today with the introduction of quick, mechanized transport. For example, people generally move from one village to another on foot which involves a certain amount of time. The smaller towns have bus facilities so that the inhabitants can also move from one centre to another more quickly. Then the bigger towns have train facilities for travel between them. The development of airways has connected one city level centre to another. Hence travel by the aforementioned means of transport though involving money, does not consume much more time than the movement from one village to another on foot. This shows the expansion in the zone of influence as well as the spatial pattern of an urban centre based on transport facilities, which also control the rank and the number of different order of urban places. The larger centres have wider spacing and are therefore, fewer in number while the small towns are larger in number with decreasing distances. This regularity has proved that as the nodality/centrality of places increases, the number of urban places decreases according to the rank-size rule.

According to Berry and Garison (1958) rank-size regularity is a trivial geographical problem and it is the systems which deviate from it that are of greater interest. So far as the operating units of the system are concerned, urban transport workers must live near other urban dwellers, sugar mill workers near the factory, and so on. There is a vast web of economic structural relations owing to discontinuities in technological scale. The ordering of urban places will reflect that technical and social structure requires continuity and thus affects the size of units by lowering the value of N (number of people). Von Forester[21] has suggested a measure:

$$R = 1 (H^1/H)$$

where both H^1 and H are maximum entropies and both consider the same number of people, N, but H has no structural properties, considering only individuals in isolation, while H^1 pleasures all the structural relations occurring and requiring contiguity in the system. Clearly, if no structure exists, H and H^1 are equal and R is zero. On the other hand, if the system develops into a single tightly clustered web of activities, one city, H^1 would become zero and R would equal unity indicating complete order.

THE LAW OF PRIMATE CITY

There are some studies about the primacy of cities and the levels of development of different countries. While investigating the urban systems of various countries Berry (1961)[22] hypothesized that 'primacy was a feature of underdeveloped countries and a normal rank-size distribution one of the developed world El-Shaks (1974)[23] has also analysed the primacy of urban systems for 75 countries of the world, and has discussed the relationship between primacy and development. In primacy of all urban places of a country, it has been found that there is a curvilinear relationship between primacy and development. Even in Tanzania, and in other countries of the world it has been found that in the primary stage of urban development primacy tends to be comparatively low; in the intermediate stage it has maximum development and a the last stage of development it goes down again. This finding has been supported by the historic analysis of development of the urban systems of USA and Great Britain. According to Haggett (1979)[24] the countries with rank-size urban systems tend to be large, with a long history of urbanization; they are economically and politically complex, "whereas primate distributions appear to be the product of urbanization processes in countries that are smaller than average, have a short history of urbanization, and have simple economic and political structure. Hence primate distributions typify the impact of few rather strong forces."

Primacy represents a pattern of urbanization especially found in developing countries where there is one city having a population in excess of those next in size. Such primate, "supereminent" cities dominate the urban system. Quite often primate cities grow at a faster rate than the rest of the urban centres, reinforcing its primateness in many ways. One value of primate cities is the rapid industrial progress. Some scientists believe that primacy in underdeveloped countries is a necessary stage in urban development.

Brutzkus[25](1973) has discussed the following eight basic factors which are generally found in primate cities such as Dar es Salaam in the developing countries of the world:

1. Agglomeration of manufacturing and tertiary sector.
2. Harbour for sea part and airport facilities of international standing besides commandable site and situation for originating transport and communication lines to the interior part of the country.
3. Presence of technical infrastructure and services.
4. Banking facility and proximity to government offices.
5. Relatively large local markets with a purchasing power as well as a commanding location for national markets.
6. Availability of large sums of labour force including specialized skills.
7. Superiority in educational, cultural and entertainment facilities.
8. A social environment attractive to foreign investors, enterpreneurs and specialists.

Developing and underdeveloped nations have a few centres where there is concentration of population owing to the growth of manufacturing. This has given rise to an agglomerated settlement having the characteristics of a primate city. However, primate cities like Dar es Salaam are often faced with the problems of overcrowding, poor quality of housing, development of slums, increasing heterogeneity of people and income, and disparities of development. The primate city of Dar es Salaam on the edge of the country is causing severe complications in areas of its hinterland where the increasing distance from one place to another is already a factor of impeding integration, and hence the rest of the country is out of touch in terms of development from the primate city of Dar es Salaam.

As in the case of other primate cities it has been found that the percentage increase of population in Dar es Salaam is very high (Table 16.1).

TABLE 16.1 **Dar es Salaam Percentage Increase of Population (1867 - 1983)**

Year	Total population	Percentage increase	Percentage growth rate
1867	900	-	-
1887	5,000	455.55	22.77
1894	10,000	100.00	14.28
1900	20,000	100.00	16.66
1913	22,500	13.00	1.00
1921	24,600	9.33	1.16
1931	34,300	39.43	3.94
1948	69,277	101.98	6.00
1957	1,28,742	86.00	9.55
1967	2,72,821	111.91	11.19
1978	7,69,447	182.04	16.54
1983	11,20,000	46.85	9.37

Source: Calculated by the author

Table 16.1 shows that the rate of population growth in the primate city of Dar es Salaam was high in 1887, very low in 1913 and 1921, but again high (16.54%) in 1978. During they fears 1913 and 1921 population growth was either negative or very low throughout the world owing to war, famine, disease and drought; but since then, population has increased slowly and perceptibly up to the present day owing to factors such as natural increase, improved health facilities and excessive migration from rural to urban areas. In this way, Dar es Salaam an outstanding primate city is leading the destiny of Tanzania.

DYNAMIC RADIUS OF RANK SIZE RULE

In 1948 the first-ranking town Dar es Salaam had a population of 69,227 while the twenty fifth last ranking town of Songea had a population of 612 only. These two first and last ranking towns show a gap of 68,615 persons. In 1978 the first-ranking town of Dar es Salaam had a population of 769,445 against the last ranking ninety-eight urban centre of Manda having a population of 527. There was a total difference of 768,918 persons. What is apparent is that in between 1948 and 1978 the population size and economic development of Dar es Salaam had gone up 11.20 times whereas in case of the last ranking centres the population had gone down by - .14 times only. The last ranking centre had a rank of 25th in 1948, while it had gone up to 98th by creating a great margin in between the first and last ranking urban centres in terms of population concentration, economic development and transportation linkages. But this change in spatio-temporal dimensions of resource development is a clear cut sign of progress and prosperity in future if this growth has been channelized in a systematic, scientific and planned way, instead of being haphazard and lopsided as it is at present.

The rank-size curve of urban centres for the 2978 Census is S-shaped which is a sign of primacy and a more rational distribution of urban size class of towns in Tanzania in comparison with the 1948 Census. In the rank-size curve of the 1978 census several steps are to be found. Harris (1970)[26] in his work on the cities of the Soviet Union, suggested that "steps in a rank-size curve may indicate separate sub-systems of cities or relatively independent regions with little functional integration". But in case of Tanzania poor transportation linkages, functional independence owing to rough terrain conditions and socio-economic backwardness are some of the major factors responsible for different steps on the rank-size-curve.

RATIONALITY OF RANK SIZE RULE

The relationship between the actual population (1978) and the estimated population of urban centres in relation to the first ranking city of Dar es Salaam in Tanzania. It has been found that second, third, fourth, 91st and higher ranking urban centres have very low actual population in comparison with the primate city of Dar es Salaam in terms of rank-size rule.

Urban centres with ranks ranging from 7th to 90th also have a lesser number of actual population according to the rank-size rule, but here the discrepancy is low in comparison with trans Tanga, Zanzibar, Mwaza besides the 92st and higher ranking small towns

(Table 16.2).

The placing of all the points for actual and estimated population of urban centres above the line of actual rank-size distribution show a sign of an underdeveloped economy. In case of a developed economy all these points should run along the line or below the line in case of an overdeveloped economy. This represents the paucity of service facilities, poor transportation linkages with the Zanzibar island, unbalanced regional development, the availability of meagre income and low labour productive in most of the urban centres of Tanzania in relation to the primate city of Dar es Salaam.

SIZE CLASS DISTRIBUTION OF URBAN CENTRES

The analysis of rank-size rule of urban places involves the problem of hierarchical ordering, the distributional pattern of the centres of various sizes as well as the causes for such a distribution.

So far as the size class is concerned Dar es Salaam accounts for 32 per cent of the country's urban population. In general the urban pattern in Tanzania is most diffused. Four Class I cities, namely Dar es Salaam, Mwanza, Tanga and Zanzibar have 45.33.

TABLE 16.2 **MARGIN OF ACTUAL AND ESTIMATED POPULATION IN RELATION TO PRIMATE CITY OF SOME MAJOR AND SMALLER URBAN PLACES, 1978**

Rank	Urban centre order	Actual population (O)	Estimated population (E)
2	Mwanza	1,10,553	3,84,722
3	Zanzibar	1,10,506	2,56,481
4	Tanga	1,03,399	1,92,361
5	Mbeya	76,601	1,53,889
6	Tabora	67,388	1,28,240
91	Kibaya	2,621	84,553
92	Monduli	2,248	8,363
93	Vwawa	1,585	8,273
94	Kisarawe	1,434	8,185
95	Mkokotoni	1,170	8,099
96	Koani	832	8,015
97	Karagwe	644	7,932
98	Manda	527	7,851

Source: Estimated by the author.

per cent of the country's urban population and the balance is found in dispersed urban places of medium and smaller sizes. In Tanzania, 63 per cent of the urban areas are of smaller population size, that is below 10,000 persons in the 1978 census (Table 16.3).

TABLE 16.3 **Size Class Distribution of Urban Centres in Tanzania (1978)**

Number of centres	Population size	Total popul-ation	Percentage of Urban population	Size class of towns
1	Over 5,00,000	769,445	32	I
3	5,00,000-100,000	324,458	13	I
6	1,00,000-50,000	419,279	19	II
27	50,000-10,000	533,701	21	III
61	Below 10,000	365,917	15	IV
Total (98)		2,412,800	100%	-

Source: Calculated by R. B. Mandal.

In Tanzania urban places have served as the nodes of transportation, regional development and inducement of administrative efficiency ever since the colonial era of the Dutch, Arab and German. Although the evolution of towns took place a thousand years ago, [27] increase in the size of towns is truly a recent urban development. In the years prior to the twentieth century most of the towns were confined to the eastern coast but during the twentieth century towns have sprang up even in the interior too, in particular town such as Tabora, Mpwapwa and Ujiji. The development of Ujiji has been the outcome of the activities of the Arab traders in East Africa. These towns were established in the interior during the colonial rule not only to spread Islam and but also to popularise the Kiswahili language.

During the 1948 Census only four towns with a population of over 10,000 each were identified. These were Dar es Salaam, Tanga, Tabora and Mwanza. The urban places of second order were Dodoma, Lindi, Morogoro and Moshi as those were trading centres with population ranging from 10,000 to 8000. All these towns were capitals of the seven provinces of the colonial administration.[28] Iringa and Arusha were European settlements having a population of 5,000, whereas Bagamoyo, a port town, had a population of 4,162 only. The smallest towns in 1948 were Lushoto (662) and Songea (612).

In the 1957 Census two twin towns of Mtwara/Mikindani and Kigoma/Ujiji were added, today, they are small commercial centres besides pre-colonial indigenous settlements.[29] The towns which retained their former ranks are Dar es Salaam, Tanga, Iringa, Musoma, Mbeya and Bukoba. In 1957 Bagamoyo's population declined from 4,162 to 3,861 and Chunya's population from 1,716 to 1,664 (Table 16.4).

In the 1967 Census owing to the formation of regions and districts the dimensions of urban centres have changed, and some new towns, such as Kondoa, Nansio, Mpwapwa and Mwadui were included. Mwadui was a minor settlement pin 1957, but in 1967 it became a fullfleged town. While in the 1957 Census there were 31 urban centres in Tanzania there were 32 in 1967 and 98 in 1978. In 1967 the city of Dar es Salaam had a population of 272,821 which was four times higher than the second major town of Tanga (61,658).

In 1978 Census Tanzania showed a more than 100 per cent increase in the number of urban centres in comparison with the 1967 Census. Dar es Salaam the capital and primate city has a population of 769,445 followed by the second ranking city of Mwanza with a population of 110,553 which is more than seven times smaller in size than Dar es Salaam. The last ranking town is Manda with a population of 527 ranking 98th but its population is 1,460 times smaller than it is in Dar es Salaam. This clearly represents that the transportation and trade relations are in perpetuity in between the first and the last ranking urban centres.

So far as the population size distribution of towns is concerned most of the large sized and closely spaced towns are found on the eastern sea shore and along the transportation lines which connect most of the port towns with the western-up-country. This clearly represents the colonial impact of export of raw goods and import of finished products and machineries, through different channels of transport.

Further it may be seen that the areas north-east of Lake Rukwa, and north-east of the Songea and Serengeti Plains are completely devoid of urban centres owing to the infection of tse-tse fly in the river basins, no supply of drinking water, low population density, lack of transportation lines and poor agricultural development. This sort of regional inequality could only be removed when the main arteries of transport connect one urban centre with the other, instead of running only towards the port.

TABLE 16.4 **Trends of Number and Size of Urban Centres in Tanzania (1948-78)**

Population Size Class	Number of Centres			
	1948	1957	1967	1978
Less than 1,000	2	1	-	3
1,00-2,500	7	7	4	4
2,500-5,000	8	8	8	24
5,000-10,000	6	4	6	30
10,000-15,000	2	5	2	11
15,000-20,000	1	4	1	7
20,000-25,000	-	-	5	2
25,000-50,000	-	1	4	5
50,000-1,00,000	1	-	1	7
Over 1,00,000	-	1	1	4
Total	27	31	32	98

Source: Tanzania: Population Census, Vol.2.
Dar es Salaam, 1970-1978.

CHANGING RANK OF TOWNS

The rank of towns depends on the population size and the rate of population growth. Dar es Salaam, Mwanza, Zanzibar and Tanga have maintained their leading positions during the four censuses. Mwanza which replaced Tabora for the third position in 1957 retained the third rank in 1967 and again changed to the second rank in 1978. Tanga which was second in rank during the 1948, 1957 and 1967 censuses came down to 4th rank in 1978 after Mwanza and Zanzibar. Bukoba, Mbeya and Musoma have interchanged their ranks but Mbeya emerged 5th in 1978 from 14th in 1967. Lindi's position is continuously declining from being 6th rank in 1948 to 10th in 1957, 13th in 1967, and 17th in 1978. Arusha's rank was 10th in 1948, 11th in 1957, 4th in 1967 and 9th in the 1978 Censuses.

In some cases the increase in population size and change in rank have been more on account of the extension of town boundaries than owing to the natural increase in population or the encoming of migrants, such as in the towns of Arusha and Mbeya. Since 1948 the rank of Bagamoyo is also continuously declining from 17th to 18th, 18th to 20th, and 20th to 24th in the 1948, 1957, 1967 and 1978 censuses respectively. In the 1967 Census Kimamba which ranked 31st and Lushoto 32nd have gone down to 43rd and 90th ranks, respectively in the 1978 Census. This showed that although the population of the towns increased their ranks declined in most of the cases owing to the addition of newer towns to the list.

RANK SIZE AND SPACING OF TOWNS

According to the 1978 Census Tanzania has an area of 886,090 sq kms over which 98 urban centres are found in different parts of the country. These urban centres have grown as a result of the slow and continuous process of grown and development. In such a situation with the increasing number of centres decreasing complexity is a rule (Table 16.5) in case the process of urbanization, economic growth, industrialization and development are taking place leading to the overall integrated development of the whole country.

TABLE 16.5 **Rank and Spacing of Urban Places in Tanzania (1978)**

Rank/ size of Towns	Spacing in kms
1	1007
10	318
20	225
30	184
40	159
50	142
60	129
70	120
80	111
90	106
98	102

Source: By the author

Spacing by Mather's Formula $1.07\sqrt{\frac{A}{N}}$

Table 16.5 shows that when there is just one urban centre the spacing is as high as 1007 kilometres. When there are 50 urban centres, the spacing is reduced to 142 kilometres and in case of the addition of up to the 98th centre the inter-distance of urban centres in the country as a whole has been reduced to only 102 kilometres. All these spatial patterns show the diffused character and greater distance of one centre from another where one cannot think of performing any work of economic value by travelling on foot. This also represents the physical barrier and social hindrance in the economic development of the country.

LOG NORMAL RELATIONSHIP

The log normal distribution appears as a straight line on a logarithmic normal probability graph. The cumulative percentage of the number of urban centres are plotted on the Y axis and the city size on the X axis. The Y axis should be graduated to the normal probability scale and the X to a logarithmic scale. The straight line drawn with the help of the above two sets of data shows the log-normal distribution which is in effect a rank-size distribution.[30]

TABLE 16.6 **The Log normalcy of Urban Centres in Tanzania (1978)**

Population (X)	Number of urban centres	Percentage of total number of urban centres	Cummulative percentage (Y)
Below 5,000	32	32.66	32.66
5,000-9,999	30	30.62	63.28
10,000-19,999	18	18.36	81.64
20,000-49,999	7	7.14	88.78
50,000-99,999	7	7.14	95.92
1,00,000 and above	4	4.08	100.00
Total	98	100.00	

Source: Calculated by R.B.Mandal

with the help of X and Y data in Table 16.6, on probability paper the vertical scale has been adjusted so that any normal distribution will appear as a straight line if it is in cumulative percentage form. The horizontal axis can be divided arithmetically or logarithmically depending on whether or not the data needs to be transformed to achieve a straight line.[31]

CONCLUSION

Ultimately it can be said that the rank-size rule does not fully operate in Tanzania. Berry and Garison (1958) remarked that rank-size rule is certainly not the answer to all city size problems. The reasons are several such as inadequate development of trade, transportation lines, industries, establishment of ports, administrative centres besides landscape features as carriers and barriers of urban development. The rule would, however, be applicable if the urban centres develop on isotropic plain surface without artificial incentives to chosen centres, or limitations to the growth of other centres. It may be concluded that the urban centres of Tanzania are log-normally distributed.

REFERENCES

1. F. Auerbach, "Das Gestz der Bevolkungs Konzedtration", *Petermannas Geographie che Mittilungen,* Vol. 59, Part I, pp. 74-76.
2. J. Clarke, Population Geography, Oxford: Porgamon Press, 1966.
3. G.K. Zipf, National Unity and Disunity, Bloomington: Principia Press, 1941.
4. C.T.J. Stewart, *The Size and Spacing of Cities"* Reading in Urban Geography (Edt. H.M. Mayer and Clyde F. Kohn), Allahabad, 1967 p.241
5. R.B. Mandal, *Introduction to Rural Settlements.* New Delhi: Concept, 1979.
6. P. Haggett, Locational Analysis in Human Geography, London: Edward Arnold, 1965.
7. F.W. Boal, and D.B. Johnson, "The Rank-Size Curve, A Diagnostic Tool," *The Professional Geographer* X VII; No. 5, 1965.
8. B.J.L., Berry, and W.L. Garrison, "Alternative Explanations of Urban Rank-Size Relationship," *Annals of the Association of American Geographers* 48 (1958) 83.
9. B.J.L. Berry, *Geography of Market Centres and Retail Distributions,* Prentice Hall, 1967.
10. R. Hankal, "The Urban Systems of Kenya, Tanzania, Zambia and Zimbabwe." Paper presented to South Africa Conference of the Commonwealth Geographical Bureau, Lusaka, June 1982.
11. K.E. Rosing, "A Rejection of the Zipf Model (Rank-Size Rule) in Relation to City Size", *The Professional Geographer* 18 (1966) 75-82.
12. J. Stewart, "Emperical Mathematical Rules Concerning the Distributional Equilibrium of Population," *Geographical Review* 37 (1947) 461-85.
13. J.H. Von Thunen, Der isolierite Staat in Beziehung auf Landwrtschaft and Nationale konomie, Rostok, 1826.
14. A. Weber, Uberden Standart der Industrier, Riene Theories standarts, Tubinzen, 1900.
15. M. Jefferson, "The Law of Primate City," *Geographical Review* (1939) 226-232.
16. Christaller W., Central Places in Southern Germany. Translated by C.W. Baskin. Englwood Cliffs, Prentice Hall, 1966.
17. Losch. A., The Economics of Location. Translated by W. Stolper. New Haven: Yale University Press, 1954.

18. Berry, B.J.L., "Cities as systems within systems of cities", Papers of the Regional Science Association, 13, (1964) 147-164.
19. King L.J., *Statistical Analysis in Geography*. Englewood Cliffs: Prentice Hall, 1959.
20. Berry,B.J.L. and W.L. Garsison, op. cit. 1958.
21. Von Foerster H., On Self-Organizing Systems and their Environments in Self Organizing System. Edited by M.C. YO Vitts and S. Cameron. New York: Pergamon Press, 1960.
22. Berry, B.J.L,"City Size Distributions and Economic Developments and Cultural Change 9 (1961) 573-587. 23 El Shaks. S. "Development, Primacy and Systems of Cities," *Journal of Developing Areas* 7 (1972) 11-36.
24. Haggett, P "Geography, a Modern Synthesis, 3rd ed, New York: Harper and Row, 1979.
25. Brutzkus E. "Centralized Versus Decentralized Pattern of Urbanization in Developing Countries," Tijdschrift Voor Econo. In *Soc. Geografie* 64 No. 1 (1973) 11-23.
26. Harris,C.D. *Cities of the Soviet Union: Studies in their Functions, Size, Density and Growth*. Chicago: Rand Mcnally, 1970.
27. R. Coupland, East Africa and Invadors, Oxford, 1965.
28 The provinces and capitals of 1957 are as follows: Central province (Dodoma), Eastern (Dar es Salaam), Lake (Mwanza) Northern (Arusha), Southern (Mwanza), Southern Highlands (Mbeya) and Tanga (Tanga).
29. Kigoma the Port and Administrative centre was proclaimed a town in 1921 *(Tanzania Gazette* Vol. 2, p. 319). Ujiji was declared as a minor settlement in 1933 *(Tanganyika Ordinance*, Vol. XII, P. 22).
30. Reddy N.B.K., "Comparative Study of the Urban Rank-Size Relationship in the Krishna and Godavari Deltas and South Indian states," *The National Geographical Journal of India* XV Part II, (1969) 63-90.

Index